KISSING THE TRAIL

KISSING THE TRAIL

NORTHWEST & CENTRAL OREGON MOUNTAIN BIKE TRAILS

SECOND EDITION

JOHN ZILLY

ADVENTURE PRESS
SEATTLE, WASHINGTON

At Adventure Press, we strive to produce sustainable books.
They're always printed in the US on recycled paper using earth-friendly inks.

Researcher: Spencer Harris
Cover and interior design: Peter D'Agostino
Layout and design: Dave Caplan, Feedback Graphics
Cover photograph: Colin Meagher
Interior photographs: John Zilly, Spencer Harris, Greg Strong
Maps: John Zilly
Copy editor: Erin Moore

Cover photo: Chris Sheppard rips it on the Metolius-Windigo Trail.
Backcover photo: Dave Baldwin at Newberry Caldera.

ISBN 978-188158312-7

Adventure Press
PO Box 14059
Seattle, Washington 98114
206.200.2578, www.adventurepress.com

For Dova and Pablo
Let your hearts choose the trail

Thank you Spencer Harris. Your work and companionship were essential ingredients, and the book is much better because of your help. Thanks to my First Kiss Marea, and also to Alan Bennett, Dave & Cinda, David Dodge, Doobie, Jim Emery, Eric, Mark Flint, Gravey, Angela Reid, Rick & Holly, and Greg Strong.

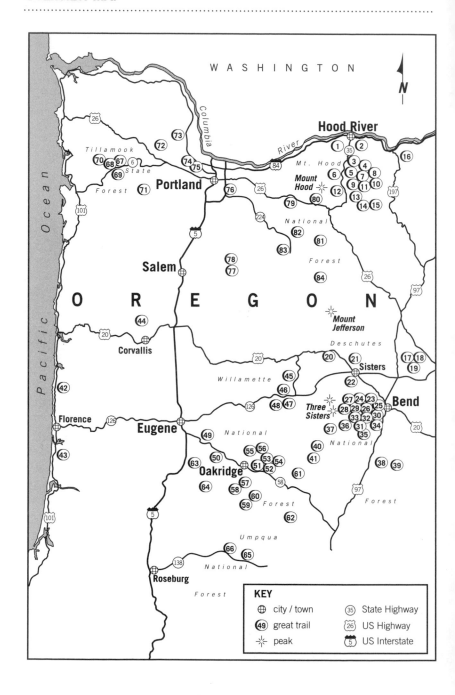

CONTENTS

RIDES BY DIFFICULTY

As I sit here writing this at 5:30 a.m. on a Sunday morning, my mind keeps drifting off to the trails. Zippy ones, steep ones, dark and mysterious ones, fast and butter smooth, root-strewn and rocky. And I want to go. Now. I want to leave this stupid computer and get on my bike. Perhaps head out to the winding maze of singletrack and freeride features at Scappoose. Or maybe sample Molalla or Post Canyon or even the lower half of the North Umpqua, which are all open in April. If I left right now, how long would it take to get there? And who could I call at this last minute? But it's raining and I have obligations, and that's when the daydreams of summer riding begin. When's the trip to Hood River to ride the East Mount Hood Epic? While I'm at it I'll need to ride Eightmile to Fifteenmile, new to this second edition, with its two spectacular descents, descents rivaling Bend's Mrazek Trail. And what about Bend? Damit, shouldn't I have at least six weeks of vacation? That would be a lot more civilized. Because there are so many new trails in Bend, as well as old, must-ride classics. Farewell, North Fork to Flagline, Storm King, Phil's, C.O.D, and of course Newberry Caldera. What's that, a week's worth of riding?

Then on to Oakridge and Eugene. McKenzie still sets an unreal standard. Waldo, too. I've included another ride at Alpine out of Westfir. But perhaps the best thing about this second edition is the infamous North Umpqua Trail, rides 65 and 66. That trail rocks, and the descriptions here will tell you the best way to ride it. There are new rides near Portland as well, in Tillamook State Forest and in the Scappoose wonderland. Time to call in sick for a month.

I'm nearly done with this second edition of KTTO, as some call it. I shitcanned a few of the first edition dogs. I added about 13 new rides. And most of the others have been checked and rechecked. You'll find new features, photos, phone numbers, web addresses, and stuff I can't remember at 5 in the morning. One thing I do know is that this book has some trails no other mountain bike guide gets to. Eighty-four rides in all. Okay, I need to go pack my stuff now and pick-up a new bike. Want to go?

John Zilly
April 2008

First, *Kissing the Trail* makes it easier for you to pick out a great ride. Second, it'll get you to the trailhead and around the route without getting lost. Pretty simple. I've arranged the 84 rides in this book into four geographic regions—Hood River and East Mount Hood, Bend and Central Oregon, Oakridge and Eugene, and Portland and Beyond. Keeping rides grouped in regions makes it easier to plan multiday trips. What follows describes the book's rating system, explains how the information is presented, and provides an annotated look at some of the conventions I use to detail each ride.

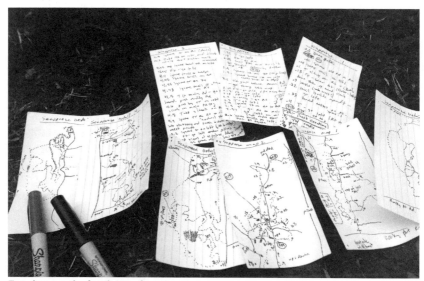

Two days worth of trail notes from Scappoose

Each route's overall difficulty rating, measured in wheels, is displayed at the top of each ride. One wheel is easiest; five, hardest. The rating is based on three factors: distance, elevation gain, and the level of bike-handling skill needed to ride enjoyably and safely.

⊙ (easy): Just about anyone can make it through a ride rated as one wheel. These rides are short and flat, have well-packed (sometimes paved) riding surfaces, and are perfect for families.

⊙ ⊙ (intermediate): Two-wheel rides primarily traverse dirt roads and rail-trails, although they occasionally venture onto easily negotiated doubletrack and singletrack. These rides are somewhat longer and may involve more elevation gain than those rated one wheel. However, two-wheel rides never demand a high skill level, so even beginners should be able to ride the whole way.

⊙ ⊙ ⊙ (difficult): More rides in this book receive this rating than any other. These routes—all of which contain some singletrack—travel less than 18 miles and have moderate elevation gains, generally less than 1,600 feet. A typical three-wheeler combines a dirt-road climb with a singletrack descent. Be prepared for at least a few steep climbs as well as a few rough, technical sections of trail. Some hike-a-biking may be required.

⊙ ⊙ ⊙ ⊙ (most difficult): If a ride is long, hilly, and chock-full of challenging singletrack, I've rated it four wheels. Some riders may have to push or carry their bikes for long distances. You'll gain big chunks of elevation and have your bike-handling skills tested on every four-wheel route. Of course, if you're not hiking, you're not really mountain biking.

⊙ ⊙ ⊙ ⊙ ⊙ (epic): Only a few rides in this book are sufficiently difficult to warrant the extreme, epic rating of five wheels. These rides are very long, technical, and hilly, and may require lots of walking or hike-a-biking. Then there's the fourth factor—less-than-intuitive route-finding. Not to sound overly cautious or anything, but you probably shouldn't attempt these trails unless you are a good mountain biker, in great physical condition, and enjoy pinning your physical limits for long periods of time.

RIDE STATISTICS

Distance

This information is given in miles, along with the ride's format: either loop, out-and-back, one-way, figure eight, or lollipop.

Route

Is this on singletrack? Paved rail-trail? Dirt-road climb followed by single-track descent? Get your snapshot here. If the word "views" appears on this line, then on clear days you should expect to see a snow-capped volcano, a spectacular mountain lake, a panoramic vista, or all of the above.

Climbs

Here, in a word or two, I describe the ascents. This is followed by the route's high point and elevation gain from the bottom of the ride to the top.

Duration

Okay, how many hours it takes to ride the route depends on your skills, stamina, and map-reading abilities, as well as the number of mojitos you downed the previous night. Trail conditions and weather can also drastically alter the time it takes to complete a ride. Before you leave, call to find out about current trail and weather conditions (you'll find the contact listed in the ride description under "Manager"). There's another factor too: riders are out there for different reasons—some like to hammer while others like to chat and gawk at the scenery. So I've listed one duration estimate for Fitness Riders and another for Scenery Riders. All of these routes can each be done in a day.

Travel

The driving distance from nearby towns or cities is listed.

Skill

Rides are rated for beginner, intermediate, or advanced, depending on the minimum bike-handling ability a rider ought to have before attempting a particular trail. This rating has little to do with fitness; you may be a fine athlete, but I wouldn't recommend an expert trail if you have never mountain biked before.

Season

The best time of year to be out on this trail.

Maps

Supplementary maps are extremely helpful, unless you enjoy bivouacking. I typically recommend United States Geological Survey (USGS) topographical maps, United States Forest Service (USFS) ranger district maps, or Green Trails maps.

Rules

Here I note which trailheads require parking and trail-use passes. Seasonal trail closures and one-way trails are also noted. Call the managing agency for current trail conditions and restrictions.

Manager

You have a question about a trail? Here's who to call, the responsible agency or land manager. You should always call ahead, too, for current conditions, maintenance schedules, snow levels, permit information, and any other information.

Web

Here's where you'll find the best beta on a given trail.

RIDE DESCRIPTION

Who Will Like This Ride

In a few words I try to match up rider and trail.

The Scoop

Each ride begins with a descriptive overview, including trail notes and other anecdotes.

Driving Directions

Find your detailed driving instructions here. In most cases, I've indicated a point at which you should set the trip odometer in your car to zero, a helpful feature because the starts for many of these rides can be challenging to find.

The Ride

In addition to notes about the terrain and the scenery, plus an occasional random quip, the ride section contains a detailed description of the route—up or down, left or right. These paragraphs note the mileage—in bold—for most intersections, hills, tricky sections of trail, vistas, and other significant landmarks. Riding with an odometer is highly recommended.

What follows is an annotated listing of some of the conventions I use in describing the trails in Kissing the Trail: Northwest & Central Oregon. **WHOA!** signifies a dangerous section of trail or a turn easily missed, and warns the rider to pay close attention. **WOOF!** identifies the top of a particularly difficult climb. Stay on the main trail/road means that other trails or roads exit from the main route—use good judgment to continue on the primary trail or road. When the trail dead-ends at another trail, forcing a 90-degree turn either right or left, the resulting three-way intersection is described as a T. Other three-way intersections are usually described as forks, though sometimes I write that the trail divides. If a faint trail or lesser trail forks off the main trail, I will sometimes tell you to ignore, pass, or bypass rather than describe it as a fork. When two trails or roads cross, the result is usually referred to as a four-way intersection.

On many trails you'll have to walk or push your bike up a steep hill. If, however, a long stretch of trail requires an awkward combination of walking and riding, I describe it as a hike-a-bike. A technical section of trail—typically a narrow tread or steep slope populated by roots, rocks, or other obstacles—demands good bike-handling skills. An especially technical section of trail may be referred to as an expert section. On unmaintained or faint trails, on trails transformed by clearcutting and road building, and in areas that have mazes of trails, it's sometimes difficult to figure out which way to go. In these instances, I'll likely mention the problematic route-finding.

A number of different types of trails and roads are described in this book. A dirt or gravel road could probably be used by a car. Roads in national forests are usually identified by a number preceded by FR for forest road. Doubletracks, also know as old roads, refer to narrow, rough roads and may be either motorized or nonmotorized. Sometimes these old roads are gated to keep out motor vehicles. Old railroad grades, or rail-trails, are abandoned railroad lines that have no tracks or ties. Typically, rail-trails have the look and feel of dirt roads, although rail-trails are almost always nonmotorized and nearly flat. Trail and singletrack, terms that are used interchangeably, generally refer to soft-surface trails less than 36 inches wide. A wide trail refers to a path 3 to 8 feet wide. Sometimes, however, "trail" is used in a generic sense to mean any part of a route, whether paved or soft-surface, between 12 inches and 12 feet wide.

Option

For some rides, I have provided directions to modify the route, to bail out early, bag a peak, catch a nice view, or just noodle along an extra stretch of singletrack.

Gazetteer

Each ride concludes with information on nearby campgrounds and services. The information on the nearest town helps you pinpoint the ride's location and identify the nearest gas station, and lets you know which direction to head to satisfy that cheeseburger craving. Use the information under Gazetteer to plan weekend trips and extended excursions.

MAPS AND GPS FEATURES

The start and finish of each ride are clearly visible, and the highlighted route prevents map face—squinted eyes and a furrowed brow. Bold arrows indicate the direction of travel, and intermediary trail mileages are noted between the triangular ridepoints. Key elevations are highlighted, and elevation profiles show all of the ups and downs.

I recorded the route, mileage, and elevation data using a global positioning system (GPS) receiver, a cycle computer, a couple altimeters, and a whole bunch of Sharpies. Using these tools, I wrote the text and created the maps for *Kissing the Trail: Northwest & Central Oregon*.

After recording the twists and turns of every route, I then used that track data to create the maps. In some cases, the maps in *Kissing the Trail* are more accurate than any other existing map. In addition to recording the track data, I used the receiver to make a series of waypoints (GPS lingo for an exact location) for each ride, which I call ridepoints. Individual ridepoints are marked on the maps by numbered triangles at key junctures along the ride; you'll also find a complete list of ridepoints—a route—for each ride in a small box on the map.

The numbers in the GPS Ridepoints box are latitude and longitude coordinates (WGS 84 map datum; dd°mm.mmm format). Ridepoint 1 △ is the trailhead. To use the ridepoints, punch the coordinates into your GPS receiver the night before a ride. The following day, your receiver will point toward each successive ridepoint for the entire loop and tell you where you are in relationship to the other ridepoints. The ridepoints are all referenced in the trail descriptions as well.

At the top of an epic descent, a friend turned to me and said, "Have fun and keep the rubber side down." As he pedaled away his smile indicated he was having fun, but he didn't heed his second piece of advice. And at the bottom he didn't say, "You should try that skin-side-down technique sometime."

Though driving to the trailhead is probably the most dangerous part of any trip, bicycling injuries such as cracked collarbones, dislocated shoulders, and fractured wrists are all too common. Thankfully, you can shake off most crashes. If, however, you've sustained a serious injury, extra clothes and a first-aid kit could save your life. But the danger of mountain biking isn't just the spectacular crash. A simple mechanical failure, a sore knee, a wrong turn, or exhaustion can strand you miles from the trailhead and force an unplanned night in the woods. If you don't have the proper supplies and a friend to plan strategy with, you could be in trouble. And the worst trouble is often self-inflicted: panic and hysteria. If you stay calm, if you have enough to eat and drink, and if you have an extra layer of clothing to put on, you will probably be fine.

Before You Leave
- How's the trail? Is it hunting season? Call the managing agency.
- Check out the mountain weather.
- Let someone know where you plan to ride and when you plan to return.

During the Ride
- Don't ride alone.
- Always wear a helmet and eye protection.
- Have fun, but always stay aware of other trail users.
- First-aid kits are good.
- Carry extra clothes and a hat, no matter how nice the weather seems.
- Pack sunscreen, a lighter, a pocket knife, extra food, and a flashlight.
- Drink! And not just alcohol. Don't count on finding water.
- Carry a map of the area and bring a compass.
- Use a cycle computer.

Recommended Tools
- pump
- patch kit
- extra tube
- tire irons
- spoke wrench
- chain tool
- multi-tool with allen wrenches and phillips screwdriver

Other trail users, sometimes even other mountain bikers, will tell you to get off the trail—you shouldn't be there, it's a "local" trail, mountain bikes are bad for the environment, there are too many conflicts. I've been told to not write about local trails lest I be killed. Okay, that attitude closes a lot of trails, and mountain bikers have borne the brunt of those closures. But when bicyclists ride smart, they don't hurt the environment and they don't cause conflicts. So ride smart. If you tear up the trail, toss wrappers into the woods, or frighten other trail users, then you shouldn't be there.

Most bicyclists search out the magic tucked around the trail's next bend—an old growth cedar, a gurgling creek. We can't deny that mountain biking is great fun. Why should we? Being out in the woods should be a joyous, not solemn, occasion. But you can be joyous without abusing the trail or any other users. How? A little courtesy goes a long ways. Yield the trail to hikers, equestrians, and uphill riders. Say hello to other trail users. And when approaching from behind, give hikers and equestrians a friendly "hello" before you startle them.

Cyclists have been a central part of the conservation movement for years—commuting, vacationing, and doing errands on bicycles. Bicyclists have been building and sharing soft-surface trails in the West for more than 100 years. In fact, bicyclists helped invent the idea of outdoor recreation. For that good tradition to continue, we need to keep searching for that magic, yielding the path to others, riding gently, maintaining trails, and acting green in the rest of our lives.

Guidelines

- Leave no trace.
- Try not to skid. Take it easy on trails that are poorly constructed, mucky and wet, or otherwise vulnerable. Walk around all delicate areas.
- Respect all other trail users. Yield the right-of-way to everyone, including hikers, runners, other bicyclists, motorcyclists, and equestrians.
- Stop and dismount when you encounter horses. Stand on the downhill side of the trail, and talk to the horse and rider as they pass.
- Ride in control.
- Respect wildlife (you are in their home!) and livestock (they can't help it!).
- Turn around if you reach a "No Trespassing" sign.
- Help with trail maintenance.

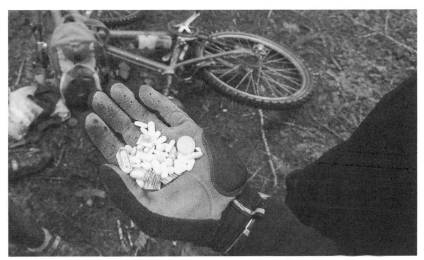

Tip Number 1: Remember which pill is which

Eating

Eating is more important than training and way more effective at holding that bonk at bay than all the titanium components your bank account can afford. I usually start out with a couple thousand calories of food in my pack: candy bars and energy bars, as well as peanuts, Fig Newtons, and at least one piece of fruit to avoid "energy-bar stomach," from which no amount of Tums can save you.

Drinking

Always bring plenty of water and electrolytes to consume. Two quarts a day is the minimum. I've quaffed five quarts of water on really long, hot days. Even early in your training cycle when you are not yet quite up to speed, eating and drinking enough can get you up a lot of hills and home before dark.

Walking

Most riders will push their bikes during some part of the three-, four-, or five-wheel rides included in *Kissing the Trail: Northwest & Central Oregon*. But walking your bike is nothing to be ashamed of—it's part of the sport. Walk to avoid getting hurt, walk to save your legs for the remainder of the ride, and walk around muddy areas to save delicate sections of the trail.

Cadence

As a rule, it's best to pedal 70 to 100 rotations per minute while riding a bike. This can seem awkwardly fast if you're not used to "spinning." But a healthy cadence is the easiest way to keep your legs fresh for the longest time possible. Slow, laborious pedal strokes strain muscles, tiring them for the miles ahead. On rough trails, the cadence rule doesn't always apply, but it's good to keep in mind in order to stay smooth and loose.

Descents

The header, digger, cartwheel, auger, and endo are bad. Whips, flips, drops, and pinballing can also be bad unless you're freeriding. Then they're good. Riding sideways toward small children is also bad. Riding upside down? Again bad. Either ride in control or walk down the steep sections. Sit back to lower your center of gravity, and keep your arms and legs slightly bent. Keep your fingers on the brakes. Don't use your front brake suddenly or erratically. The conundrum of braking: The front brake does most of the real braking, but you have more precise steering and you're less likely to take a header if less pressure is applied to the front brake. Remember that speed is the most hazardous bicycling condition. It's difficult to get hurt at 1 mile per hour; at 20 miles per hour, it's all too easy.

Climbs

The idea is to get to the top without hurling or passing out. Ride at a pace you can sustain for the length of the climb, concentrating on deep, relaxed breathing. Locomotive breathing—bad. Generally, it's best to stay seated so your rear wheel doesn't spin out. If traction is not a problem, try pedaling in a standing position occasionally to save your butt and use different muscles. Remember: It's okay to take a rest break (unless you're a Fitness Rider).

Freeriding

A trail builder I know once told me that freeriding wasn't scary, but free-riding on a front-suspension-only cross-country bike was terrifying. Cross-country bikes are too light and twitchy, and they never have enough front travel for the job. So if you plan to catch air, pull stunts, repeat trail features, or just rip a downhill, get on an all-mountain bike, at least. And don't stop there: A full wrap-around helmet, shin guards, and other gear can keep you alive, and that's a good thing. If you're just starting out, sign up for a clinic, class, or week-long camp to get it right from the start.

Training

Do some. Of course, if you're already out riding, then it's too late for me to do much sermonizing, but you'll have a better time if you've put some miles in before a tough ride. More importantly, carefully select the route and your riding partner. Don't ride an epic with an über-biker if you'd rather be following first-gear Freddy on a three-wheeler.

Maintenance

You'll have more fun out on the trail if your bike rolls smoothly, doesn't skip gears, and doesn't screech when you hit the brakes. Think about it: All week long you have to deal with copy machines that don't copy, computers that crash, and coworkers who skip gears and screech—so doesn't it make sense that when you are spending your hard-earned free time, you use something that works the way it's supposed to? Keep your bike in good working order. It'll keep your riding partners happy as well.

Insects

During the summer, mosquitoes can be a lot more than a nuisance in the central Oregon Cascades. Repellant is your friend. Then there are those bad years, when aggressive mosquitoes can ruin a trip, even when you've slathered on the repellant. Keep pedaling. Immediately after the snow melts and then again after the first hard freeze are often the best times to go to avoid insects. If there's a lake nearby, I'd suggest not riding the trail in July. Call the ranger station and ask for a BSR (bug status report).

Poison Oak

This stuff sucks. It's also all over the place, at least at elevations under 4,000 ft. I have tried to mention it in the descriptions or scoops where it's especially rampant. There are a few things you can do. First, know what it looks like. That's the best way to avoid it. Unfortunately, the poisonous oils can get on you even during times of the year when the plant has no leaves. Second, immediately after the ride wash with soap and water or, better yet, with a proven poison oak remover like Tecnu (try putting some on before the ride, too). Third, wash your clothes using a Tecnu-like product, because those oils can stick around and then come back to bite. Fourth, when considering a trail, call the ranger station and ask about the presence of poison oak.

For Portlanders, the 16 rides covered in this section are all within Saturday striking distance and don't require getting up at o'dark-thirty to make it a day trip—the epics excluded. With a few exceptions, these rides are single-track loops with dirt-road segments. Typically, they pass through fir forests and meadows, and offer exceptional views of Mount Hood. Expect fast, fun, switchbacking descents and technical ridgeline trails. The territory east of Mount Hood is a great place for mountain bikers.

But let's start with Post Canyon (ride 1), a fantastic freeride and cross-country area near Hood River. It's growing up. A few "non-formalized" trails in the '90s have sprouted into a full park of winding trails, skinnies, bridges, and jumps, most of which have been accepted by the powers that be. Surveyors Ridge (rides 3 and 4) is perhaps the most talked about and traveled ride in this area, but if you want a great ride—beautiful and challenging but with fewer people—try Gunsight Ridge (ride 13), High Prairie (ride 9), a combination of Knebal Springs (ride 8) and Fivemile Butte (ride 7), or Fifteenmile Creek (ride 10) for the descent. And check out Eightmile to Fifteenmile (ride 11). It has two of the best descents in the book. Mineral Creek, a confusing but classic ride from the first edition, was cut due to flood damage. Badger Lake was cut too, because, well, it sucked. Sorry if you suffered through it.

Two routes described in this section (rides 4 and 14) are epics—extra long and challenging. The East Mount Hood Epic (ride 14) is my favorite ride in this section, for its challenge and beauty.

Three of the rides—Historic Highway 30 (ride 2), East Fork Hood River (ride 6), and Lower Deschutes Rail-Trail (ride 16)—are quite easy and great for families. And since these are all out-and-backs, it's easy to tailor the length to fit your fitness level by turning around at any time.

The Hood River and Barlow Ranger Districts, both part of Mount Hood National Forest and managers of many of these trails, have done an admirable job keeping most of their non-wilderness area trails open to bicycles. They've done a good job maintaining the trails described here, as well. They have, however, neglected other trails in their district. Green Trails maps, the Hood River Ranger District map, and even the district's mountain-bike handout all list trails that aren't regularly maintained. The last time I checked, North Section Line, Bennett Pass, Crane Creek, Three Mile, and Rocky Butte Trails, to name a few, are either nonexistent or only semipassable. If you want to ride off-book and explore—and I've got to say, yes, exploring's a good thing—be prepared for anything. If you check out Fir Mountain, a bewildering maze of trails on private and unmanaged public land near Hood River, be sure to add poison oak to that "anything" list.

1 POST CANYON   ⊙⊙⊙

Distance 4 to 14 miles

Route Ups and downs, ramps and air on dirt roads and singletrack

Climbs Moderate to steep, high point: 1,700 ft, gain: 1,034 ft

Duration All riders: 1 to 5 hours

Travel Hood River—4 miles; Portland—60 miles

Skill Advanced

Season Year-round

Map USGS 7.5 minute: Hood River; Green Trails: Hood River

Rules None

Manager Hood River County, 541-387-7089

Web www.co.hood-river.or.us

Who Will Like This Ride

Freeriders, stunt seekers, and cross-country riders who dabble in extended airtime.

The Scoop

   Changes are happening at Post Canyon. It's not even called Post Canyon anymore by the county! Welcome to the Northwest Area, a name about as descriptive as calling mountain bikers "wheel users." Since the first edition of *Kissing the Trail*, trails have been built and then rerouted, forests have been cut, and land managers have changed and then changed again. As of 2008, Hood River County is coordinating the recreation effort on lands west and south of Hood River. Currently, there are about 74 miles of trail in the Northwest Area, most of which are open to motorized users (12 miles are non-motorized). When you ride from town,

Riding the chrome rooster at Post Canyon

explore the area, get lost in the not-well-signed labyrinth, and then repeat some loops, you can spin out a lot of miles, and that's good for the cross-country riders among us.

But that's not why we're talking about Post Canyon. The biggest change over the past 10 years has been the proliferation of ramps, teeters, bridges, skinnies, and jumps. It's freeride central. So while I've highlighted an introductory loop on the map, following the start of the ride, I've dispensed with my usual route description because the route specifics can change every weekend. Indeed, Hood River County is completing a master plan that includes more non-motorized trails, more loops and better routes, and plenty of features to huck your carcass all over the forest. What follows are directions to the trailhead and the start of the ride, a route where families and freeriders share the trail. But more and more, freeriders are ruling, and throwing a lot of air.

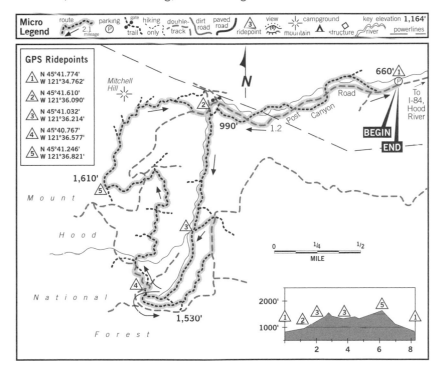

Driving Directions

From the intersection of Oak Street and Third Avenue in Hood River, set your odometer to zero and proceed west on Oak Street. Oak Street soon becomes Cascade Avenue. At 1.8 miles, turn left on County Club Road. At 3.2 miles, turn right on Post Canyon Road. When the road turns to gravel at 3.8 miles, pull over and park.

From Portland, drive east on Interstate 84. Take exit 62, the first Hood River exit. Turn right at the end of the ramp and then immediately right again on Country Club Road. Zero your odometer here. At 1.5 miles, turn right on Post Canyon Drive. When the road turns to gravel at 2.1 miles, pull over and park at a wide spot in the road. Note: The line of parked cars may begin before the road turns to dirt.

Or take the circuitous ramp option

Starting The Ride

From the start of the gravel road, spin up Post Canyon Road, climbing. Stay on the main road as you pass a dozen or more trails, on the left and on the right, some that return to the road shortly, others that head out into the Northwest Area hinterlands. Stay on the main road and warm up those legs. At **1.2** miles, reach a fork. The road on the right is gated. **WHOA!** Find an unmarked trail on the left that parallels the road. Take the trail and immediately bear right, following the meandering tread as it follows along Post Canyon Creek. This is the popular Seven Streams Trail. Now have fun.

Gazetteer

Nearby camping: Toll Bridge, Sherwood (primitive)
Nearest food, drink, services: Hood River

Distance	9-mile out-and-back
Route	Paved trail closed to vehicles; views
Climbs	Gentle rolling hills; high point: 550 ft, gain: 250 ft
Duration	Fitness rider: 30 minutes; scenery rider: 1 to 2 hours
Travel	Hood River—2 miles; Portland—65 miles
Skill	Beginner
Season	Year-round
Map	USGS 7.5 minute: White Salmon
Rules	None
Manager	Oregon State Parks, 800-551-6949
Web	www.oregonstateparks.org/park_155.php

Who Will Like This Ride

Families, beginning bicyclists, and anyone who wants to ride but doesn't want to ride in the dirt.

The Scoop

Designed by Samuel Lancaster, the Historic Columbia River Highway (Historic Highway 30), built between 1913 and 1922 and once the main thoroughfare for vehicles traversing the Columbia River Gorge, is now a state trail and closed

Columbia River from Historic Highway 30

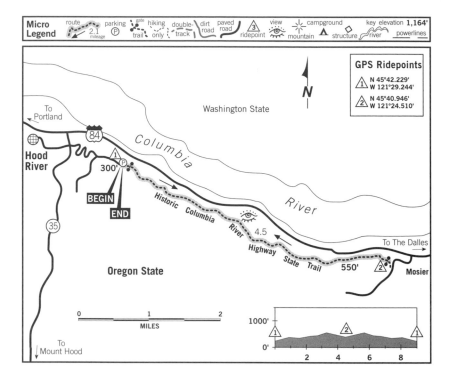

to motorized vehicles. Oregon State Parks gated the old road between Hood River and Mosier, repaired two tunnels along the route, then reopened it to hikers and bicyclists. This paved trail runs along the bluffs and basalt cliffs that form the southern wall of the gorge, affording outstanding views of the river. The ride demands little effort; however, it can be hot and windy.

Driving Directions

From Portland, drive east on Interstate 84. Take exit 64, just past Hood River. Zero out your odometer at the end of the interstate ramp and turn right. Immediately turn right again and wind up the hill. At 0.3 mile, reach a four-way intersection and turn left, following the signs for Historic Highway State Trail. Stay on the main road, which winds upward. At 1.0 mile, bear left. At 1.5 miles, reach the parking area at the Hatfield West trailhead.

. . . .

The Ride

From the western trailhead, ride east on the old paved road. The route climbs easily through pine, oak, and bigleaf maple, affording views north of the wide Columbia River Gorge and the browned hills of southern Washington. The way climbs, then rolls along the old chiseled roadway. At around the **3-mile** mark, pass through two tunnels and then descend to a white gate, the eastern end of the trail, at **4.5** miles (ridepoint 2). Turn around here and pedal back to the western trailhead to complete the ride, **9** miles.

Gazetteer

Nearby camping: Toll Bridge, Sherwood (primitive)
Nearest food, drink, services: Hood River

3 SURVEYORS RIDGE

Distance	24.3-mile loop
Route	Paved and gravel road, rugged ridgeline singletrack; views
Climbs	Moderate climb; high point: 4,260 ft, gain: 890 ft
Duration	Fitness rider: 2 to 3 hours; scenery rider: 3 to 5 hours
Travel	Hood River—17 miles; Portland—81 miles
Skill	Advanced
Season	Summer, fall
Map	USGS 7.5 minute: Hood River; Green Trails: Hood River
Rules	National Forest Recreation Pass required
Manager	Mount Hood National Forest, Hood River District, 541-352-6002
Web	www.fs.fed.us/r6/mthood/recreation/trails/hood-river-conditions

Who Will Like This Ride

Cross-country riders who want views and a challenge but no epic.

The Scoop

Surveyors Ridge is one of the most well-known mountain bike rides in Oregon, and for good reason—badass views of Mount Hood around many a corner, a riot of wildflowers in the meadows and clearcuts, and a fun, challenging trail. But what's the best way to ride this point-to-point ridge trail? Let us count the ways: Many stronger riders enjoy it as an out-and-back, beginning from the south end of the trail along FR 44 or from the north end along FR 17 (either north of Bald Butte or just south of the butte under the powerlines). Adventurers may begin at the ranger station along Hwy 35, ride north to FR 17, ride south on Surveyors to FR 44, descend Dog River, and finish by pedaling north on Hwy 35 (Ride 4). Epic seekers might combine it with Gunsight Ridge (Ride 13), which I actually prefer. Or you can follow the ride below, which is the easiest way to ride Surveyors (though not entirely easy). The route winds up forest roads to start, then scampers down the trail, over root and rock and across meadowed hillsides. As with most ridge trails, incessant and unpredictable ups and downs prove both exhilarating and draining. It's good, whichever way you ride it.

Driving Directions

From Portland, drive east on Interstate 84 and take exit 64, just past Hood River. Zero out your odometer at the end of the interstate ramp. Turn right and then immediately right again, following signs for State Highway 35. Proceed straight through the intersection at 0.3 mile, now heading south on Hwy 35. At 10.9 miles, after milepost 92, turn left on Pine Mont Drive (FR 17). Stay on the main road. At 17.3 miles, just after passing under some powerlines, turn right and follow the sign for Surveyors Ridge Trail. Find the trailhead parking on your left at 17.7 miles.

The Ride

From the small parking area at the trailhead, ride back down the dirt road to FR 17 and turn right. Stay on the main road, sometimes paved, sometimes gravel, as it climbs gently. At **2** miles, pass through Long Prairie. At **3.2** miles, ride straight through a four-way intersection. Crest a high point around **5.5** miles. Reach a fork at **8.9** miles

Surveyors Ridge Trail near Rim Rock

and bear right. Crest another high point, and then reach a T at **9.7** miles. From the T, turn right, following the sign for FR 44. At **10.2** miles (ridepoint 2), FR 17 ends—bear right on FR 44. The road descends, then climbs. At **11.9** miles (ridepoint 3), turn right onto FR 620. Immediately find Surveyors Ridge Trail 688 on the right.

Ride around the white gate and head east. The trail, hard-packed and fast, descends slightly to a fork, **13.3** miles. Bear left, cross Dog River, and then climb through Cooks Meadow. At **13.9** miles, stay to the left (ignoring a doubletrack on the right) and cross a small creek. From here, follow the doubletrack around a clearcut hillside. In June and July, fireweed, paintbrush, lupine, and shooting star line the route. The doubletrack is dusty and

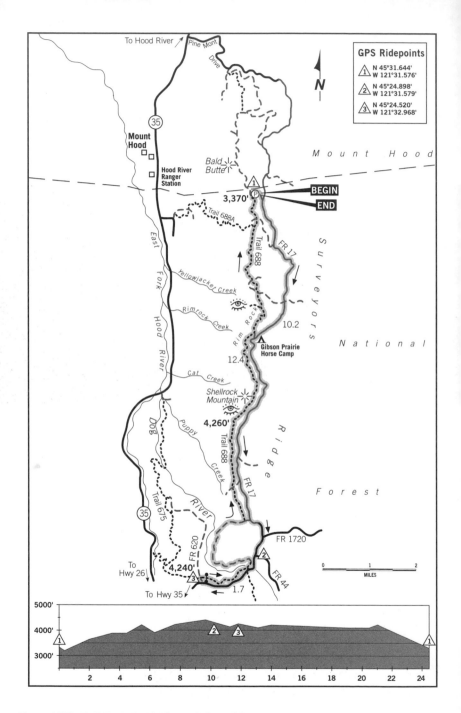

rocky in sections. **WHOA!** At **15.8** miles, leave the doubletrack by turning left onto Trail 688. This turn is easily missed. Cross a dirt road at **16.6** miles. Pass through stands of fir that alternate with clearcuts filled with fireweed. Starting at about **18.1** miles, there's a tough climb to the top of an open knoll, which affords awesome views of Mount Hood to the west.

Mount Hood from Surveyors Ridge

From the knoll, the trail descends, churning through the forest, to a fork at **18.7** miles—bear right and continue down before climbing again. At **19.3** miles, when the trail kisses a dirt road on the right, stay to the left. After a few more pedal strokes, stay left again onto the singletrack. From here, the trail winds around some dramatic rock outcrops and traverses a series of hillside meadows that afford more Mount Hood views. Rocks, some embedded, some loose, combine with a tricky side slope to make the riding quite technical at times. At a fork, **20.6** miles, bear to the left and climb. At **21.2** miles, pass a short trail to a lookout on the left. Cross gravel roads at **21.3** and **21.7** miles. When the trail forks at **22.4** miles, bear right and descend the rocky trail. Reach a fork at **23.3** miles, go right, then cross another gravel road. At **24.3** miles, the trail dumps out at the trailhead under the powerlines to complete the loop.

Gazetteer

Nearby camping: Eightmile Crossing (primitive), Sherwood (primitive)
Nearest food, drink, services: Parkdale, Hood River

Distance	33.2-mile loop
Route	Tough ridgeline singletrack, paved start and finish; views
Climbs	Steep ups and downs; high point: 4,260 ft, gain: 2,810 ft
Duration	Fitness rider: 4 to 6 hours; scenery rider: 6 to 8 hours
Travel	Hood River—15 miles; Portland—78 miles
Skill	Advanced
Season	Summer, fall
Map	Green Trails: Hood River, Mount Hood
Rules	None
Manager	Mount Hood National Forest, Hood River District, 541-352-6002
Web	www.fs.fed.us/r6/mthood/recreation/trails/hood-river-conditions

Who Will Like This Ride

Endurance riders who really wanted to ride the East Mount Hood Epic but couldn't organize a shuttle and didn't want to buck up for an extra 25 miles to make it a loop.

The Scoop

Here's a way to ride the fabled Dog River descent without succumbing to a two-car shuttle, which, let's face it, is weak. Besides, riding thirty-three miles is better than riding six. With ten miles of paved road and less than 3,000 feet of elevation to gain, this loop straddles the epic fence, but the southbound route up Surveyors Ridge is challenging, and the climb up Bald Butte strenuous. Surveyors Epic serves up a sampling of the best riding in the Hood River Ranger District, with a tough ridgeline singletrack, incredible views of Mount Hood, and, of course, the romping Dog River descent. If you are up for an epic and have never ridden east of Mount Hood, this trail is a great place to start.

Driving Directions

From Portland, drive east on Interstate 84 and take exit 64, just past Hood River. Zero out your odometer at the end of the interstate ramp. Turn right and then immediately right again, following signs for State Highway 35. At

0.3 mile, proceed straight through the intersection, now heading south on Hwy 35. At 14.4 miles, just beyond milepost 85, turn right and park at the Hood River Ranger Station.

The Ride

From the dirt parking area at the ranger station, ride out to the highway and turn left, riding north. Pass the Hood River General Store, then descend to the ride's low point around **3** miles. Climb gently to Pine Mont Drive (FR 17), **3.5** miles, and turn right. The road, still paved but rising more steadily now, winds up the open, north end of Surveyors Ridge, bearing southeast. At **5.4** miles, turn right on a gravel road. Just after a bend, **5.6** miles (ridepoint 2), the road forks. Take the unmarked trail that begins between the two prongs of the fork. This is gut-check time—the route gains 1,600 feet over the next two and one-half miles. The trail is smooth and hard-packed but very steep.

At **6.6** miles, the trail ends at a T—turn right onto the dirt road. Reach another T at **6.9** miles, and again turn right. When the road forks at **7.1** miles, bear left, climbing, then descending, then climbing steeply—perhaps walking—toward the summit of Bald Butte. *WOOF!* Take a break at the top, **8.2** miles, and wait until your hyperventilating becomes run-of-the-mill gasping so you can appreciate the views of Mount Hood. Mount Adams and Mount St. Helens are also visible to the north. From the top, continue south, descending a steep, ragged dirt road covered with loose rock death-cookies. At **9.1** miles, ride under a set of powerlines. As the road bends to the left (ridepoint 3), find the singletrack on the right and take it: Surveyors Ridge Trail 688.

Cross a gravel road at **9.9** miles. When the trail forks at **10.1** miles, stay to the left on Trail 688 toward Clinger Springs. From here, through stands of fir and brushy clearcuts, the trail climbs, its tread embedded with rocks and roots. Cross gravel roads at **11.7** and **12.1** miles. Reach a fork at **12.3** miles and stay to the left. (The right prong leads to an old fire lookout along Rim Rock—a great spot for a break.) The way descends quickly—a rocky, open, west-facing traverse—to a fork at **12.8** miles. Bear right, continuing toward Clinger Springs on Trail 688.

After passing across the top of some cliffs, the trail kisses a road on the left: Bear right. Several trail undulations farther, cross a gravel road, **16.7** miles. At **17.6** miles, the trail ends at a T with a doubletrack—turn right.

Fireweed along Surveyors Ridge Trail

Follow the doubletrack, rocky and steep in spots, around a long bend through lily and lupine, columbine and shooting star, to a creek crossing at **19.8** miles. After crossing the creek, bear right, riding singletrack again through Cooks Meadow. At **20** miles, cross Dog River and immediately reach a fork—go right. From here, the trail is smooth, hard-packed, and fast. At **21.5** miles (ridepoint 4), ride around a white gate. This is the end of Surveyors Ridge Trail. Pedal across the dirt spur that acts as an ad hoc trailhead and head down Dog River Trail 675.

Let the fast descent begin. Reach a fork at **22.4** miles and bear right, continuing down Dog River Trail. Wheee! (though it can be dusty, in which case the exclamation might be uggh!) Traversing north across a steep slope, the trail occasionally skirts the edge of a cliff. **WHOA!** At an unmarked fork, **24** miles, take a sharp, switchbacking left (if you reach a dirt road, you've gone too far). At **24.5** miles, ignore the trail back on the right. After a long switchback to the southeast, cross Dog River and continue north again along the east side of the river. At **27.7** miles, the trail ends at a dirt road—turn left. At **28.1** miles (ridepoint 5), reach the trailhead along Hwy 35. Turn right and pedal down the highway. At **33.2** miles, reach Hood River Ranger Station on the left to complete the loop.

Gazetteer

Nearby camping: Eightmile Crossing (primitive), Sherwood (primitive)
Nearest food, drink, services: Parkdale, Hood River

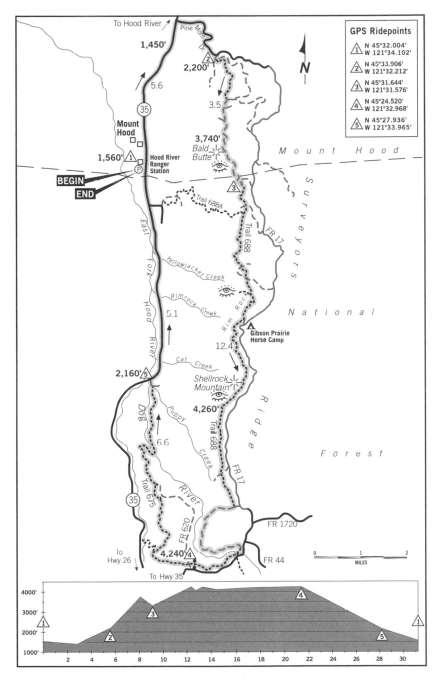

GPS Ridepoints

1. N 45°32.004'
   W 121°34.102'
2. N 45°33.906'
   W 121°32.212'
3. N 45°31.644'
   W 121°31.576'
4. N 45°24.520'
   W 121°32.968'
5. N 45°27.936'
   W 121°33.965'

To Hood River

Pine Mont Dr.

1,450'

2,200'

5.6

3.5

35

Mount Hood

3,740'
Bald
Butte

Mount Hood

1,560'

BEGIN

END

Hood River Ranger Station

Trail 6884

Trail 688

FR 17

Surveyors

East Fork Hood River

Yellowjacket Creek

Rimrock Creek

National

Rim Rock

Gibson Prairie Horse Camp

5.1

12.4

Cat Creek

Shellrock Mountain

2,160'

4,260'

Ridge

Forest

Dog

Puppy

River

6.6

Trail 688

Trail 675

FR 17

FR 620

35

FR 1720

FR 1720

FR 44

To Hwy 26

4,240'

To Hwy 35

0   1   2
        MILES

N

4000'

3000'

2000'

1000'

1

2

3

4

5

1

2   4   6   8   10   12   14   16   18   20   22   24   26   28   30

Distance	6.6-mile one-way shuttle
Route	Bomber singletrack descent
Climbs	More like a freefall; high point: 4,240 ft, loss: 2,085 ft
Duration	Fitness rider and scenery rider: 1 hour
Travel	Hood River—31 miles; Portland—73 miles
Skill	Advanced
Season	Summer, fall
Map	Green Trails: Mount Hood
Rules	National Forest Recreation Pass required at both trailheads
Manager	Mount Hood National Forest, Hood River District, 541-352-6002
Web	www.fs.fed.us/r6/mthood/recreation/trails/hood-river-conditions

Who Will Like This Ride
Dust-breathing, downhill-only, speed seekers.

The Scoop

The thrilling Dog River descent has been described as better than sex. Stop hyperventilating and hold on a minute. While this description is on the right track, it's a wee bit overheated. Advanced riders love the tight switchies and hair-raising, open-it-up traverses. No doubt. But this trail gets hammered in the summer from riders skidding around each switchback and blind corner, and the tread gradually transforms from dirt to dust to a fine powder that's oh-so-good for your bike's moving parts (not to mention your nasal passages). Have at it, just watch out for other trail users.

Driving Directions

From Portland, take US Highway 26 eastbound about 56 miles, past Ski Bowl and Government Camp, to its junction with State Highway 35. Set your odometer to zero, and turn north onto Hwy 35. At 6.2 miles, cross Bennett Pass. At 13.4 miles, pass Forest Road 44 on the right. At 20.9 miles, drop a car off at the Dog River trailhead on the right. Then turn around and drive

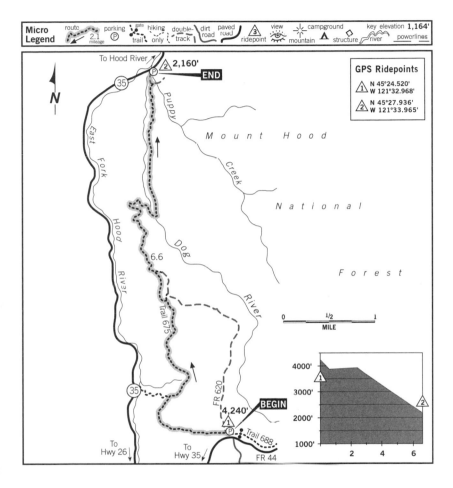

south on Hwy 35, back to FR 44. Turn left onto FR 44, and again set your odometer to zero. At 3.8 miles, turn left onto FR 620 and immediately park.

From Hood River (exit 64 off Interstate 84), set your odometer to zero and drive south on Hwy 35. At 19.5 miles, drop a car off at the Dog River trailhead on the left, then continue south on Hwy 35. At 27 miles, just past milepost 71, turn left onto FR 44. At 30.8 miles, turn left onto FR 620 and immediately park.

The Ride

Facing away from FR 44, you'll find Dog River Trail 675 on the left. Let the fast descent begin. Reach a fork at **0.9** mile and bear right, continuing down Dog River Trail. Wheee! Traversing north along a steep slope, the trail occasionally skirts the edge of a cliff. **WHOA!** At an unmarked fork, **2.5** miles, take a sharp, switchbacking left (if you reach a dirt road, you've gone too far). At **3** miles, ignore the trail back on the right. After a long switchback to the southeast, cross Dog River and continue north again along the east side of the river. At **6.2** miles, the trail ends at a dirt road—turn left. At **6.6** miles (ridepoint 2), reach the trailhead along Hwy 35 to complete the ride.

Gazetteer

Nearby camping: Eightmile Crossing (primitive), Sherwood (primitive)
Nearest food, drink, services: Parkdale, Hood River

Fine-tuning the velocity near Dog River

Distance	10.8-mile out-and-back
Route	Wide, fast singletrack
Climbs	Short but tough; high point: 3,450 ft, gain: 500 ft
Duration	Fitness rider: 1 hour, scenery rider: 2 hours
Travel	Hood River—25 miles; Portland—71 miles
Skill	Intermediate
Season	Summer, fall
Map	Green Trails: Mount Hood
Rules	National Forest Recreation Pass required
Manager	Mount Hood National Forest, Hood River District, 541-352-6002
Web	www.fs.fed.us/r6/mthood/recreation/trails/hood-river-conditions

Who Will Like This Ride

Gung-ho families or riders who have to be back at the car in an hour.

The Scoop

This trail, wide and smooth, travels along the East Fork of Hood River. While it's not listed as a views ride, the trail often runs right next to the river, and it's quite picturesque. East Fork Hood River Trail is a fence sitter between a two- and three-wheel rating. Most of the trail is easy, wide singletrack, however several climbs and a few sandy sections may pose a challenge for less adventurous mountain bikers or families with kids. Just turn around early if you have trouble or aren't inclined to ford Newton Creek, which is near the old Robinhood Campground close to the turn-around point.

Driving Directions

From Portland, take US Highway 26 eastbound about 56 miles, past Ski Bowl and Government Camp, to its junction with State Highway 35. Set your odometer to zero, and turn north onto Hwy 35. At 6.2 miles, cross Bennett Pass. At 15.1 miles, just past milepost 72 and Sherwood Campground, turn left into the gravel parking area and trailhead alongside the highway.

From Hood River (exit 64 off Interstate 84), set your odometer to zero at the end of the interstate ramp and head south on Hwy 35. At 14.4

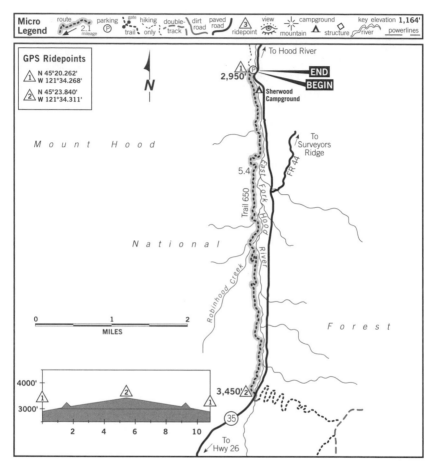

miles, pass the Hood River Ranger Station on the right. At 25.3 miles, after milepost 73, turn right into the gravel parking area and trailhead alongside the highway (just before Sherwood Campground).

The Ride

From the highway, the trail, which isn't well marked, immediately drops down to the river. Just across a narrow bridge, the trail forks—turn left. Heading upriver now, the trail climbs through a dark fir forest. At **1.3** miles, the trail switchbacks up the bank, then drops back to the river again

Racing the river on Trail 650

one-half mile farther. The forest opens up as you proceed upriver. At about **4.7** miles, you'll have to ford Newton Creek. Depending on the flow of the creek and who's riding with you, you may want to turn around here. After a few more ups and downs, the grade of the trail evens out and follows close to the river all the way up to where the Robinhood Campground used to be before being flooded out, **5.4** miles (ridepoint 2). Turn around here and ride back to the trailhead parking, **10.8** miles.

Gazetteer

Nearby camping: Sherwood (primitive)
Nearest food, drink, services: Parkdale, Hood River

Distance	6.3-mile loop
Route	Singletrack; views
Climbs	Moderate; high point: 4,800 ft, gain: 1,000 ft
Duration	Fitness rider: less than 1 hour; scenery rider: 1 to 2 hours
Travel	Hood River—35 miles; Portland—77 miles
Skill	Intermediate
Season	Summer, fall
Map	Green Trails: Flag Point
Rules	National Forest Recreation Pass required
Manager	Mount Hood National Forest, Barlow District, 541-467-2291
Web	www.fs.fed.us/r6/mthood/recreation/trails/barlow-conditions

Who Will Like This Ride

All riders who like it short and good, with a dash of challenge.

The Scoop

This singletrack loop begins with a rolling climb to Fivemile Lookout, then descends a furious set of switchbacks before finishing with a lovely, meandering climb along Eightmile Creek. It's a short ride but a fun one, perfect for the second ride of the day or simply a lazy day. When it's clear, views from the lookout are outstanding. The trail, open only to hikers and mountain bikers, is in good shape, although it can get dusty later in the summer. This is a great route for families, especially if you're camping at Eightmile Crossing. Take the trail up from the campground to the 3.8-mile mark. It's less than one-half mile. Then turn left. Ride the entire loop, or just an out-and-back on Trail 459. Note that the switchbacks down from Fivemile Butte Lookout may be too steep and technical for some.

Trail 459 along Eightmile Creek

Driving Directions

From Portland, take US Highway 26 eastbound about 56 miles, past Ski Bowl and Government Camp, to its junction with State Highway 35. Set your odometer to zero, and turn north onto Hwy 35. At 6.2 miles, cross Bennett Pass. Pass milepost 70, then at 13.4 miles turn right onto Forest Road 44. At 18.9 miles, turn right to stay on FR 44 (to the left is FR 17). At 21.3 miles, turn left on FR 120 and park immediately.

From Hood River (exit 64 off Interstate 84), drive south on Hwy 35. After about 27 miles, just past milepost 71, turn left onto FR 44 and set your odometer to zero. At 5.5 miles, turn right to remain on FR 44 (to the left is FR 17). At 7.9 miles, turn left on FR 120 and park immediately.

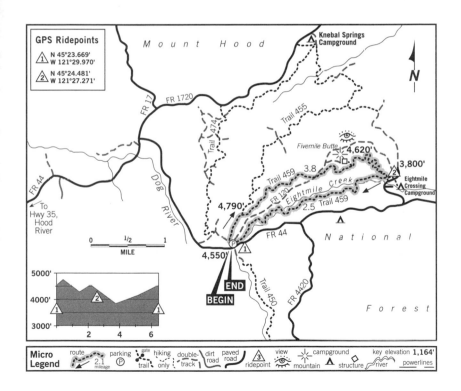

The Ride

On a wide, rough trail, ride away from FR 44 and FR 120, bearing left. After about fifty yards, reach a fork and turn right, following the sign to Trail 459. The trail narrows and climbs. At **0.5** mile, the trail forks again: Go right on Eightmile Loop Trail 459. The trail traverses to a high point and then cruises down the pine- and fir-covered hillside to the saddle between Eightmile Creek and the head-waters of Fivemile Creek where, at **1.5** miles, it crosses a dirt road and begins climbing Fivemile Butte. After a short ascent through fireweed and pines, reach a fork at **2.2** miles. The trail on the left leads to Fivemile Butte Lookout, less than one-quarter mile away; it's a must-do side trip, with views of Mount Hood, Mount Adams, Mount St. Helens, and even Mount Rainier on clear days.

Fivemile Butte Lookout

To continue the loop, bear right at the fork at **2.2** miles. After a short sputter, the trail switchbacks steeply down the dusty east edge of the butte. It's a fun descent. At **3.8** miles (ridepoint 2), arrive at a four-way and turn right. From here, the trail winds gently upstream along Eightmile Creek, which gurgles among grand fir, spruce, Canadian dogwood, and fern. At **6.3** miles, reach FR 120 to complete the loop.

Gazetteer

Nearby camping: Eightmile Crossing (primitive)
Nearest food, drink, services: Parkdale, Hood River

Distance	9.2-mile loop
Route	Singletrack with paved road section
Climbs	Difficult; high point: 5,000 ft, gain: 1,340 ft
Duration	Fitness rider: 1 to 2 hours; scenery rider: 2 to 3 hours
Travel	Hood River—35 miles; Portland—77 miles
Skill	Advanced
Season	Summer, fall
Map	Green Trails: Flag Point
Rules	National Forest Recreation Pass required
Manager	Mount Hood National Forest, Barlow District, 541-467-2291
Web	www.fs.fed.us/r6/mthood/recreation/trails/barlow-conditions

Who Will Like This Ride
You love varied terrain, zippy trails, and a modicum of adventure, but you don't need to ride all day.

The Scoop
I like this loop a lot. Take is as it is, or combine it with Fivemile Butte (ride 7) for a great 15.5-mile ride. Not much for views (unless you take the short spur out to Perry Point for an expansive look out into the rolling, hazy brown void of eastern Oregon), this loop provides a tour of sorts though fir and pine forests, clearcuts, thickets of manzanita, and high meadows on a variety of trails from fast slalom to loose technical to pine-needle grinder. Stretches of the trail become quite dusty as summer progresses, and the

No pain on Trail 459

fine powder functions as an attractive eyeliner on riders who follow too close. Horses add to the dusty conditions—with more than just churned-up dirt. At a rest stop on this ride, my riding partner's pack tipped off his handlebars and made a direct hit in a pile of horse pucky. Score one for the trail gremlins.

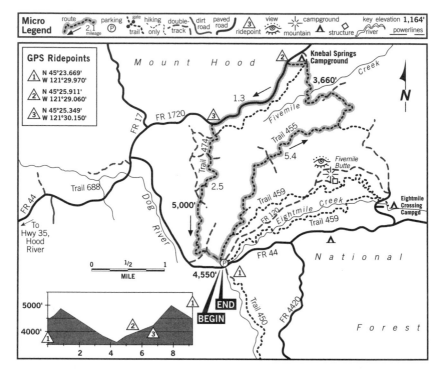

route parking gate hiking double- dirt paved view campground key elevation **1,164'**
2.1 mileage ℗ trail only track road road ridepoint mountain structure river powerlines

GPS Ridepoints

⚠ N 45°23.669'
   W 121°29.970'

⚠ N 45°25.911'
   W 121°29.060'

⚠ N 45°25.349'
   W 121°30.150'

M o u n t   H o o d

Knebal Springs Campground

3,660'

Creek

Fivemile

1.3

FR 1720

FR 17

Trail 4741

Trail 455

5.4

Fivemile Butte

N

Trail 688

FR 44

Dog River

5,000'

2.5

Trail 459

FR 120

Eightmile Creek

Trail 459

Eightmile Crossing Campgd

To Hwy 35, Hood River

0   1/2   1
MILE

4,550'

FR 44

N a t i o n a l

END
BEGIN

Trail 450

FR 4420

F o r e s t

5000'

4000'

2   4   6   8

Driving Directions

From Portland, take US Highway 26 eastbound about 56 miles, past Ski Bowl and Government Camp, to its junction with State Highway 35. Set your odometer to zero, and turn north onto Hwy 35. At 6.2 miles, cross Bennett Pass. At 13.4 miles, after passing milepost 70, turn right onto Forest Road 44. At 18.9 miles, turn right to stay on FR 44 (to the left is FR 17). At 20.9 miles, ignore a dirt road and the Knebal Springs Trail sign on the left. At 21.3 miles, turn left on FR 120 and park immediately.

From Hood River (exit 64 off Interstate 84), drive south on Hwy 35. After about 27 miles, just past milepost 71, turn left onto FR 44, and set your odometer to zero. At 5.5 miles, turn right to remain on FR 44 (to the left is FR 17). At 7.5 miles, ignore a dirt road and the Knebal Springs Trail sign on the left. At 7.9 miles, turn left on FR 120 and park immediately.

....

The Ride

On a wide, rough trail, ride away from FR 44 and FR 120, bearing left. After about fifty yards, reach a fork and turn right, following the sign to Trail 455. The trail narrows and climbs. At **0.5** mile, the trail forks—bear left on Bottle Prairie Trail 455. Continue ascending to a fork at **0.8** mile—bear left again (one-quarter mile to the right you'll find Perry Point). From here, whiz down a twisting, frolicking, dusty descent. Cross a dirt road at **2.5** miles. Reach a fork in the trail at **3.5** miles, and bear left on Knebal Springs Trail 474.

At **3.8** miles, reach a dirt road and turn left. After a few pedal rotations, regain the trail on the right. From here, the trail becomes rocky and loose as it descends to cross Middle Fork Fivemile Creek. Beyond the creek, the trail, still dusty, climbs up through a corridor of manzanita.

Some riders will likely hike-a-bike this stretch. As the hillside levels, bear left to remain on the trail. Reach Knebal Springs Campground at **5** miles. (Note: A relatively new, though steep, trail connects the campground to Trail 474 near the **7**-mile mark of this ride, and it avoids the paved-road section ahead.) Ride along the campground road, staying to the left. At **5.1** miles, take the singletrack on the left. When the trail ends at a paved road, **5.4** miles (ridepoint 2), turn left on the road and continue climbing.

At **6.7** miles (ridepoint 3), find Knebal Springs Trail 474 on the left. Take the trail, pushing your bike to begin. The trail crosses a dirt road on a jog to the right, climbs relentlessly, then crosses another dirt road on a jog to the left, **7.2** miles. **WOOF!** At **7.6** miles, reach a T at a dirt road and turn right. At **7.7** miles, bear left to return to the singletrack. Cross another dirt road, then noodle across a high meadow. At **8.4** miles, back into the woods now, begin a fast descent. Cross a dirt road at **8.9** miles. Pass by a trail on the left, and reach the trailhead at **9.2** miles to complete the ride.

Gazetteer

Nearby camping: Eightmile Crossing (primitive), Pebble Ford (primitive)
Nearest food, drink, services: Parkdale, Hood River

Distance	16.1-mile loop
Route	Singletrack with some gravel and paved roads; views
Climbs	Tough; high point: 6,000 ft, gain: 1,780 ft
Duration	Fitness rider: 2 to 3 hours; scenery rider: 3 to 5 hours
Travel	Hood River—31 miles; Portland—73 miles
Skill	Advanced
Season	Summer, fall
Map	Green Trails: Mount Hood, Flag Point
Rules	National Forest Recreation Pass required
Manager	Mount Hood National Forest, Barlow District, 541-467-2291
Web	www.fs.fed.us/r6/mthood/recreation/trails/barlow-conditions

Who Will Like This Ride
Dedicated cross-country riders and people who crave views.

The Scoop

The singletrack climbs and descents are challenging, though not murderous, and the views of Mount Hood from High Prairie are hard to beat. The ride begins with a short stretch of singletrack followed by several miles of paved forest road. After the warm-up, a demanding trail climbs most of the way to High Prairie. A road-to-trail conversion links High Prairie with Cooks Meadow Trail, a raucous descent.

Driving Directions

From Portland, take US Highway 26 eastbound about 56 miles, past Ski Bowl and Government Camp, to its junction with State Highway 35. Set your odometer to zero, and turn north onto Hwy 35. At 6.2 miles, cross Bennett Pass. At 13.4 miles, after passing milepost 70, turn right onto Forest Road 44. At 17.2 miles, turn left onto FR 620 and immediately park.

From Hood River (exit 64 off Interstate 84), drive south on Hwy 35. After about 27 miles, just after passing milepost 71, turn left onto FR 44 and set your odometer to zero. At 3.8 miles, turn left onto FR 620 and immediately park.

The Ride

Facing away from FR 44, take the trail on the right, Surveyors Ridge Trail 688. The smooth, hard-packed trail roller-coasters, rising slightly. At **1.4** miles (ridepoint 2), reach a fork and turn right on Cooks Meadow Trail 639. Almost immediately, the trail hits FR 44: Turn left on this paved road and begin climbing. At **1.7** miles, bear right to remain on FR 44. At **4.1** miles (ridepoint 3), reach FR 120 on the left and an unmarked doubletrack on the right. Turn right and ride south on the doubletrack, gently climbing along Eightmile Creek. The way quickly narrows to singletrack. At **5.4** miles, the trail levels somewhat and meanders through a forest of grand fir, lodgepole pine, and larch. Ignore an unmaintained trail on the left at **5.9** miles, and continue toward Upper Eightmile Meadow on Trail 450. From here, the trail noodles through a thick stand of fir, finally emerging into Eightmile Meadow at a fork, **6.8** miles. Take the right fork.

From Eightmile Meadow, the trail ascends at a hectic rate, crossing dirt roads at **7** and **7.2** miles. **WOOF!** The worst of the climbing is over at **8** miles. Reach FR 4420, which has been converted to a wide trail, at **8.1** miles and

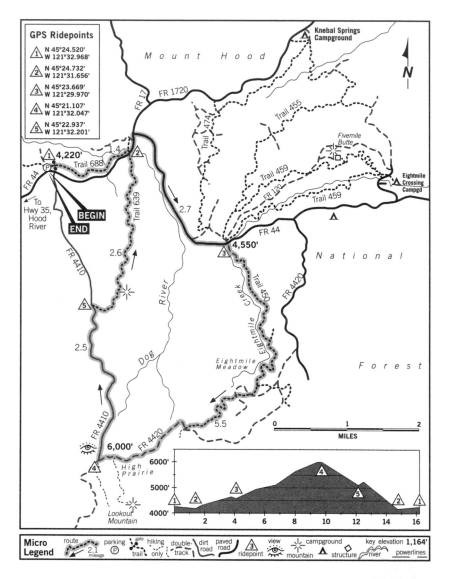

GPS Ridepoints

⚠1 N 45°24.520'
W 121°32.968'

⚠2 N 45°24.732'
W 121°31.656'

⚠3 N 45°23.669'
W 121°29.970'

⚠4 N 45°21.107'
W 121°32.047'

⚠5 N 45°22.937'
W 121°32.201'

M o u n t   H o o d

Knebal Springs
Campground

FR 1720

FR 17

Trail 455

Trail 474

Fivemile
Butte

Trail 459

FR 120

Trail 459

Eightmile
Crossing
Campgd

1 4,220'

.4

2

Trail 688

FR 44

FR 4410

To
Hwy 35,
Hood
River

Trail 639

2.7

BEGIN
END

N a t i o n a l

FR 44

3 4,550'

Trail 450

FR 4420

Dog

River

2.6

2.5

5

Eightmile Creek

Eightmile
Meadow

F o r e s t

FR 4410

FR 4420

6,000'

4

High
Prairie

5.5

Lookout
Mountain

0   1   2
MILES

6000'
5000'
4000'

1 2   3   4   5   2 1

2   4   6   8   10   12   14   16

**Micro
Legend**

route
2.1
mileage

parking
Ⓟ

gate
trail

hiking
only

double-
track

dirt
road

paved
road

3
ridepoint

view

campground

mountain

structure

river

key elevation **1,164'**

powerlines

turn right (the trail across the road enters Badger Creek Wilderness). The climb continues up the wide trail, but at an easier grade. At **8.9** miles, the trail, which designates the border of the wilderness area, levels out and cuts through High

Prairie, a lovely, wildflowered meadow just north of Lookout Mountain. The trail, alas, reverts to dirt road. Reach a fork in the road at **9.6** miles (ridepoint 4) and turn right on FR 4410. Before bombing down the road, check out the four-volcano view from this intersection.

Trail 450 giving it up

FR 4410, gravelly and at times washboarded, winds down the top of the ridge that connects Gunsight Ridge to the south with Surveyors Ridge to the north. Watch out for vehicles on the road during this fast descent. **WHOA!** At **12.1** miles (ridepoint 5), turn right onto Cooks Meadow Trail 639, which is unmarked, and immediately begin climbing again. Through a light fir forest accented by small meadows, the trail soon bends left and rounds the west side of the hill, **12.6** miles. From here, the trail, twisted and root-strewn, hardscrabble in spots, launches furiously down the hillside toward Cooks Meadow. Cross a dirt road at **13.7** miles and continue the fast, sometimes technical descent. The trail crosses FR 44 at **14.7** miles (ridepoint 2). Immediately after crossing the paved road, the trail forks—turn left onto Trail 688. Ride the fast hard-pack to the trailhead at **16.1** miles to compass the route.

Gazetteer

Nearby camping: Eightmile Crossing (primitive), Pebble Ford (primitive)
Nearest food, drink, services: Parkdale, Hood River

Distance	10.9-mile lollipop (17.9-mile option)
Route	All singletrack, baby
Climbs	Nasty; high point: 4,600 ft, gain: 1,800 ft
Duration	Fitness rider: Less than 2 hours; scenery rider: 2 to 4 hours
Travel	Hood River—39 miles; Portland—82 miles
Skill	Advanced
Season	Summer, fall
Map	Green Trails: Flag Point
Rules	None
Manager	Mount Hood National Forest, Barlow District, 541-467-2291
Web	www.fs.fed.us/r6/mthood/recreation/trails/barlow-conditions

Who Will Like This Ride
Descent junkies who appreciate trippy rock escarpments.

The Scoop
Short for a four-wheel ride, this loop makes up for it with a half-mile hair-ball drop and a grueling singletrack climb. The descent here is one of the best, though if you have more time and like your descents, you really should be riding the extended version (ride 11). First through a mixed fir forest, then—lower on the ridge between Cedar and Fifteenmile Creeks—through ponderosa pine meadows punctuated with goblinlike rock formations, the spirited trail drops and weaves and drops some more. It's fun, exciting, and fast. The final drop, rocky and loose, may be a walk for less skilled riders. As for direction of travel, counterclockwise (as described here) is potentially ridable the entire loop for very strong riders, whereas riding clockwise forces a three-quarter-mile hike but is an easier ride for the rest of the loop. Either way, this is one of those gee-whiz descents that you'll dream about in dark January.

Driving Directions
From Portland, take US Highway 26 eastbound about 56 miles, past Ski Bowl and Government Camp, to its junction with State Highway 35. Turn

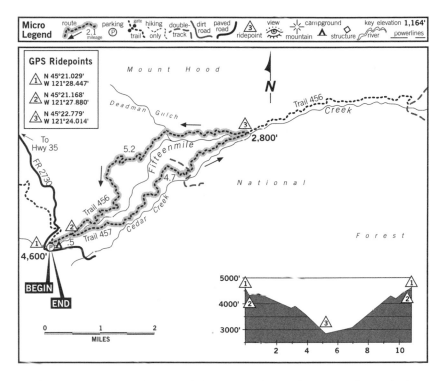

north onto Hwy 35, and proceed about 13 miles to Forest Road 44, which is past milepost 70. Turn right onto FR 44, and zero out your odometer. At 5.5 miles, bear right to remain on FR 44. At 8.9 miles, turn right onto FR 4420. Stay on the paved road. At 11.2 miles, stay left onto FR 2730. At 13.2 miles, reach Fifteenmile Creek Campground. Don't park in a camp spot. Find a place on the road or in the small day-use parking area.

From Hood River (exit 64 off Interstate 84), drive south on Hwy 35. After about 27 miles, just after passing milepost 71, turn left onto FR 44 and set your odometer to zero. At 5.5 miles, bear right to remain on FR 44. At 8.9 miles, turn right onto FR 4420. Stay on the paved road. At 11.2 miles, stay left to FR 2730. At 13.2 miles, reach Fifteenmile Creek Campground. Don't park in a camp spot. Find a place on the road or in the small day-use parking area.

The Ride

The trail exits the small campground next to the toilet. Bear right at the immediate fork and descend Fifteenmile Trail 456. When the trail forks at **0.5** mile (ridepoint 2), take a sharp right, drop to the creek, and cross the bridge on Cedar Creek Trail 457. After a short climb away from the creek, follow the bouncing singletrack, tricky in spots, as it descends and corkscrews (with a couple short middle-ring climbs) from a mixed stand of fir and pine down through an open forest of scattered ponderosa pine, winding across dry, yellow-meadowed knolls and past variously shaped rock hoodoos.

At **3.7** miles, the trail crosses a doubletrack and continues down. From the **4.5**-mile point, the trail is gnarled—loose, rocky, and very steep. At **5.2** miles (ridepoint 3), reach the ride's low point when you cross Fifteenmile Creek. Immediately reach a T and turn left (for a longer ride, see "Option" below). The trail is good and gradually climbs. After **7** miles, though, the trail seems to head straight up, gaining huge chunks of elevation. It's a probable hike-a-bike. *WOOF!* By **9.6** miles, the torture is largely over, as the trail winds across an open, rocky hillside. Reach a fork in the trail at **10.4** miles (ridepoint 2) and stay to the right. At **10.9** miles, arrive back at the campground and trail-head to complete the ride.

Option

At the T at **5.2** miles, turn right and ride **3.5** miles, gradually descending, to the end of Trail 456. Turn around and ride back. This 7-mile addition creates the rare upside-down lollipop ride format. Reason to take this spur: It extends the descent and drops into a completely new ecosystem, one of pure oak. Reason not to take it: It doesn't go anywhere, and it just ensures that you definitely will bonk on the climb back out.

Paying your Fifteenmile Creek dues

Gazetteer

Nearby camping: Fifteenmile Creek (primitive), Pebble Ford (primitive)
Nearest food, drink, services: Parkdale, Hood River

11 EIGHTMILE TO FIFTEENMILE

Distance	27.5-mile amoeba
Route	Awesome singletrack descent, some dirt road
Climbs	Nasty and tough; high point: 5,720 ft, gain: 2,920 ft
Duration	Fitness rider: 3 to 5 hours; scenery rider: 5 to 8 hours
Travel	Hood River—37 miles; Portland—80 miles
Skill	Advanced
Season	Summer, fall
Map	Green Trails: Flag Point, Mount Hood
Rules	National Forest Recreation Pass required
Manager	Mount Hood National Forest, Barlow District, 541-467-2291
Web	www.fs.fed.us/r6/mthood/recreation/trails/barlow-conditions

Who Will Like This Ride
You like to work for your descents, and be richly rewarded.

The Scoop

At 27 miles, this loop doesn't quite achieve epic 5-wheel status. But be afraid, be very afraid. The ride's three long, tough climbs add up, and you'll have wished you'd done a few more training rides before the day is over. The reward, however, is a couple of the best descents in the book—packaged together in one ride. They'll put a smile on even the most over-tired, curmudgeonly rider. For reference, this route includes parts of High Prairie (ride 9), Fivemile Butte (ride 7), and the entire length of Fifteenmile Creek (ride 10).

Driving Directions

From Portland, take US Highway 26 eastbound about 56 miles, past Ski Bowl and Government Camp, to its junction with State Highway 35. Turn north onto Hwy 35, and proceed about 13 miles to Forest Road 44, which is past milepost 70. Turn right onto FR 44, and zero out your odometer. At 5.5 miles, bear right to remain on FR 44. At 8.9 miles, pass FR 4420 on your right. At 10.4 miles, turn left on FR 4430, toward Eightmile Crossing Campground. At 10.7 miles, turn right into the campground. Park in the day-use area.

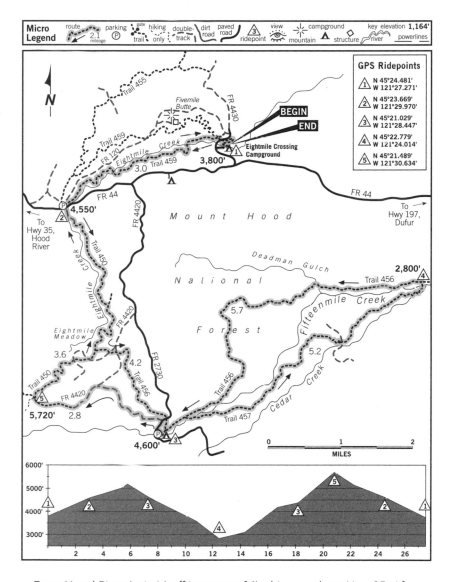

Micro Legend
route 2.1 mileage | parking (P) | gate, hiking trail only | double-track | dirt road | paved road | (3) ridepoint | view, mountain | campground | structure | key elevation **1,164'**, river, powerlines

GPS Ridepoints

1. N 45°24.481'
   W 121°27.271'
2. N 45°23.669'
   W 121°29.970'
3. N 45°21.029'
   W 121°28.447'
4. N 45°22.779'
   W 121°24.014'
5. N 45°21.489'
   W 121°30.634'

From Hood River (exit 64 off Interstate 84), drive south on Hwy 35. After about 27 miles, just after passing milepost 71, turn left onto FR 44 and set your odometer to zero. At 5.5 miles, bear right to remain on FR 44. At

Trail 450 kisses Eightmile Creek

8.9 miles, pass FR 4420 on your right. At 10.4 miles, turn left on FR 4430, toward Eightmile Crossing Campground. At 10.7 miles, turn right into the campground. Park in the day-use area.

The Ride

Find the trail on the north side of the campground. It switchbacks up the hillside to a dirt road, FR 4430. (If you can't find this trail, ride out to FR 4430, turn right, and ride up the hill.) The trail from the campground crosses FR 4430. Just after crossing the road, **0.5** mile, reach a four-way and turn left onto Trail 459. From here, you'll climb gently through the shade along Eightmile Creek. At **3.0** miles (ridepoint 2), reach FR 120. Turn left and immediately reach FR 44. Cross over the paved road to a doubletrack on the opposite side. The doubletrack soon narrows to singletrack, Trail 450. Though heading south now, you're still ascending Eightmile Creek. Pay attention to the bermed corners, you'll be descending this trail later in the day.

At **4.8** miles, ignore a lesser trail on the left. After noodling through a thick stand of fir, reach a fork at Eightmile Meadow, **5.7** miles, and turn left. The trail crosses a dirt road right at a fork—keep going until you find the trail on the opposite side. From here, the trail, rough in places, climbs to a high point, then rips down a hillside. At **6.9** miles, cross a paved road (FR 2730). At **7.2** miles (ridepoint 3), reach a T at Fifteenmile Campground and turn left.

The trail follows Fifteenmile Creek on Trail 456. When the trail forks at **7.7** miles, take a sharp right on Cedar Creek Trail 457, and drop down to cross a bridge. After a short climb away from the creek, follow the bouncing singletrack, tricky in spots, as it descends and corkscrews (with a couple short middle-ring climbs) from a mixed stand of fir and pine down through an open forest of scattered ponderosa pine.

At **10.9** miles, the trail crosses a doubletrack and continues down. From the **11.7**-mile point, the trail is gnarled—loose, rocky, and very steep. At **12.4** miles (ridepoint 4), reach the ride's low point when you cross Fifteenmile Creek. Immediately reach a T and turn left. After about **14** miles, the trail seems to head straight up, gaining huge chunks of elevation. It's a probable hike-a-bike. *WOOF!* By **16.8** miles, the suffering is largely over, as the trail winds across an open, rocky hillside. Reach a fork in the trail at **17.6** miles and stay to the right. At **18.1** miles (ridepoint 3), arrive back at Fifteenmile Campground.

From the campground, pedal up to the paved road and turn right. After a short ascent, turn left onto an unmarked and not-so-maintained dirt road. The road heads west, climbing, and it's kind of a grunt. At **19.5** miles, reach a T at another dirt road (FR 4420) and turn left. The ascent continues. At **20.1** miles, the dirt road ends in a berm. From here, FR 4420 has been converted to trail. Continue on. At **20.9** miles (ridepoint 5), find Trail 450 on the right. Take it, but not before putting on an extra layer.

The descent down Trail 450 is all joy and no pain. There's no need for six inches of travel or body armor, but it's fast and fun. Cross a couple of dirt roads. At **22.3** miles, reach a fork and bear left, continuing down Trail 450. At **24.5** miles (ridepoint 2), after an optional rock drop, you'll pop out at FR 44. Cross the road and find Trail 459 immediately on the right. The smiles and tears continue as you hurtle down the smooth trail. At **27** miles, reach a four-way and turn right. Immediately cross a dirt road. From here, the trail switchbacks down to Eightmile Crossing Campground to complete the trip, **27.5** miles.

Gazetteer

Nearby camping: Fifteenmile Creek (primitive), Pebble Ford (primitive)
Nearest food, drink, services: Parkdale, Hood River

12 UMBRELLA FALLS

Distance	4.4-mile loop
Route	Mountain singletrack, technical at times
Climbs	Some steep pitches; high point: 5,280 ft, gain: 820 ft
Duration	Fitness rider: 30 minutes; scenery rider: 1 to 2 hours
Travel	Hood River—33 miles; Portland—64 miles
Skill	Intermediate
Season	Summer, fall
Map	Green Trails: Mount Hood
Rules	Forest Service Recreation Pass required
Manager	Mount Hood National Forest, Hood River District, 541-352-6002
Web	www.fs.fed.us/r6/mthood/recreation/trails/hood-river-conditions

Who Will Like This Ride

Cross-country riders who don't have much time, don't have a shuttle, and happen to be at Mount Hood Meadows.

The Scoop

Umbrella Falls, wide and rippling, highlights this short loop. Besides the falls and the beautiful high-mountain singletrack, there aren't a lot of other reasons to go. The entire ride takes less than two hours, and that's if you take a leisurely picnic at the falls. Sections of the loop are quite steep, so it's not a great ride for families. And if you're in any sort of good condition, it's probably too short. (Perhaps a double feature on a long July day?) On the other hand, if you're not in good shape, it may be steeper than you want, and still too short. Despite the awkward combo of short distance and steep terrain, it is a lovely mountain trail; well, except for the chairlifts. And in summer, when you can ride, the trail is heavily traversed by hikers. So ride with caution, especially on weekends.

Driving Directions

From Portland, take US Highway 26 eastbound about 56 miles, past Ski Bowl and Government Camp, to its junction with State Highway 35. Set your odometer to zero, and turn north onto Hwy 35. At 6.2 miles, cross

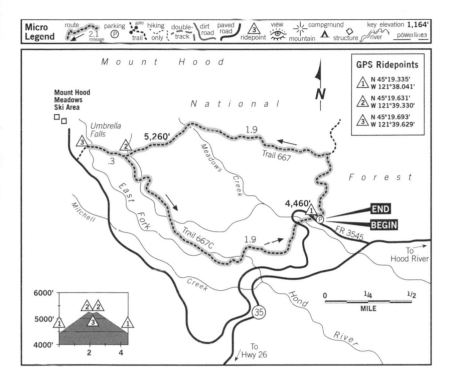

Micro Legend: route, 2.1 mileage, parking ℗, gate, hiking trail, double-track, dirt road, paved road, ridepoint ③, view, mountain, campground, structure, river, power lines, key elevation 1,164'

GPS Ridepoints
- △1 N 45°19.335' W 121°38.041'
- △2 N 45°19.631' W 121°39.330'
- △3 N 45°19.693' W 121°39.629'

Bennett Pass. At 7.5 miles, between milepost 66 and 65, turn left on Forest Road 3545, following signs for Mount Hood Meadows and Sahalie Falls Loop. At 7.9 miles, park at the trailhead on the right.

From Hood River (exit 64 off Interstate 84), drive south on Hwy 35. After about 33 miles, immediately past milepost 65, turn right on FR 3545, following signs to Mount Hood Meadows and Sahalie Falls Loop. Set your odometer to zero. At 0.3 mile, park at the trailhead on the right.

The Ride

Take the trail that exits from the right side of the road. At **0.3** mile, ignore a faint trail back on the left. Reach a fork at **0.4** mile and turn left on Umbrella Falls Trail 667. The trail begins a steady ascent with a few switchbacks. After crossing a ski run, **0.9** mile, the way becomes quite steep. Hit a doubletrack at **1.1** miles, bear left, and continue up. Cross under a ski lift, **1.4** miles, and continue the thigh-burning climb, past the ski area boundary,

Umbrella Falls

to a crest at **1.7** miles. At **1.9** miles (ridepoint 2), reach a fork and stay to the right, continuing on Umbrella Falls Trail.

At **2.2** miles (ridepoint 3), reach a bridge at Umbrella Falls. (For a great view of Mount Hood, continue down the trail to a paved road, turn right, and ride a short distance up to the ski area parking lot.) For this loop, turn around at Umbrella Falls and ride back to the previous fork. Turn right on Sahalie Falls Trail 667C at **2.5** miles (ridepoint 2). The trail, smooth and hard-packed, with enough roots and narrow alleys to keep it interesting, descends now before zipping precariously along the top of a ravine. At **4.2** miles, the trail dumps out onto a paved road. Turn left on the road, ride for a short distance, then turn right at the intersection to return to the trailhead, **4.4** miles.

Gazetteer

Nearby camping: Sherwood (primitive)
Nearest food, drink, services: Government Camp

13 GUNSIGHT RIDGE

Distance	Distance 16.5-mile loop
Route	Tough ridgeline singletrack, paved and dirt roads; views
Climbs	Steady then very hard; high point: 5,920 ft, gain: 2,320 ft
Duration	Fitness rider: 2 hours; scenery rider: 3 to 5 hours
Travel	Hood River—30 miles; Portland—67 miles
Skill	Advanced
Season	Summer, fall
Map	Green Trails: Mount Hood
Rules	Forest Service Recreation Pass required
Manager	Mount Hood National Forest, Hood River District, 541-352-6002
Web	www.fs.fed.us/r6/mthood/recreation/trails/hood-river-conditions

Who Will Like This Ride

Strong cross country riders who crave subalpine zones and want to ride the snappiest switchback descent east of Mount Hood.

The Scoop

During some summers, stubborn snow patches tucked in Gunsight Ridge's coves and swales refuse to melt until August. Be prepared. But in the six weeks or so after melt-out, the ridge lights up in a riot of wildflowers that swirl around the sparse noble fir and mountain hemlock forest. The views of Mount Hood are epic, as is the trail: a typical ridge trail that rises and drops with steep, jagged unpredictability. Much like its better known but lesser cousin to the north, Surveyors Ridge, making a loop using Gunsight Ridge can be problematic, thus the unfortunate stretch of riding along State Highway 35. Just remember, the loop described here offers an awesome ridge trail, an interesting dirt-road climb, and the descent from Gumjuwac Saddle—a freaking switchie clinic; so grin and bear the first four and a half paved miles. If you have a shuttle and more time—the East Mount Hood Epic (ride 14) is your best bet in the area.

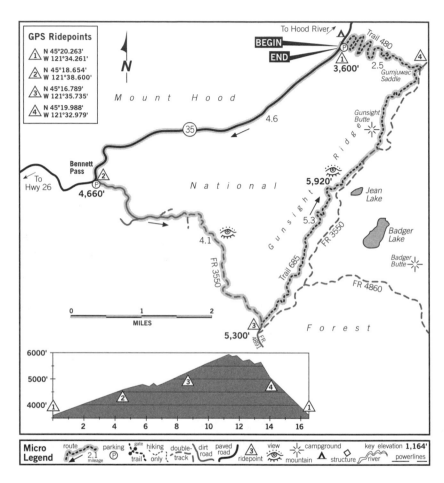

GPS Ridepoints

1. N 45°20.263'
   W 121°34.261'
2. N 45°18.654'
   W 121°38.600'
3. N 45°16.789'
   W 121°35.735'
4. N 45°19.988'
   W 121°32.979'

To Hood River
BEGIN
END
3,600'
2.5
Gumjuwac Saddle

Trail 480

Mount Hood

35

4.6

Gunsight Butte

Gunsight Ridge

5,920'

Jean Lake

5.3

Badger Lake

Bennett Pass

To Hwy 26

4,660'

National

Forest

4.1

FR 3550

Trail 685

FR 3550

Badger Butte

FR 4860

0   1   2
MILES

3
5,300'

FR 4881

Micro Legend — route 2.1 mileage · parking (P) · gate/hiking trail · hiking only · double-track · dirt road · paved road · 3 ridepoint · view · mountain · campground · structure · river · key elevation 1,164' · powerlines

Driving Directions

From Portland, take US Highway 26 eastbound about 56 miles, past Ski Bowl and Government Camp, to its junction with Hwy 35. Set your odometer to zero, and turn north onto Hwy 35. At 6.2 miles, cross Bennett Pass. At 10.8 miles, park at Gumjuwac trailhead on the right, across the highway from the old Robinhood Campground location.

From Hood River (exit 64 off Interstate 84), drive south on Hwy 35. After about 27 miles, pass FR 44 on the left and set your odometer to zero. At 2.6

miles, park on the left at Gumjuwac trailhead, across the highway from the old Robinhood Campground location.

The Ride

From the trailhead, ride south on Hwy 35, climbing. At **4.6** miles (ridepoint 2), immediately before reaching Bennett Pass, exit to the right, following signs for Bennett Pass SnoPark. Turn left to cross over the highway, then pedal through the parking area and up Bennett Pass Road (FR 3550), which becomes dirt just after the parking area. From here, the climbing continues, with a few short descents thrown in for good measure. When the road forks at **5.7** miles, bear left. At **5.9** miles, the road divides again—bear right and

Grunting toward the top of Gunsight Ridge

continue up. (Note: Some maps show Trail 684 paralleling the road from this point on, but Trail 684 has not been maintained in years and doesn't exist. Unlike me, don't spend any time searching for it.) Rougher, steeper, and narrower now, the road forks at **6.4** miles—go left, continuing up the ridgeline. The narrow ridge affords excellent views of Mount Hood and East Fork Hood River Valley. Pass around the dramatic rocky crown of the ridge, descend for a short distance, then climb again.

At **8.7** miles (ridepoint 3), just before the road reaches a T, turn left on Gunsight Ridge Trail 685. The trail, rocky and technical at times, follows the

Switchie practice on Gumjuwac Trail 480

ridgeline up, paralleling FR 3550, which runs just to the east of the ridge. **WOOF!** Crest a high point, then at **11.4** miles pass a rocky viewpoint on the left. At **11.7** miles, the trail kisses the road, then climbs to another high point before noodling across a small subalpine meadow. Views: Mount Hood to the west, Mount Jefferson to the east. At **12.1** miles, when the trail drops to FR 3550, bear left and ride along the road. The singletrack begins again on the left at **12.3** miles.

From here, the trail climbs around the east side of Gunsight Butte, another high point, before bombing down the blade of the ridge to Gumjuwac Saddle, **14** miles (ridepoint 4). At the saddle, the route kisses FR 3550. Find Gumjuwac Trail 480 on the left. The trail gains some serious momentum here, dropping more than 1,600 feet in just over two miles. After the **14.5**-mile mark, the switchies come fast and furious. **WHOA!** Watch for hikers, who use this trail to access Badger Creek Wilderness. At **16.4** miles, the trail ends at a dirt road—turn right. At **16.5** miles, reach Hwy 35 and the trailhead parking area to complete the loop.

Gazetteer

Nearby camping: Sherwood (primitive)
Nearest food, drink, services: Government Camp, Hood River

Distance	31.6-mile one-way shuttle
Route	From dirt roads to rigorous ridge trails, it's all here; views
Climbs	More than you think; high point: 6,000 ft, loss: 4,000 ft
Duration	Fitness rider: 4 to 6 hours; scenery rider: 6 to 9 hours
Travel	Hood River—34 miles; Portland—98 miles
Skill	Advanced
Season	Late summer, fall
Map	Green Trails: Mount Hood, Hood River
Rules	None
Manager	Mount Hood National Forest, Hood River District, 541-352-6002
Web	www.fs.fed.us/r6/mthood/recreation/trails/hood-river-conditions

Who Will Like This Ride
The more trails you can pack into a day, the better.

The Scoop

Don't let the mammoth elevation loss fool you—the cumulative gain on this ride logs in at more than 5,000 feet. The East Mount Hood Epic begins with a 1,500-foot dirt-road and singletrack climb, and tosses in another 1,000-foot climb after ten miles. Most of the rest of the ride consists of the jagged ups and downs of difficult ridge-trail riding. Is this the top? Not yet. After thirty-one miles, you'll find yourself walking up a minefield of death-cookies toward the top of Bald Butte. Who signed me up for this? But this ridgeline trail, my favorite east of Mount Hood, affords almost continuous views of the mountain, and the high meadows and wildflowers will dazzle you. Just get in shape and bring plenty of food and water. In case of the unexpected bonk, four bailout points are noted in the ride description. The bailouts don't significantly reduce the mileage, but they do offer easier road routes back to the car. Perhaps the most enticing bailout comes at 26.4 miles, though it's actually more of a reroute. Check out the map for this: Start the ride by parking your first vehicle at the ranger station rather than the spot along Pine Mont Drive. When you reach the fork at 26.4 miles, turn left on Oak Ridge Trail 688A. From there, drop down to Highway 35, and pedal north to the ranger station to complete the ride. It's a nice alternative and avoids the pain of Bald Butte.

Driving Directions

From Portland, drive east on Interstate 84 and take exit 64, just past Hood River. Zero out your odometer at the end of the interstate ramp. Turn right and then immediately right again, following signs for State Highway 35. Proceed straight through the intersection at 0.3 mile, now heading south on Hwy 35. At 10.9 miles, turn left on Pine Mont Drive (Forest Road 17). At 12.3 miles, drop off a car at the gravel pullout on the right. With all the bikes in one car, return to Hwy 35, turn left, reset your odometer to zero, and continue south. At 23.3 miles, immediately after milepost 64 and just before the top of Bennett Pass, take the exit on the right, following signs to Bennett Pass Sno-Park. Turn left to cross over the highway, then park in the paved Sno-Park lot east of the highway.

The Ride

From Bennett Pass, ride up FR 3550, climbing moderately but with a few short descents. When the road forks at **1.1** miles, bear left. At **1.3** miles, the road divides again—bear right and continue up. (Note: Maps show Trail 684 paralleling the road from this point on, but Trail 684 has not been maintained in years and doesn't exist. Don't spend any time searching for it.) Rougher, steeper, and narrower now, the road forks at **1.8** miles—go left, continuing directly up the ridgeline. On a clear day, Mount Hood is so close it seems you can reach out and grab a handful of snow off Newton Clark Glacier. Pass around the dramatic rocky crown of the ridge, descend for a short distance, then climb again.

At **4.1** miles (ridepoint 2), just before the road reaches a T, turn left on Gunsight Ridge Trail 685. The trail, rocky, technical, and steep at times, follows the ridgeline. *WOOF!* Crest a high point, then at **6.8** miles pass a rocky viewpoint on the left. At **7.1** miles, the trail kisses the road. From here, climb to another high point and noodle across a small subalpine meadow, where you'll see views of Mount Hood to the west and Mount Jefferson to the east. At **7.5** miles, when the trail drops to FR 3550, bear left and ride along the road. The singletrack begins again on the left at **7.7** miles.

The trail climbs around the east side of Gunsight Butte, another high point, before heading down the steep edge of the ridge to Gumjuwac Saddle, **9.4** miles. (Bailout 1: Turn left on Gumjuwac Trail 480 and ride down to Hwy 35. Turn right on Hwy 35 and ride to Pine Mont Drive.)

Mount Hood from FR 3550 near High Prairie

From the saddle, continue north on FR 3550. Stay on the main road. The serious climbing begins at **9.6** miles as you grind up the open, west-facing bowl of Lookout Mountain. *WOOF!* At **11.3** miles, reach a fork—the ride's crest—at High Prairie. Bear left on FR 4410. Before bombing down FR 4410, though, check out the four-volcano view from this intersection.

FR 4410, gravelly and washboarded, winds down the ridge that connects Gunsight Ridge to the south with Surveyors Ridge to the north. Watch out for vehicles during this fast descent. *WHOA!* At **13.8** miles (ridepoint 3), turn right onto Cooks Meadow Trail 639, which is unmarked and easily missed, and immediately begin climbing. *WHOA!* number two: This trail is low on the forest service's priority list, and sometimes isn't cleared out until August. Call ahead for current conditions. If the trail hasn't been cleared, you can detour around via FR 4410. The trail soon bends left and rounds the west side of the hill, **14.3** miles. From here, the trail, twisted and root-strewn, hardscrabble in spots, launches down the hillside toward Cooks Meadow. Cross a dirt road at **15.4** miles and continue down. The trail crosses FR 44 at **16.4** miles. (Bailout 2: You can turn left and take FR 44 to Hwy 35 to Pine Mont Drive, or you can turn right and take FR 44 to FR 17 to Pine Mont Drive, or you can grab Dog River Trail 675 to Hwy 35 to Pine Mont Drive.) Immediately after crossing the

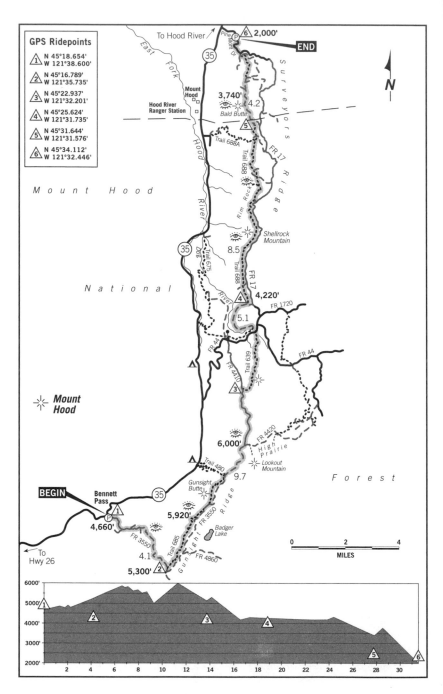

GPS Ridepoints

1. N 45°18.654'
   W 121°38.600'
2. N 45°16.789'
   W 121°35.735'
3. N 45°22.937'
   W 121°32.201'
4. N 45°25.624'
   W 121°31.735'
5. N 45°31.644'
   W 121°31.576'
6. N 45°34.112'
   W 121°32.446'

To Hood River

Pine Hollow Dr.

END

6 2,000'

35

East Fork

Mount Hood

Hood River Ranger Station

Surveyors Ridge

3,740'

4.2

Bald Butte

5

Trail 688A

Trail 688

FR 17

Mount Hood National

Rim Rock

Hood River

Shellrock Mountain

8.5

Trail 675

35

Trail 688

FR 17

4,220'

4

FR 1720

5.1

FR 44

Trail 663

FR 4410

3

FR 44

FR 4420

6,000'

High Prairie

Lookout Mountain

Forest

Trail 480

9.7

Mount Hood

BEGIN

Bennett Pass

35

Gunsight Butte

5,920'

4,660'

1

FR 3550

Trail 685

Gunsight Ridge

FR 3550

Badger Lake

To Hwy 26

4.1

5,300'

2

FR 4860

0   2   4
MILES

paved road, the trail forks—turn right onto Surveyors Ridge Trail 688, cross Dog River, and climb through Cooks Meadow.

At **17** miles, stay to the left (ignoring a doubletrack on the right) and cross a small creek. From here, follow the doubletrack through a cleared area. The doubletrack is dusty and rocky in sections. *WHOA!* At **18.9** miles (ridepoint 4), turn left onto Trail 688— it's easily missed. Cross a dirt road at **19.7** miles. Pass through stands of fir alternated with clearcuts and fireweed. Starting around **21.2** miles, there's a tough climb to the top of an open knoll, which affords awesome views of Mount Hood.

The trail descends, churning through the forest, to a fork at **21.8** miles—bear right and continue down before climbing again. At **22.4** miles, when the trail kisses a doubletrack, bear to the left. After a few more pedal strokes, bear left again onto the singletrack. (Bailout 3: Take the doubletrack 50 yards to FR 17, turn left, and ride north to the end of the ride.) From here, the trail traverses a series of hillside meadows. Past rock outcrops, the trail is technical and tricky in places, with embedded rocks and a side slope. At a fork, **23.7** miles, bear to the left and climb. At **24.2** miles, pass a trail on the left that leads to the site of an old lookout. After a short traverse, descend. Cross gravel roads at **24.4** and **24.8** miles. When the road forks at **25.5** miles, bear right and descend the rocky trail. Reach a fork at **26.4** miles and go right. (A left here heads west on Oak Ridge Trail 688A, a switchie fest down an exposed hillside to Highway 35. This isn't a good bailout if you've left a car on Pine Mont Drive. But it's by far the best choice if you parked at the ranger station—see The Scoop, above.) Cross another gravel road.

At **27.4** miles (ridepoint 5), the trail dumps out at the trailhead under the powerlines. (Bailout 4: Turn right at the powerlines and take the dirt road one-half mile to FR 17. Turn left on FR 17 and ride north to the end of the ride.) From here, cross under the powerlines, veering left, and climb the horrible, ogreish road to the top of Bald Butte. Don't be deceived by the false summit or the I-think-I-lost-a-lung sensation you have during the ascent. At **28.3** miles, reach the top. Do you care about views any more? Descend northward down the doubletrack. At **29.4** miles, stay to the right. When the doubletrack forks again, **29.6** miles, bear left. *WHOA!* At **29.9** miles, turn left to find an easily missed singletrack. The trail rips down the north slope of

Let's see your trail shimmy

Surveyors Ridge, a nice ride through fir forest. At **30.9** miles, the trail dumps out at an intersection of three roads: Go straight, downhill. At **31.1** miles, reach Pine Mont Drive, which is paved, and turn left. At **31.6** miles (ridepoint 6), reach the gravel pullout on the left to complete the ride.

Gazetteer

Nearby camping: Sherwood (primitive)
Nearest food, drink, services: Government Camp, Hood River

Distance	17.7-mile lollipop (6.4-mile option)
Route	Dirt roads and singletrack; views
Climbs	Moderate to tough; high point: 5,240 ft, gain: 885 ft
Duration	Fitness rider: 2 to 3 hours; scenery rider: 3 to 5 hours
Travel	Hood River—34 miles; Portland—62 miles
Skill	Advanced
Season	Late summer, fall
Map	Green Trails: Mount Hood, Mount Wilson
Rules	None
Manager	Mount Hood National Forest, Barlow District, 541-467-2291
Web	www.fs.fed.us/r6/mthood/recreation/trails/barlow-conditions

Who Will Like This Ride
Explorers more interested in new places than perfectly fantastic trails.

The Scoop
   The simple elevation gain listed for this ride, 885 feet, is deceptive. Since you reach the route's high point around the middle of the ride and then drop again, the cumulative gain on this route tops 3,000 feet. Still, it's more exploratory than difficult, with more than two-thirds on various dirt roads. The trail down to the lake is a technical challenge; it's also used extensively by hikers. Boulder Lake, plunked into a large, rocky cirque east of Bonney Butte, makes for a great picnic stop. The views of Mount Hood from the road climb are icing.

Driving Directions
   From Portland, take US Highway 26 eastbound about 56 miles, past Ski Bowl and Government Camp, to its junction with State Highway 35. Set your odometer to zero, and turn north onto Hwy 35. At the top of Bennett Pass, 6.2 miles, exit to the right, following the signs for Bennett Pass Sno-Park. Park immediately in the paved Sno-Park lot.
   From Hood River (exit 64 off Interstate 84), set your odometer to zero at

the end of the interstate ramp and drive south on Hwy 35. At 34.2 miles, immediately after milepost 64 and just before the top of Bennett Pass, take the exit on the right, following signs to Bennett Pass Sno-Park. Turn left to cross over the highway, then park in the paved Sno-Park lot east of the highway.

The Ride

From Bennett Pass, ride up FR 3550, climbing moderately. When the road forks at **1.1** miles, bear left. At **1.3** miles, the road divides again—bear right and continue up. Rougher, steeper, and narrower now, the road forks at **1.8** miles—go left, continuing up the ridgeline. On a clear day, Mount Hood is so close it seems you can reach out and grab a handful of snow off Newton Clark Glacier. Pass over the rocky crest of the ridge, descend for a short distance, then climb again.

Pass Gunsight Ridge Trail on the left, **4.1** miles, and immediately reach a T. Turn right on FR 4891 toward Bonney Meadow and continue ascending. After a crest, reach a fork and bear left at **5.1** miles. At **5.3** miles (ridepoint 2), turn left on FR 120 toward Bonney Meadow Campground. Just after entering the campground at **5.6** miles, stay left and find an unmarked trail on the left next to a campsite. A sign soon assures you that you're on Boulder Lake Trail 463. At **5.8** miles (ridepoint 3), reach a fork and bear left toward Boulder Lake. After a short noodle, the trail switchbacks down a steep hillside and then traverses south across several rockfalls.

Boulder Lake

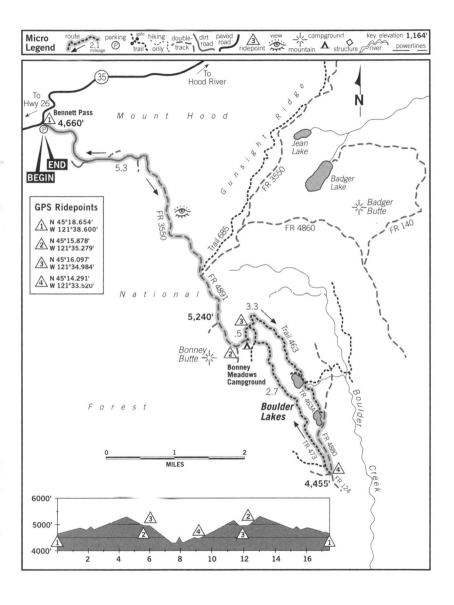

Micro Legend — route 2.1 mileage, parking P, gate, hiking trail only, double-track, dirt road, paved road, ridepoint, view, mountain, campground, structure, river, key elevation 1,164' powerlines

35 To Hood River

To Hwy 26

Bennett Pass 4,660'

M o u n t   H o o d

G u n s i g h t   R i d g e

Jean Lake

Badger Lake

FR 3550

Badger Butte

FR 4860

FR 140

END
BEGIN

5.3

FR 3550

Trail 685

FR 4891

GPS Ridepoints

1. N 45°18.654'
   W 121°38.600'
2. N 45°15.878'
   W 121°35.279'
3. N 45°16.097'
   W 121°34.984'
4. N 45°14.291'
   W 121°33.520'

N a t i o n a l

5,240'

3.3

Trail 463

.5

Bonney Butte

Bonney Meadows Campground

2.7

Boulder Lakes

FR 463A

Boulder Creek

F o r e s t

TR 473

FR 4880

4,455'

FR 124

0   1   2
MILES

6000'
5000'
4000'

2   4   6   8   10   12   14   16

After a short cannonball, reach Boulder Lake and a fork at **7.4** miles. Stay to the left, pass through several campsites, then reach a fork at **7.5** miles. Turn right on Little Boulder Lake Trail 463A. The narrow trail climbs a ridge, tops out, and then drops to Little Boulder Lake, **8.1** miles. Turn left, away from the lake. Almost immediately the trail ends at FR 4880—turn right and pedal south. On sunny days, FR 4880 affords hazy views south of the low hills and

Boulder Creek

plains, bare and mottled, of eastern Oregon. **WHOA!** Immediately after passing FR 124 on the left, **9.1** miles (ridepoint 4), find a faint trail on the right, marked by a small cairn and an ancient sign: Loop.

The trail, which may need brushing, climbs north at a moderate grade, skirting close to the edge of the ridge on occasion and offering views down to Boulder Lakes and into the Boulder Creek valley. Reach a T at **11.6** miles (ridepoint 3) and turn right toward Bonney Meadow Campground. At **11.8** miles, arrive at another T and turn left. When the trail ends at the campground road, **12.1** miles, turn right and retrace your path to Bennett Pass. Reach a T at **12.4** miles and turn right on FR 4891. Stay on the main road, climbing and then descending to a fork at **13.6** miles. Turn left onto FR 3550, following the sign toward Hwy 35. Reach Bennett Pass at **17.7** miles to complete the ride.

Option

With a four-wheel-drive vehicle, you can drive to Bonney Meadow Campground and begin riding from there. This slashes 11.2 miles of dirt-road riding from the ride, but now it may not be long enough given the effort it takes to get there.

Gazetteer

Nearby camping: Bonney Meadow (primitive), Sherwood (primitive)
Nearest food, drink, services: Government Camp, Hood River

Distance	22.2-mile out-and-back (longer and shorter options)
Route	Wide, sometimes loose rail-trail; views
Climbs	Nearly flat (two short hills); high point: 260 ft, gain: 110 ft
Duration	Fitness rider: 2 to 3 hours; scenery rider: 3 to 4 hours
Travel	Hood River—36 miles; Portland—100 miles
Skill	Beginner
Season	Year-round
Map	USGS 30x60 minute: Goldendale
Rules	None
Manager	Oregon State Parks, 800-551-6949
Web	www.oregonstateparks.org/park_37.php

Who Will Like This Ride
Fishermen and lovers of those golden, treeless, eastern Oregon hillsides.

The Scoop
This ride follows the wide canyon views of the winding Deschutes River, a National Wild and Scenic River, green in spring, golden in summer and fall. If

Harris Ranch

you do go in summer, try this ride at dawn or be prepared for a scorching, 100-degree day. Like most rail-trails, this one is wide and level. And some sections are sandy. Be sure to turn around well before you get tired or run low on water. Most of the time there are more folks

fishing on the river below the trail than biking on it. While most of the trail is on BLM land, Oregon State Parks offers the most up-to-date information.

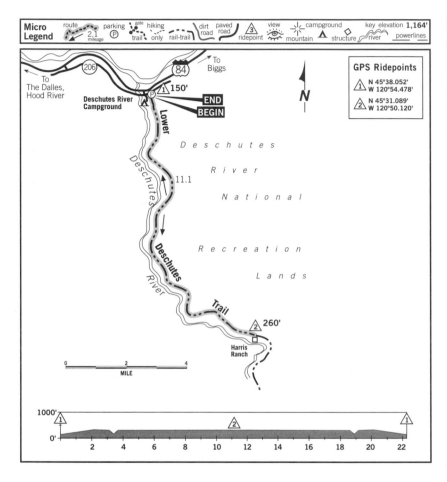

Driving Directions

From Portland, drive east on Interstate 84 past The Dalles and take exit 97 at Celilo. Set your odometer to zero at the end of the interstate ramp. Turn right, then immediately turn left onto State Highway 206, following the signs toward Deschutes Park. At 3.1 miles, turn right and park in the dirt parking area on the left next to Deschutes River State Park Campground.

Sunrise hits the lower Deschutes River canyon

The Ride

From the trailhead parking, take the trail next to the campground's entrance road. The trail starts out steep and sandy, but after less than one-quarter mile it flattens out and begins meandering along the river. Lined with sage and low brush, dominated by expansive golden-brown hillsides and high, rocky escarps, the wide trail winds above the Deschutes River. Ignore the numerous trails on the right that lead down to the river. Pass occasional thickets of blackberry. At **3.1** miles, the trail drops steeply to a low point and then climbs back up to the level grade. *WHOA!* Take care on this rocky section of trail.

From here the trail is sandy in sections, rough and bumpy in others, as it matches the river's long, languorous turns. At **11.1** miles (ridepoint 2), reach the weathered-gray derelicts that comprised Harris Ranch. Though the trail continues much farther south, turn around here and ride back to the trailhead, **22.2** miles, to complete the ride.

Option

From Harris Ranch, the trail continues another 4.9 miles to a signed turnaround, making the entire out-and-back 32 miles. And of course you can always go short by just turning around whenever you want.

Gazetteer

Nearby camping: Deschutes River State Park
Nearest food, drink, services: The Dalles, Biggs

Tired of the rain, mud, and overcast skies of western Oregon? (And why wouldn't you be.) Bend, one of the West's finest mountain-bike destinations, combines dry weather with awesome trails—many of them user-built, which basically means they're perfect. Just two hours from Eugene and three hours from Portland, these 25 Bend-area rides provide great fodder for winter bike dreams and easy summer weekend tripping for most Oregonians. The riding is best early in the summer when the trails aren't too dusty and the thermostat isn't too high, or after the first nighttime freeze around mid-August, which rids the land of many mosquitoes.

Farewell Epic (ride 27) and North Fork to Flagline (ride 28) constitute new epics to this second edition. Both should be on the "ride once a year" list. I've also added C.O.D. (ride 30), Swampy Lakes (ride 36) and a new ride at Phil's Trail.

The routes at Phil's trail system (rides 31, 32, 33) epitomize Bend riding—fast, smooth, and dream-like—as well as being riding distance from town, another typical attribute. And with all the recent trail connections emanating out from Phil's, it may be the center of the mountain bike universe. Indeed, from Phil's trailhead, you can ride on dirt to 14 of the rides in this section.

For my gas money, though, the most outstanding trail near Bend is the circuit around Newberry Caldera (ride 39)—one of the best trails in the West. It's tough, exciting, and spectacular. Combine it with Paulina Creek (ride 38), and you've got your hands on a nice epic. But before you think this place can do no wrong, know there are shabby trails even in Bend. Forget about Lower Black Butte Trail—and even the upper trail at Black Butte, ride 21, is hanging onto this book by a thread. And while some of the trails near Skeleton Cave look interesting on the map, manzanita-shredded arms and unstable, horse-trodden trails are what you have to look forward to.

The Central Oregon Trails Alliance, COTA, is the mountain bike club to thank for trails and access near Bend. Their tireless work and political savvy have opened up riding here like no other place in the nation. Thank them, buy them beer, become a member!

Distance	4.2-mile out-and-back
Route	Short dirt-road descent, casual singletrack; views
Climbs	Nearly flat; high point: 2,840 ft, gain: 190 ft
Duration	Fitness rider: 30 minutes; scenery rider: 1 hour
Travel	Bend—25 miles; Eugene—131 miles
Skill	Intermediate
Season	Late spring, summer, fall
Map	USGS 7.5 minute: Redmond
Rules	Oregon State Parks Day-use Permit required
Manager	Oregon State Parks, 800-551-6949
Web	www.oregonstateparks.org/park_51.php

Who Will Like This Ride

Anyone interested in the scene and stark beauty of Smith Rock, plus riding a sinewy singletrack.

The Scoop

Out on the edge of Eastern Oregon's high desert just northeast of Terrebonne, the Crooked River snakes around a humongous prow of rock known as Smith Rock. Carabiners, harnesses, and climbing rope fill the old Subaru wagons and air-cooled Westfalias that haul in underfinanced pilgrim climbers from all over the world. The mountain-bike trails that begin from Smith Rock State Park are less well known but offer an exciting range of experience and scenery. This route sticks to the short, easy trail that cuts around the base of Smith Rock alongside the Crooked River. Families should note that there are a few advanced sections of trail, so some riders may want to push their bikes for short distances. Looking for a more difficult ride? Check out Gray Butte (ride 18) or Burma Road (ride 19).

Driving Directions

From Bend, drive about 22 miles north on US Highway 97. In Terrebonne, turn right on B Avenue toward Smith Rock State Park, and set your

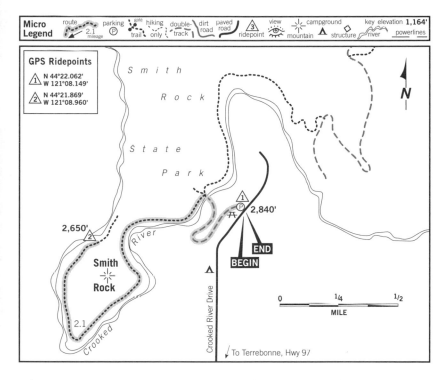

Micro Legend: route 2.1 mileage, parking, gate hiking trail only, double-track, dirt road, paved road, 3 ridepoint, view mountain, campground, structure, key elevation 1,164', river, powerlines

GPS Ridepoints
1 N 44°22.062' W 121°08.149'
2 N 44°21.869' W 121°08.960'

Smith Rock State Park

2,840'
END
BEGIN
2,650'
2.1
Smith Rock
Crooked River
Crooked River Drive
To Terrebonne, Hwy 97

0   1/4   1/2
MILE

N

odometer to zero. B Avenue becomes Northeast Smith Rock Way. At 0.6 mile, turn left on First Street Northeast, which soon becomes Wilcox Avenue. At 2.7 miles, turn left on Crooked River Drive. At 3.2 miles, reach the day-use parking area for Smith Rock State Park.

The Ride

From the day-use parking area, take the paved trail toward Smith Rock. At the edge of the bluff, the trail becomes a ragged, gravelly road as it descends toward the river, possibly requiring a short walk. Ignore the trail on the right as you descend; stay on the road. At the bottom, cross a wooden bridge over Crooked River. At the four-way just across the bridge, turn left onto the wide dirt trail, and pedal along the base of the towering rocks. Stay along the river, ignoring numerous climbers' trails on the right. At the **1**-mile point, walk up a set of stairs. From here the trail traverses the hillside above the river.

The Crooked River winds through Smith Rock State Park

Cross between some big rocks on the left and Smith Rock on the right. The sandy trail winds through low brush. At **1.7** miles, traverse a difficult, loose scree slope. The trail soon widens and zips again, running for a short distance right along the river. At **2.1** miles (ridepoint 2), the trail becomes quite technical, loose and rocky. Turn around here and retrace your route along Crooked River and then back up to the parking area, **4.2** miles.

Gazetteer

Nearby camping: Smith Rock State Park (primitive)
Nearest food, drink, services: Terrebonne, Redmond

Distance	18.6-mile figure eight
Route	Dirt-road ascent, singletrack climbs and descents; views
Climbs	A long slog; high point: 4,380 ft, gain: 1,540 ft
Duration	Fitness rider: 2 to 3 hours; scenery rider: 3 to 5 hours
Travel	Bend—25 miles; Eugene—131 miles
Skill	Advanced
Season	Late spring, summer, fall
Map	USGS 30x60 minute: Bend
Rules	Oregon State Parks Day-use Permit required
Manager	Oregon State Parks, 800-551-6949
Web	www.oregonstateparks.org/park_51.php

Who Will Like This Ride
Strong climbers who appreciate wide open spaces.

The Scoop

This figure-eight route travels over the same dirt roads and singletrack as Burma Road (ride 19), but then adds a big loop around Gray Butte. It's a more challenging ride than Burma Road, and the singletrack's much better, with some sections that dance and fly and others that trip and stumble. Whatever: If it's singletrack, it's all good. The ride begins at Smith Rock State Park and, during the course of three separate climbs, ascends into Crooked River National Grasslands, which is managed by the BLM, as well as some sections of private property. It can be hot out there, so drink plenty of water.

Driving Directions

From Bend, drive about 22 miles north on US Highway 97. In Terrebonne, turn right on B Avenue toward Smith Rock State Park, and set your odometer to zero. B Avenue becomes Northeast Smith Rock Way. At 0.6 mile, turn left on First Street Northeast, which soon becomes Wilcox Avenue. At 2.7 miles, turn left on Crooked River Drive. At 3.2 miles, reach the day-use parking area for Smith Rock State Park.

The Ride

From the day-use parking area, take the paved trail toward Smith Rock. At the edge of the bluff, the trail becomes a gravelly road as it descends toward the river. Ignore a trail on the right as you descend. At the bottom of the road, cross a wooden bridge over Crooked River. At the four-way just across the bridge, turn right onto a dirt trail that runs along the river.

When the trail forks at **1.4** miles, turn left and walk up the steep, loose trail. At **1.6** miles, the trail ends at the Burma Road: Turn left and climb. The road, steep and exposed to the sun, switchbacks at **2** miles and continues up. Woof! Crest the ridge at **2.5** miles (ridepoint 2), ignoring the singletrack on the right, and gear up for a fast descent. Views: Three Sisters, Broken Top, and Mount Jefferson. **WHOA!** At **3.5** miles (ridepoint 3), just as you've attained top speed, reach a fork and take a sharp right onto Sherwood Road, which is unmarked (if you haven't turned and you start climbing, you've gone too far).

Sherwood Road climbs gently at first. At **4.5** miles, ignore a lesser double-track on the right, then pass through a gate and bear right. When the road forks at **4.8** miles, turn right and continue up. After a steep quarter-mile climb, reach Gray Butte Trail at **6** miles (ridepoint 4), immediately before a four-way junction in the road. Turn left onto the trail. At **6.3** miles, turn right at the fork. The trail immediately crosses a dirt road and descends, past a corral and down into a narrow drainage. When the trail dumps out to a road, **7.7** miles, bear left and continue down, passing through Skull Hollow. When the road ends at a T, turn left on Forest Road 5710.

The road is covered with large rocks, and this makes the otherwise moderate climb more challenging. Reach a fork at **9.2** miles and go left on FR 57, following the sign to Gray Butte trailhead. The road plateaus a quarter-mile farther, crosses a cattle grate, and descends. At **9.8** miles (ridepoint 5), reach a fork in the road. **WHOA!** Turn left onto the unmarked singletrack here and climb gently. At **10** miles, ignore a trail back on the right. From here the trail rounds the back side of Gray Butte, ascending in fits and starts. Ignore another trail on the right, then cross an old doubletrack.

At **10.8** miles, pass through a gate—as with all gates, leave them the way you found them, either open or closed. Top out a quarter-mile farther

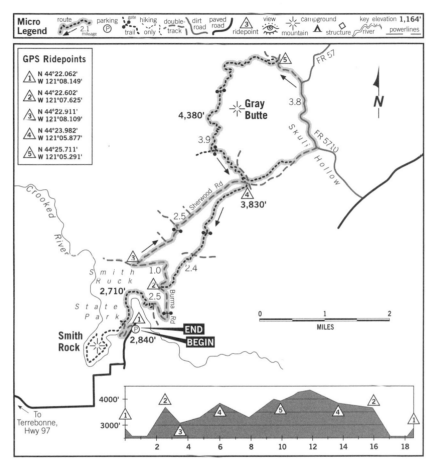

to spectacular views to the right; Gray Butte is high to the left. The trail rolls across the west flank of the butte. The descent begins at **11.9** miles, fast and sometimes rough. Reach a T at **12.6** miles. Turn left, pass through another gate, and continue descending. As the trail approaches a dirt road, **13.3** miles, stay to the right on the trail. At **13.5** miles, bear right at the fork. At **13.7** miles (ridepoint 4), the trail crosses the road at the top of Sherwood Canyon. From here, stay on the main trail, ignoring numerous lesser trails. Zip down a long traverse on a steep, sage-covered hillside toward Three Sisters.

Traversing the ridge toward Burma Road

Pass through a gate at **14.7** miles. At **15.2** miles, pass straight through a four-way, then immediately turn left to return to the singletrack. After another fast descent, the trail ends at the crest of Burma Road, **16.1** miles (ridepoint 2). Turn left and cruise down the steep road toward Smith Rock State Park. At **17** miles, turn right onto the unmarked singletrack that drops precipitously down to Crooked River. At the bottom of the hill, turn right and meander back to the wood bridge, **18.1** miles. Cross the river and climb back to the day-use parking area to complete the ride, **18.6** miles.

Gazetteer
Nearby camping: Smith Rock State Park (primitive)
Nearest food, drink, services: Terrebonne, Redmond

19 BURMA ROAD

Distance	11-mile lollipop
Route	Dirt-road ascents and descents, singletrack descent; views
Climbs	Brutal; high point: 3,830 ft, gain: 1,120 ft
Duration	Fitness rider: 1 to 2 hours; scenery rider: 2 to 3 hours
Travel	Bend—25 miles; Eugene—131 miles
Skill	Intermediate
Season	Late spring, summer, fall
Map	USGS 30x60 minute: Bend
Rules	Oregon State Parks Day-use Permit required
Manager	Oregon State Parks, 800-551-6949
Web	www.oregonstateparks.org/park_51.php

Who Will Like This Ride
You like the classic tough dirt-road climb followed by a singletrack descent.

The Scoop
Let's face it: Burma Road sounds like it might be a cool ride, kind of exotic, off into who-knows-where land. Well, this ride isn't that extraordinary, but it does include two sections of nice singletrack and starts out from Smith Rock State Park, which is awesome. The zippy singletrack along the Crooked River that begins the ride is terrific but over altogether too soon. That's where Burma Road begins, a First-gear Freddie climb that, on hot summer days, will sauté your brain in olive oil and garlic if you don't drink enough water. After a descent and another dirt-road climb, the route takes a fast singletrack back to Burma Road and then returns to the state park.

Driving Directions
From Bend, drive about 22 miles north on US Highway 97. In Terrebonne, turn right on B Avenue toward Smith Rock State Park, and set your odometer to zero. B Avenue becomes Northeast Smith Rock Way. At 0.6 mile, turn left on First Street Northeast, which soon becomes Wilcox Avenue. At 2.7 miles, turn left on Crooked River Drive. At 3.2 miles, reach the day-use parking area for Smith Rock State Park.

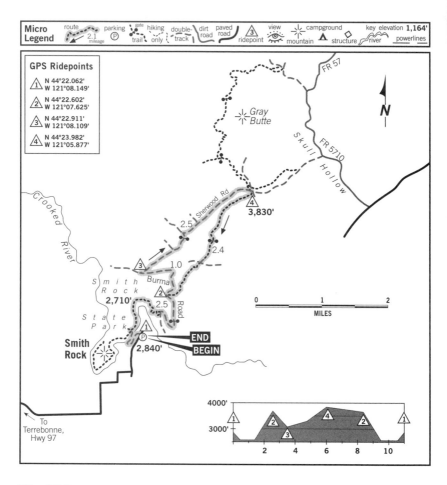

Micro Legend — route 2.1 mileage, parking (P), gate hiking trail, hiking only, double-track, dirt road, paved road, ridepoint, view, mountain, campground, structure, river, powerlines, key elevation **1,164'**

GPS Ridepoints

1. N 44°22.062' W 121°08.149'
2. N 44°22.602' W 121°07.625'
3. N 44°22.911' W 121°08.109'
4. N 44°23.982' W 121°05.877'

FR 57

Gray Butte

Skull Hollow

FR 5710

Crooked River

Sherwood Rd

2.5

4 3,830'

2.4

3 1.0

Burma

2.5 2

Road

END

BEGIN

Smith Rock State Park 2,710'

1 2,840'

Smith Rock

To Terrebonne, Hwy 97

0   1   2
MILES

4000'

3000'

2   4   6   8   10

The Ride

From the day-use parking area, take the paved trail toward Smith Rock. At the edge of the bluff, the trail becomes a ragged, gravelly road as it descends toward the river. Ignore the trail on the right as you descend. At the bottom of the road, cross a wood bridge over Crooked River. At the four-way intersection immediately across the bridge, turn right onto a dirt trail that spins along the river through pine and sage and rocky crags.

When the trail forks at **1.4** miles, turn left and walk up the steep, loose trail. At **1.6** miles (ridepoint 2), the trail ends at the Burma Road: Turn left

The Three Sisters from Highway 97

and climb. The road, steep and exposed to the sun, cuts a switchback at **2** miles and continues up. **WOOF!** Crest the ridge at **2.5** miles, ignoring the singletrack on the right, and click in to a bigger gear for the fast descent. Views: the Three Sisters, Broken Top, and Mount Jefferson. **WHOA!** At **3.5** miles (ridepoint 3), just as your speed has peaked, reach a fork and take a sharp right onto Sherwood Road, which is unmarked (if you haven't turned and you start climbing, you've gone too far).

Sherwood Road climbs gently at first. At **4.5** miles, ignore a lesser double-track on the right, then pass through a gate and bear right. When the road forks at **4.8** miles, turn right and continue up. After a steep quarter-mile climb, reach Gray Butte Trail on the left and right (immediately before a four-way intersection), **6** miles (ridepoint 4). Turn right onto the trail. From here, stay on the main trail, ignoring numerous lesser trails. The way zips down a long traverse across a steep, sage-covered hillside toward the Three Sisters.

Pass through a gate at **7** miles—leave the gate the way you found it, either open or closed. At **7.5** miles, pass straight through a four-way, then immediately turn left to return to the singletrack. After another full-throttle descent, the trail ends at the crest of Burma Road, **8.4** miles (ridepoint 2). Turn left and cruise down the steep road back toward Smith Rock State Park. At **9.3** miles, turn right onto the unmarked singletrack that drops precipitously down to Crooked River. At the bottom of the hill, bear right and noodle along the riverside trail to the wood bridge on the left, **10.4** miles. Cross the river and climb back to the day-use parking area to complete the ride, **11** miles.

Gazetteer
Nearby camping: Smith Rock State Park (primitive)
Nearest food, drink, services: Terrebonne, Redmond

Distance	13.2-mile lollipop
Route	Rolling singletrack, wide in spots; views
Climbs	Gentle; high point: 3,460 ft, gain: 140 ft
Duration	Fitness rider: 1 to 2 hours; scenery rider: 2 to 3 hours
Travel	Bend—33 miles; Eugene—93 miles
Skill	Intermediate
Season	Late spring, summer, fall
Map	U.S. Forest Service: Sisters Ranger District
Rules	None
Manager	Deschutes National Forest, Sisters District, 541-549-7700
Web	www.fs.fed.us/r6/centraloregon/recreation/trails/54094-suttletie

Who Will Like This Ride
Riders not ready for a climb today.

The Scoop

From the trailhead on a roads-to-trails conversion, this route noodles and winds—it's not quite zippy—across the flats between Cache Mountain and Black Butte following the northwestern slant of US Highway 20. Although you can't see the highway from the trail, you can hear the occasional traffic noise. The trail around Suttle Lake is fun and popular with families, fishermen, and campers out for a walk, so ride with care. Not the place to ride fast and impress your friends with those new crossovers and super whips, this is a nice intermediate ride with no tough climbing and lots of fine views of the lake.

Driving Directions

From Bend, drive northwest on US 20 through Sisters. At the west end of Sisters, set your odometer to zero as you pass the Sisters Ranger Station on the right, continuing northwest on US 20. At 9.9 miles, turn left onto Forest Road 2060, and immediately park at the small trailhead on the right. (Note: There is additional parking directly across US 20.)

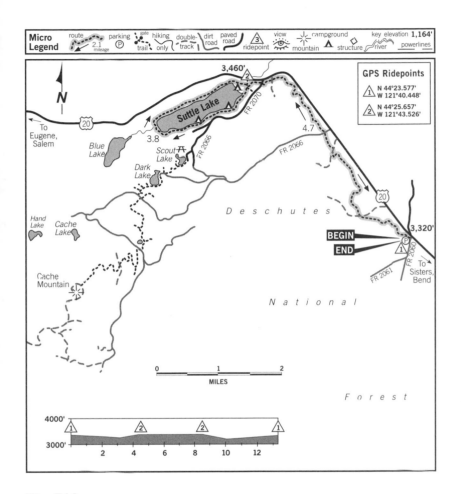

route 2.1 mileage parking ℗ gate hiking trail only double-track dirt road paved road 3 ridepoint view mountain campground structure river key elevation **1,164'** powerlines

GPS Ridepoints

1 N 44°23.577' W 121°40.448'

2 N 44°25.657' W 121°43.526'

The Ride

From the trailhead, ride north, following the Roads to Trails signs, along Suttle Tie Trail 4094. The trail, which fumbles between doubletrack and singletrack, crosses a dirt road at **0.9** mile. When the trail forks at **2.2** miles, bear right on FR 700. But at **2.3** miles, bear left onto a singletrack, again following the Roads to Trails sign. Cross a dirt road at **2.6** miles. The way ascends moderately from here. Cross a dirt road again at **4.3** miles, then cross over a paved road a short distance farther. From here, stay on the main

Onward toward Suttle Lake

trail, first ignoring a trail on the left and then bearing left at a fork. Reach a five-way intersection at **4.7** miles (ridepoint 2) and go straight on the main trail, Suttle Lake Trail 4030, that wraps clockwise around Suttle Lake.

WHOA! Since the trail around the lake is popular with families, ride conservatively. As you ride, stay to the right, ignoring the spur trails on the left. The trail, which is mostly wide with a few roots and tight corners thrown in for good measure, passes several boat launches and campgrounds as it traverses the south side of the lake. At the west end of the lake, the trail crosses several bridges. As you reach a campground on the northeast end of the lake, **8.2** miles, follow the trail signs up to the left onto a paved road. Follow the paved road to an intersection at **8.4** miles and cross this intersection, veering right, to the singletrack that continues on the far side. Cross a bridge. At an intersection of trails, **8.5** miles (ridepoint 2), bear left and ride back toward the trailhead following the Roads to Trails signs. Reach the trailhead at **13.2** miles.

Gazetteer

Nearby camping: Indian Ford, South Shore
Nearest food, drink, services: Sisters

Distance	15.9-mile lollipop
Route	Rocky roads, wide and narrow trails; views
Climbs	Persistent and tough; high point: 4,130 ft, gain: 750 ft
Duration	Fitness rider: 2 to 3 hours; scenery rider: 3 to 4 hours
Travel	Bend—29 miles; Eugene—97 miles
Skill	Intermediate
Season	Late spring, summer, fall
Map	U.S. Forest Service: Sisters Ranger District
Rules	None
Manager	Deschutes National Forest, Sisters District, 541-549-7700
Web	www.fs.fed.us/r6/centraloregon/recreation/trails/54026-blackbt

Who Will Like This Ride

It's not whether you like it or not, it's whether the shadow force made you ride it.

The Scoop

With none of the irregular crags and ridges and late-summer snow that characterize most other mountains near Bend, Black Butte looms out of the ponderosa pine distance like a foreboding shadow. An apparition. And its looming nature, along with a perfect cone-shaped symmetry, makes this is the best-formed lollipop route in *Kissing the Trail*. Without any of the zippy singletrack, however, and only a few of the snowcapped views that this area is known for, the mountain-bike routes on Black Butte—both upper and lower—don't rate among my top choices in the Bend-Sisters area. The tread is sometimes ragged and horse-torn, sometimes steep and scattered with loose rocks, and there's very little real singletrack. But if you pass Sisters with any frequency, your mountain bike latched to the top, that shadow can lure you in, so at last you'll be able to say you've circled Black Butte, the most perfectly shaped lollipop route in Oregon.

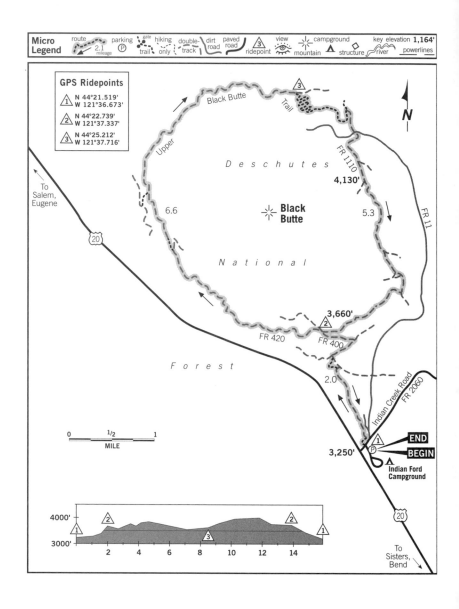

Micro Legend — route 2.1 mileage, parking Ⓟ, gate, hiking trail only, double-track, dirt road, paved road, ③ ridepoint, view, mountain, △ campground, structure, river, key elevation **1,164'**, powerlines

GPS Ridepoints

① N 44°21.519'
W 121°36.673'

② N 44°22.739'
W 121°37.337'

③ N 44°25.212'
W 121°37.716'

Black Butte Trail

Upper

③

D e s c h u t e s

FR 1110

4,130'

To Salem, Eugene

20

6.6

☼ **Black Butte**

5.3

FR 11

N a t i o n a l

3,660'
②

FR 420

FR 400

2.0

Indian Creek Road

FR 2060

F o r e s t

0 1/2 1
MILE

3,250'

①
Ⓟ

END

BEGIN

△
Indian Ford Campground

20

To Sisters, Bend

4000' ② ③ ②
3000' ①   ①
  2 4 6 8 10 12 14

....

Driving Directions

From Bend, drive northwest on US Highway 20 to Sisters. At the west end of Sisters, set your odometer to zero as you pass the Sisters Ranger Station on the right, and continue northwest on US 20. At 9.9 miles, turn left onto Indian Creek Road (Forest Road 2060), and immediately park at the trailhead on the right.

The Ride

From the trailhead parking area next to the entrance to Indian Ford Campground, cross Indian Creek Road to a narrow trail. Descend slightly, then bear left on a doubletrack, following wood posts marked Roads to Trails. Stay left. The doubletrack, sandy and horse-worn, ascends slightly, through old-growth ponderosa pine. At **1** mile, bear left onto a narrow trail. At **1.3** miles, the trail ends at a dirt road: Turn left, then immediately right, following the sign toward Upper Black Butte Trail. When you reach a fork in the road at **1.6** miles, turn up to the left on FR 400. The climb is short but can be brutal: hot, loose, rocky, and steep.

Reach a four-way at **2** miles (ridepoint 2) and turn left on FR 420. The route, alternating between doubletrack and wide singletrack, through open pine forests and tight corridors of manzanita, rounds the southwestern slope of Black Butte, climbing and falling and, at times, affording glimpses of the Three Sisters and Mount Washington. *WHOA!* At **4.7** miles, turn left on an unmarked singletrack; it's easily missed. At **4.8** miles, when the trail ends, continue straight on the doubletrack. At **5.6** miles, ignore a singletrack back on the left that connects with Lower Black Butte Trail. Continue straight on Upper Black Butte Trail.

At **6** miles, the doubletrack begins rounding the north slope of the butte, descending slightly. Through the fir and pine, you can occasionally see Three Finger Jack and Mount Jefferson. *WHOA!* At **8.6** miles (ridepoint 3), turn right onto a singletrack; it's an easy turn to miss. The trail climbs steadily, switchbacking up the hillside. At **9.3** miles, the trail bends left, alternating between singletrack and doubletrack. Reach a fork at **10** miles and go right, following the Roads to Trails sign. After a tough climb, cross a gravel road. The route follows FR 1110 now, and it's doubletrack the rest of the way. At **10.5** miles, reach a fork and bear right. When the road divides at **10.9**

Circling the foreboding shadow

miles, bear left. To the southeast, you'll see long views into the mottled expanse of eastern Oregon.

At **11.8** miles, stay to the right on FR 190. At **12.1** miles, reach a fork and bear left, twice. At **12.5** miles, reach a fork and go right, following the Roads to Trails sign. Reach a four-way at **13.9** miles (ridepoint 2) and turn left. The road descends steeply; the surface is loose and rocky. Reach a T at **14.4** miles—turn right. At **14.7** miles, reach a four-way: Turn left and then immediately right onto a singletrack, following the trail sign. Bear right at **14.9** miles and also at **15.8** miles. Turn right at **15.9** miles and climb slightly. At **15.9** miles, reach the end of the trail across the road from the trailhead to complete the ride.

Gazetteer

Nearby camping: Indian Ford, South Shore
Nearest food, drink, services: Sisters

Distance	14.8-mile loop
Route	Paved-road ascent, doubletrack and singletrack descent; views
Climbs	Moderate; high point: 3,860 ft, gain: 640 ft
Duration	Fitness rider: 1 to 2 hours; scenery rider: 3 to 4 hours
Travel	Bend—23 miles; Eugene—103 miles
Skill	Intermediate
Season	Late spring, summer, fall
Map	U.S. Forest Service: Sisters Ranger District
Rules	None
Manager	Deschutes National Forest, Sisters District, 541-549-7700
Web	www.fs.fed.us/r6/centraloregon/recreation/trails/54090-sisters

Who Will Like This Ride

You like zippy cross-country descents; but climbing, not so much.

The Scoop

Peterson Ridge, also known as Sisters Mountain Bike Trail, a local favorite, serves up the kind of riding that makes Bend-area mountain biking famous— fast, whorling, hard-packed trails with banked corners, through an open pine forest. It's such a fun loop, in fact, that when you're done you may want to ride it a couple more times. To this end, you can make it longer and more difficult by riding out and back on the trail rather than using the paved forest road to loop it. Equestrians are discouraged from using this trail, so it stays smooth and fast.

Driving Directions

From Bend, drive northwest on US Highway 20 to Sisters. In Sisters, turn left (south) on Elm Street. After a couple of blocks, find the Village Green—a town park—on the left, opposite the town's fire station. Park here on the left.

The Ride

From the Village Green, pedal south on Elm Street. At **0.4** mile, pass the Sisters Mountain Bike Loop/Peterson Ridge trailhead on the left and continue south. Elm Street becomes Forest Road 16. After a gentle climb,

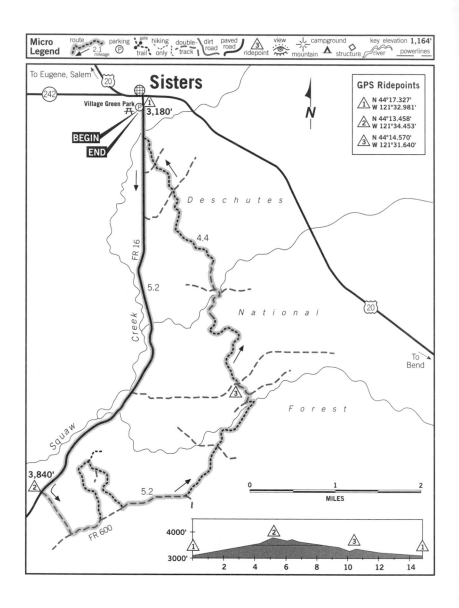

Micro Legend

route 2.1 mileage | parking Ⓟ | gate • hiking trail only | double-track | dirt road | paved road | ▲3 ridepoint | view 👁 mountain | campground △ structure | river | key elevation **1,164'** powerlines

To Eugene, Salem

㉔²

㉔²

Sisters

Village Green Park
🌲 Ⓟ ①
3,180'

BEGIN

END

D e s c h u t e s

4.4

FR 16

5.2

N a t i o n a l

US 20

To Bend

Creek

③

F o r e s t

Squaw

3,840'
②

5.2

FR 600

GPS Ridepoints

① N 44°17.327'
W 121°32.981'

② N 44°13.458'
W 121°34.453'

③ N 44°14.570'
W 121°31.640'

N

0   1   2
MILES

4000'   ②   ③
①   ①
3000'
2   4   6   8   10   12   14

the paved forest road rises more steeply beginning around the **4.1**-mile point. *WHOA!* Just past the crest of the hill and just before a narrow pullout on the left, turn left onto an unmarked doubletrack, **5.2** miles (ridepoint 2).

The doubletrack descends to a T at **5.7** miles. Turn left onto FR 600. Ride over a berm and continue straight on the road. *WHOA!* At **6.1** miles, turn left onto the unmarked singletrack. The smooth, hard-packed trail zips through and around ponderosa pine, juniper, and manzanita. At **6.7** miles, bear right at the fork, following the bike signs. At **6.9** miles, bear left. Stay on the main trail and follow the bike signs. Reach a T with a doubletrack, FR 600, at **7.7** miles and turn left. *WHOA!* At **8.5** miles, turn left to return to singletrack riding with the added banked-corner feature. Wheee! Cross a dirt road, then descend sharply.

Cross a creek at **10.1** miles, and turn right onto the doubletrack. After a few pedal rotations, reach a fork and turn left, continuing on double-track. At **10.4** miles (ridepoint 3), reach a four-way—ride straight across the dirt road to the wide trail opposite. The trail alternates between single- and doubletrack. Bear to the left at **11.1** miles. Near a campsite, **11.8** miles, bear right onto a doubletrack. *WHOA!* At **12.1** miles, turn left onto a narrow trail, and immediately cross over the canal. From here, turn left on the dirt road, then bear right at the fork. At **12.5** miles, follow the

Lower end of Peterson Ridge Trail

bike signs as the route crosses a dirt road to a singletrack.

Continue to follow the bike signs as the trail, which crosses a series of doubletracks, snakes frenetically through the pine forest. At **14.4** miles, reach the end of the trail. Turn right onto FR 16 (Elm Street) and spin back to the Village Green to complete the ride, **14.8** miles.

Gazetteer
Nearby camping: Indian Ford
Nearest food, drink, services: Sisters

Distance	4.8-mile loop
Route	Wide and narrow trails, with only a couple technical spots
Climbs	Easy; high point: 3,720 ft, gain: 250 ft
Duration	Fitness rider: 30 minutes; scenery rider: 1 hour
Travel	Bend—5 miles; Eugene—134 miles
Skill	Intermediate
Season	Late spring, summer, fall
Map	U.S. Forest Service: Bend Ranger District
Rules	None
Manager	Bend Metro Park and Recreation District, 541-389-7275
Web	www.bendparksandrec.org/Park_List_Hidden/Shevlin_Park/shevlin.htlm

Who Will Like This Ride
However short the trail, you need your mountain bike fix.

The Scoop
Up Tumalo Creek and down the opposite side, this short loop at Shevlin Park is intended for beginners. However, a couple of sections of the trail aren't ridable, so be prepared to carry your bike for short distances (this is why it's rated intermediate). Also, this loop is heavily used by walkers and trail runners, so pedal accordingly. Many intermediate and advanced riders begin from Bend—for the added workout—and use this loop as a jumping-off point to explore the numerous trails beyond Shevlin's borders, including Mrazek (ride 24).

Driving Directions
From the junction of US Highway 97 and Northeast Greenwood Avenue in Bend, zero out your odometer and head west on Greenwood. Stay on the arterial as Greenwood becomes Northwest Newport Avenue and then Shevlin Park Road. At 4.7 miles, turn left into the parking area for Shevlin Park. Park in the gravel area on the right, past the work shed.

The Ride

Take the trail that exits from the gravel parking area on the right. At **0.5** mile, proceed straight through the four-way intersection. Reach a fork at **0.7** mile and bear left. After a few pedal strokes, ignore the trail back on the right. The trail rises slightly, traversing the hillside above the paved road below, through ponderosa pine, juniper, and manzanita. At **2.2** miles (ridepoint 2), bear left at the fork and drop to a five-way intersection. Ride straight through the intersection down to Tumalo Creek.

Crossing Tumalo Creek

Cross over the narrow bridge and walk up the short but steep hill. At **2.6** miles, cross a doubletrack. At **2.8** miles, cross a creek and ignore a faint trail back on the right. At **3.6** miles, reach a T and turn left on the dirt road. But at **3.9** miles, turn left to return to the singletrack. The trail descends,

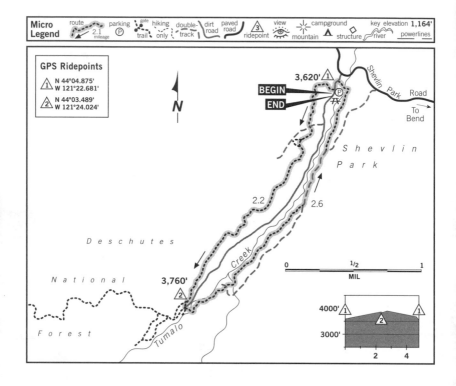

route · 2.1 mileage · parking Ⓟ · gate · hiking trail · double-track · dirt road · paved road · △3 ridepoint · view · mountain · campground · △ structure · river · key elevation **1,164'** · powerlines

GPS Ridepoints

△1 N 44°04.875'
W 121°22.681'

△2 N 44°03.489'
W 121°24.024'

N

3,620' △1

BEGIN
END

Shevlin Park Road

To Bend

S h e v l i n
P a r k

2.2

2.6

D e s c h u t e s

Creek

0   1/2   1
MIL

N a t i o n a l   3,760'
△2

4000' △1   △1
△2
3000'

F o r e s t   Tumalo

2   4

through pine and sage, then switchbacks down to Tumalo Creek. When the trail peters out, at **4.5** miles, ride across the grassy field toward the creek. Cross over the bridge and bear left. Ride to the gravel parking area to complete the loop, **4.8** miles.

Gazetteer

Nearby camping: Tumalo State Park
Nearest food, drink, services: Bend

Distance	21.4-mile out-and-back
Route	Singletrack up, Jedi down
Climbs	Gradual to steep; high point: 5,080 ft, gain: 1,660 ft
Duration	Fitness rider: 2 to 3 hours; scenery rider: 3 to 4 hours
Travel	Bend—5 miles; Eugene—134 miles
Skill	Intermediate
Season	Summer, fall
Map	U.S. Forest Service: Bend Ranger District
Rules	None
Manager	Deschutes National Forest, Bend–Fort Rock District, 541-383-4000
Web	www.fs.fed.us/r6/centraloregon/recreation/trails/trail-district-bend

Who Will Like This Ride
Any self-respecting mountain biker who has a mouth that can form a smile.

The Scoop

In the beginning there were no mountain bike trails. Mountain bikes were allowed on some trails, but they were not mountain bike trails. As the Phil's Trail system (rides 31, 32, and 33) proved, user-built trails rocked. Okay, now these are mountain bike trails! But while Phil's is fun and zippy, there were no epic descents for mountain bikes. Enter Mrazek. In the first edition of KTTO, Mrazek was relatively new, already infamous, and essentially just an out-and-back ride. Now that it's connected with Farewell (ride 27) and Metolius-Windigo (see ride 28) and made official by the Forest Service, Mrazek doesn't have so much of the renegade feel anymore. But you know what? It's still a freaking epic descent, one you will remember for a long time. Built by mountain bikers for mountain bikers.

Threading the Mrazek needle

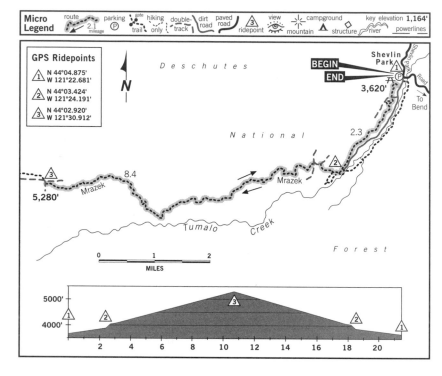

Driving Directions

From the junction of US Highway 97 and Northeast Greenwood Avenue in Bend, zero out your odometer and head west on Greenwood. Stay on the arterial as Greenwood becomes Northwest Newport Avenue and then Shevlin Park Road. At 4.7 miles, turn left into the parking area for Shevlin Park. Park in the gravel area on the right, past the work shed.

The Ride

Take the trail that exits from the gravel parking area on the right. From here, you want to traverse the hillside, never dropping to the paved road or turning away from it. While numerous trails may tempt you, try to Zen the traverse to the **2.5**-mile mark. At **0.5** mile, proceed straight through the four-way intersection. Reach a fork at **0.7** mile and bear left. After a few pedal strokes, ignore the trail back on the right. The trail rises slightly, traversing the hillside. When the trail divides, stay right. At **2.2** miles, bear

Minor Mrazek rock drop near the turnaround point

right again at the fork. At **2.3** miles (ridepoint 2), reach a fork and turn right, immediately climbing a steep, rocky, loose hill. At **2.5** miles, ignore a trail on the left and continue up through pine and thick manzanita. You'll cross a number of dirt roads and pass some lesser trails. Try to stay on the main trail.

The trail crosses a doubletrack at **2.9** miles and then again at **3.2** miles. The trail, narrower now and dusty in sections, slaloms in and around the pines, with some openings barely wider than a set of handlebars. At around **4.5** miles, the trail crosses a series of doubletracks. At **7** miles, the trail crosses a dry canal, then a doubletrack, before climbing steeply. At **7.8** miles, the grade eases and the long ridge ahead provides a perspective from the gradually sloped pine plain.

Cross several more forest roads as you climb. At **10.7** miles (ridepoint 3), the trail seems to end at a doubletrack. Beyond this there's a stretch of doubletrack before the singletrack begins again. This doubletrack at **10.7** miles makes for a reasonable turnaround point. Aimed back toward Shevlin Park, follow the galloping singletrack all the way back to the parking area, **21.4** miles. It's smiles the entire way.

Gazetteer

Nearby camping: Tumalo State Park
Nearest food, drink, services: Bend

Distance	5.4-mile out-and-back
Route	Wide wood-chip trail; easy fun
Climbs	Gentle and short; high point: 3,630 ft, gain: 30 ft
Duration	Fitness rider: 30 minutes; scenery rider: 1 hour
Travel	Bend—1 mile; Eugene—130 miles
Skill	Beginner
Season	Year-round
Map	No useful supplementary map
Rules	None
Manager	Bend Metro Park and Recreation District, 541-389-7275
Web	www.bendparksandrec.org/Park_List_Hidden/First_Street_Rapids_Park/first.html

Who Will Like This Ride

Your kids. Or perhaps you need a 30-minute micro ride to get away from them.

The Scoop

This wide trail is popular with walkers, trail runners, dog walkers, and some families. Variously known as the First Street Rapids Trail and the Bend Riverside Trail, the official name is the Deschutes River Trail—the same, unfortunately, as ride 34. One of the easiest rides in this book, this out-and-back route follows the course of the Deschutes River and affords dramatic views into the canyon.

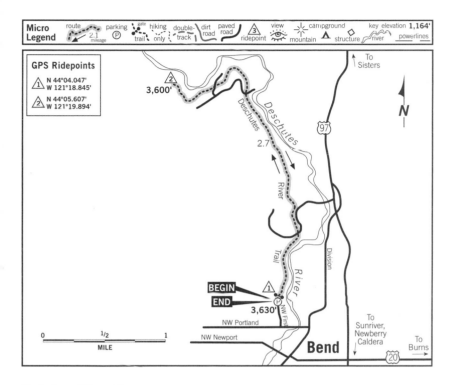

Driving Directions

From the junction of US Highway 97 and Division Street in Bend, set your odometer to zero and head south on Division. At 0.7 mile, turn right on Revere Avenue. At 0.9 mile, turn left on Hill Street. At 1.2 miles, turn right on Northwest Portland Avenue. At 1.4 miles, turn right onto Northwest First Street. At 1.6 miles, First Street dead-ends at the trailhead.

The Ride

From the trailhead, ride around the gate and descend the hill on a road. At **0.6** mile, stay to the left on Deschutes River Trail, climbing a short but steep hill to avoid the golf course on the right. After passing the golf course, stay to the right and parallel the road on a sort of wood-chip sidewalk. **WHOA!** The trail seems to end at **0.9** mile. Cross the road on the left to find the continuation of the trail. From here, stay on the main trail, ignoring spurs on the right. Cross the road twice more at **2.0** and **2.3** miles.

Deschutes River Canyon

The trail follows along the canyon rim. When the wood chips end at a T, **2.7** miles (ridepoint 2), turn around and retrace your tracks. Arrive back at the trailhead at **5.4** miles.

Gazetteer

Nearby camping: Tumalo State Park
Nearest food, drink, services: Bend

Distance	7-mile out-and-back
Route	singletrack; views
Climbs	Moderate; high point: 5,000 ft, gain: 200 ft
Duration	Fitness rider: 30 minutes; scenery rider: 2 hours
Travel	Bend—12 miles; Eugene—141 miles
Skill	Intermediate
Season	Summer, fall
Map	U.S. Forest Service: Bend Ranger District
Rules	National Forest Recreation Pass required
Manager	Deschutes National Forest, Bend–Fort Rock District, 541-383-4000
Web	www.fs.fed.us/r6/centraloregon/recreation/trails/1025a-tumalocreek

Who Will Like This Ride
Dreamers and view seekers.

The Scoop

Though you can drive a car to Tumalo Falls, riding your bike is better. And when isn't that the case? The singletrack out to the falls, first through pine then later the thick manzanita of the oddly barren Tumalo Creek canyon, rises and drops in quick bursts, reminding me of those hot days on the highway when I hold my arm out the window and fly my hand in the wind, up and down. Tumalo Falls is dramatic and beautiful, and there's a picnic area at the falls for a meditative lunch. But the trails from Skyliners Trailhead go

Tumalo Falls

well beyond the falls. They jet out toward Farewell and Mrazek (rides 27 and 24), North Fork to Flagline (ride 28), Swede Ridge (ride 29), Phil's (rides 31, 32, 33), and many others. Get in shape and check it out.

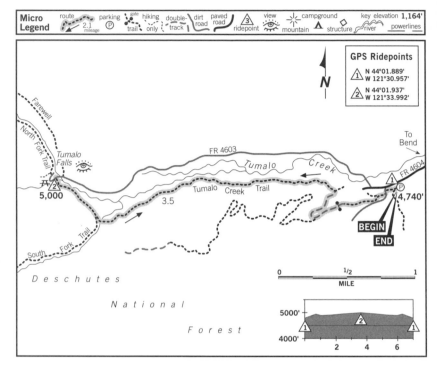

Micro Legend: route 2.1 mileage / parking Ⓟ / gate hiking trail only / double-track / dirt road / paved road / ③ ridepoint / view / mountain / campground / ▲ structure / ◇ river / key elevation 1,164' / powerlines

GPS Ridepoints

△1 N 44°01.889' W 121°30.957'

△2 N 44°01.937' W 121°33.992'

N

To Bend

FR 4603

Tumalo Creek

FR 4604

Farewell

North Fork Trail

Tumalo Falls

5,000

Tumalo Creek Trail

3.5

Tumalo Creek Trail

△1 4,740'

BEGIN

END

South Fork Trail

Deschutes

National

Forest

0   1/2   1
MILE

5000'

△1 △2 △1

4000'

2   4   6

Driving Directions

From the junction of US Highway 97 and Northwest Franklin Avenue in Bend, set your odometer to zero and head west on Franklin (which becomes Northwest Riverside Boulevard). At 1.2 miles, turn right onto Northwest Tumalo Avenue. Continue straight ahead as Tumalo becomes Northwest Galveston Avenue and then Skyliners Road. At 4.5 miles, pass Forest Road 4604 (to Phil's trailhead) on the left. At 11.9 miles, bear left into the wide, gravel Skyliners trailhead and Sno-Park.

The Ride

From the parking area, take Tumalo Creek Trail, which begins just to the right of the bathrooms. Almost immediately, ignore a trail that cuts back on the left. Cross a dirt road and reach a fork—go left, paralleling the dirt road. From here, the trail, climbing slightly, winds through second-growth forest. At **0.6** mile, pass around an old green gate and climb what used to be FR 434.

92   **KISSING THE TRAIL** *Northwest & Central Oregon*

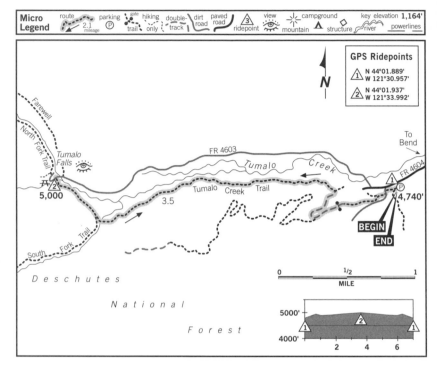

GPS Ridepoints

△1 N 44°01.889' W 121°30.957'

△2 N 44°01.937' W 121°33.992'

Driving Directions

From the junction of US Highway 97 and Northwest Franklin Avenue in Bend, set your odometer to zero and head west on Franklin (which becomes Northwest Riverside Boulevard). At 1.2 miles, turn right onto Northwest Tumalo Avenue. Continue straight ahead as Tumalo becomes Northwest Galveston Avenue and then Skyliners Road. At 4.5 miles, pass Forest Road 4604 (to Phil's trailhead) on the left. At 11.9 miles, bear left into the wide, gravel Skyliners trailhead and Sno-Park.

The Ride

From the parking area, take Tumalo Creek Trail, which begins just to the right of the bathrooms. Almost immediately, ignore a trail that cuts back on the left. Cross a dirt road and reach a fork—go left, paralleling the dirt road. From here, the trail, climbing slightly, winds through second-growth forest. At **0.6** mile, pass around an old green gate and climb what used to be FR 434.

On top of Tumalo Falls

When you reach a fork at **0.7** mile, take a hard right, continue up for a short way, then descend. At **1.1** miles, reach a fork and bear left, heading toward Tumalo Falls. From here, the trail gradually ascends in quick ups and downs along the south bank of Tumalo Creek. Scattered pines and thick manzanita line the trail, with views of the bare hillside north of Tumalo Creek. *WHOA!* Though some of the longer views are nice, the sightlines along this section suck. Head on collisions or even running into hikers is all to easy, especially when riding back toward the trailhead. It's easy to go too fast here, so watch out for other trail users. It's also an exposed stretch of trail and can be hot by late morning. At **2.1** miles, stay to the left at a fork.

Cross over a small creek at **3** miles. At **3.1** miles, reach a fork and bear right, continuing along the creek toward Tumalo Falls. At **3.5** miles (ride-point 2), arrive at the picnic area below the falls. There's a nice view of the falls from the lower picnic area, but a quarter-mile push up North Fork Trail gets you right on top of the cascade. Turn around when you're done and ride back the way you came, returning to Skyliners Sno-Park at **7** miles.

Gazetteer

Nearby camping: Tumalo State Park
Nearest food, drink, services: Bend

Distance	38.9-mile loop
Route	Big singletrack horseshoe connected by 5 miles paved; views
Climbs	Moderate with one exception; high point: 6,080 ft, gain: 2,460 ft
Duration	Fitness rider: 4 to 5 hours; scenery rider: 6 to 8 hours
Travel	Bend—5 miles; Eugene—134 miles
Skill	Intermediate
Season	Summer, fall
Map	U.S. Forest Service: Bend Ranger District
Rules	None
Manager	Deschutes National Forest, Bend–Fort Rock District, 541-383-4000
Web	www.fs.fed.us/r6/centraloregon/recreation/trails/trail-district-bend

Who Will Like This Ride
You love the smell of burning lungs in the morning.

The Scoop

What could be better than combining Phil's (rides 31, 32, 33) and Mrazek (ride 24), both Bend classics, into one ride? Here it is. And you know what, the combining part—Skyliners Trail, Tumalo, and Farewell—are awesome trails as well. By connecting the singletrack orgy with four and a half miles of paved roads, you've accessed a huge wonderful loop straight from town. Who needs a car anyway?

Driving Directions

From the junction of US Highway 97 and Northwest Franklin Avenue in Bend, set your odometer to zero and head west on Franklin. Franklin becomes Northwest Riverside Boulevard. At 1.2 miles, turn right onto Northwest Tumalo Avenue. Continue straight ahead as Tumalo becomes Northwest Galveston Avenue and then Skyliners Road. At 4.5 miles, turn left on Forest Road 4604. At 4.9 miles, you'll find the parking area for Phil's trailhead on the right.

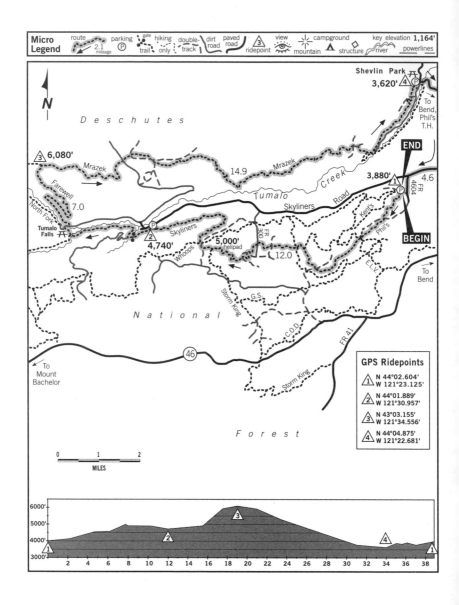

Micro Legend route — parking Ⓟ hiking trail — double-track — dirt road — paved road — ③ ridepoint — 👁 view — 🔆 mountain — campground — ▲ structure — 〜 river — powerlines — gate — 2.1 mileage — key elevation **1,164'**

N

D e s c h u t e s

🏕 **Shelvin Park** Ⓟ
3,620' ④

To Bend, Phil's T.H.

③ **6,080'**

Mrazek

Mrazek

14.9

Tumalo Creek

3,880' ① Ⓟ

END

4.6

FR 4604

Farewell

North Fork

7.0

Tumalo Falls 🏕

4,740'
②

Skyliners

Skyliners Road

Kent's

Phil's

BEGIN

E.L.V.

③

Whoops

5,000' helipad

FR 300

12.0

To Bend

N a t i o n a l

Storm King

G.S.

C.O.D.

FR 41

46

To Mount Bachelor

Storm King

F o r e s t

GPS Ridepoints

① N 44°02.604'
   W 121°23.125'

② N 44°01.889'
   W 121°30.957'

③ N 43°03.155'
   W 121°34.556'

④ N 44°04.875'
   W 121°22.681'

0   1   2
MILES

6000'
5000'
4000'
3000'

③
②
④
①   ①

2 4 6 8 10 12 14 16 18 20 22 24 26 28 30 32 34 36 38

....

The Ride

From the trailhead, take Phil's Trail. After riding straight through a four-way, the fun begins immediately, winding fast along a smooth, sometimes dusty, tread through an open pine forest. Cross a gravel road at **1** mile. At **1.6** miles, the trail braids apart for a rock drop then quickly reconnects. Reach the "Flaming Chicken" roundabout, a 5-way junction, at **2.1** miles. Essentially you need to ride straight through this intersection, which means taking the second left if you're riding clockwise around the chicken. From here the trail climbs at a gentle rate. The grade levels out before you cross a dirt road at **4.0** miles.

At **4.7** miles, reach a fork at Junction 18—go left. Ride straight through a four-way at **5** miles. Cross a doubletrack. When you reach FR 300 at **6.1** miles, turn left onto the road and then almost immediately right onto singletrack again. From here, it's a steep climb to the Phil's Helipad. The tread, through manzanita and an open pine forest, though often smooth becomes loose and rocky in sections, with a few technical step-ups and tightly wound switchbacks. **WOOF!** At **7.8** miles, reach the helipad, a collection of small rocks in a flat open circle surrounded by tall manzanita. The way descends, gradually at first. Reach a fork and bear right (a left heads down Storm King, ride 35). At **8.4** miles, the trail hits a dirt road at a T—turn right. Reach a 5-way at **8.5** miles and take a shallow left toward Skyliners trailhead.

From the 5-way, the trail pinwheels around the base of Tumalo Ridge, swinging east for nearly a mile before rounding the ridge's eastern foot and shooting off to the west. This section of the route is determinedly intermediate, with few black-diamond maneuvers and little change in elevation. The forest, however, changes radically, heading at first through low manzanita and skinny pine—allowing for lots of light and making for a dusty tread—and ending with tall firs and a rich duff trail. Skyliners is a fun trail that combines the classic Phil's meandering with a point-to-point functionality—it connects all the trails in the Phil's system with all the trail opportunities from Skyliners Road and Tumalo Creek.

After a gentle ascent followed by a fast descent, reach the trailhead at Skyliners Sno-Park, **12** miles (ridepoint 2). From the parking area, take Tumalo Creek Trail 25.1, which starts up just to the right of the bathrooms. The trail wends through a dark patch of second growth. Ignore a trail back on the left at **12.1** miles. Immediately cross a dirt road, and reach another fork—go left, paralleling the dirt road. At **12.6** miles, ride around a green gate, and climb up the wide trail. Reach an unmarked fork at **12.7** miles and take a hard right turn. First climb then drop to a fork at **13.1** miles— stay to the left. From here the trail heads west, paralleling Tumalo Creek through a hallway of high manzanita. **WHOA!** Given the poor sightlines here, watch out for hikers and oncoming cyclists. It's an exposed stretch of trail and can be hot. After numerous short ups and downs, drop to cross over a creek at **15** miles. At **15.1** miles, reach a fork and stay to the right (left climbs to Swede Ridge, ride 29).

At **15.5** miles, the trail ends at a paved road. Above you'll see Tumalo Falls. Turn right onto the road, cross the bridge over Tumalo Creek, then find Farewell Trail 26 on the left. Farewell, it should be noted, doesn't mean "see you soon." It means goodbye for a long, undetermined amount of time, perhaps forever. And, given the climb you're about to embark upon, it's an apt name for the trail. Though the trail ducks into a forested short stretch during the climb, most of the ascent is up an open, manzanita covered hillside. Not that you'll notice. You'll be busy counting the knobs on your tires as they slowly churn up the steep slope.

WOOF! The incline eases at a sweet viewpoint, **17.5** miles, but it's not until nearly **18** miles, when you enter the forest, that you'll feel like slapping it into the middle chainring. When you reach a fork at **19** miles (ridepoint 3), turn right, heading toward Shevlin Park on Mrazek Trail. (A left heads off to Happy Valley and connects, via the Metolius-Windigo Trail, to North Fork to Flagline, ride 28.)

From the fork, Mrazek swoops and dives like perhaps no other trail, and if you haven't killed yourself on the climb you have 12 straight miles of smiling bliss ahead of you. The trail crosses numerous dirt roads and doubletracks during the descent. Stay on the main trail. At **21.1** miles, find a rocky outcropping on the right—it's a nice viewpoint and better place to break than the fork at the top of Farewell. Just before the **23**-mile mark, a new downhill-only segment of trail routes around an old doubletrack. When the singletrack ends, take a right onto the doubletrack and then a left to regain singletrack. The trail is again two-way from here back to Shevlin Park.

Just try to follow the fast windies as you spin your steed toward gallop. From about **26** miles on the pine forest thins out to reveal more manzanita, fewer pines, and a dustier tread. After crossing many small dirt roads, cross a wide gravel road at **30.4** miles. A short distance farther, reach a fork and bear left. Reach the top of Shevlin Park at **31.1** miles. From here, bear left (rather than dropping to the park road) and Zen your way along the hillside, staying above the road but not climbing away from it either. Reach the parking area at the bottom (north end) of Shevlin Park at **33.9** miles (ridepoint 4).

From the parking area at Shevlin Park, ride north to the park entrance and turn right onto NW Shevlin Park Rd. At **35.6** miles, turn right onto NW Mount Washington Dr. At **36.6** miles, turn right onto NW Skyliners Rd. At **38.1** miles, turn left on FR 4604. Return to Phil's trailhead at **38.5** miles.

Gazetteer
Nearby camping: Tumalo State Park
Nearest food, drink, services: Bend

Making the turn onto Mrazek

Distance	31-mile loop
Route	All delicious singletrack; views
Climbs	Ass-kicking ascent; high point: 7,020 ft, gain: 2,280 ft
Duration	Fitness rider: 4 hours, scenery rider: 5 to 8 hours
Travel	Bend—12 miles; Eugene—141 miles
Skill	Intermediate
Season	August 15 through early October
Map	U.S. Forest Service: Bend Ranger District
Rules	National Forest Recreation Pass required; North Fork Trail is uphill only; seasonal closure
Manager	Deschutes National Forest, Bend–Fort Rock District, 541-383-4000
Web	www.fs.fed.us/r6/centraloregon/recreation/trails/trail-district-bend

Who Will Like This Ride

Since you know patience is a great virtue, you enjoy planning your long rides months in advance.

The Scoop

North Fork to Flagline was not in the first edition of KTTO, which was a big mistake as it's one of those best trails. Thank God for second editions, eh? There are several ways to check out this classic Bend loop. You can shorten it by either starting at Tumalo Falls rather than Skyliners trailhead or by finishing via the South Fork Trail from Swampy Lakes rather than the Sector 16 / Whoops / Skyliners finish described here. You can lengthen it, too, of course (since it's August and you're in shape from a summer full of riding), by starting from Phil's trailhead (ride 31) and following the first 12 miles of the Farewell Epic (ride 27). Better yet, start the journey from Bend and ride out to Phil's trailhead, which would send it well over the 50-mile mark.

But it doesn't really matter how you assemble this ride as long as you get out there and do it. This loop gets you into unbelievably beautiful country, with waterfalls and high meadows and gurgling streams. You'll like the Flagline descent, too. Note: This loop is only open between August 15 and when the snow flies at 7,000 feet, which most years means a short window of maybe only six weeks. Thus the need to plan ahead.

Driving Directions

From the junction of US Highway 97 and Northwest Franklin Avenue in Bend, set your odometer to zero and head west on Franklin (which becomes Northwest Riverside Boulevard). At 1.2 miles, turn right onto Northwest Tumalo Avenue. Continue straight ahead as Tumalo becomes Northwest Galveston Avenue and then Skyliners Road. At 4.5 miles, pass Forest Road 4604 (to Phil's trailhead) on the left. At 11.9 miles, bear left into the wide, gravel Skyliners trailhead and Sno-Park.

The Ride

From the parking area, take Tumalo Creek Trail, which begins just to the right of the bathrooms. Almost immediately, ignore a trail that cuts back on the left. Cross a dirt road and reach another fork—go left, paralleling the dirt road. From here, the trail, climbing slightly, winds through second-growth forest. At **0.6** mile, pass around an old green gate and climb what used to be FR 434. When you reach a fork at **0.7** mile, take a hard right,

continue up for a short way, then descend. At **1.1** miles, reach a fork and bear left, heading toward Tumalo Falls.

From here, the trail gradually ascends in quick ups and downs, along the south bank of Tumalo Creek. Scattered pines and thick manzanita line the trail, with views of the bare hillside north of Tumalo Creek. **WHOA!** The sightlines here are poor, so watch out for other trail users. At **2.1** miles, stay to the left at a fork. Cross over a small creek at **3** miles. At **3.1** miles, reach a fork and bear right, continuing along the creek toward Tumalo Falls. At **3.5** miles, the trail ends at a T—go left and ride a few pedal rotations to a parking area where you have a nice view of Tumalo Falls. From the parking area, take North Fork Trail 24.2 toward Happy Valley. Note: This trail is only open to bikes for uphill riding.

As you ascend, stay to the left. Three trails around the **3.8**-mile mark head out to high views of Tumalo Falls. At **4.6** miles, the trail winds out to the canyon edge for another view of the falls. After an extremely steep initial climb from the parking area, the ascent is somewhat more reasonable in its requests for suffering as it follows North Fork Creek toward Happy Valley. Cross to the north side of the creek at **6** miles. After the creek crossing, however, the trail angles up again, winding and switchbacking with a sadistic vengeance. Yet at the same time, the route rewards with views of one beautiful waterfall after another.

When the trail divides at **6.8** miles, go right. **WOOF!** The North Fork climb finally eases, though much climbing remains in your future. At **7.1** miles, bear right again at the fork to continue toward Happy Valley. Reach Happy Valley, a nondescript meadow, at **7.5** miles (ridepoint 2). The trail forks here—go left toward Todd Horse Camp (a right turn points you east toward the top of Farewell (ride 27) and Mrazek (ride 24). The way is level for a moment, but just as you think you've figured out that Happy Valley might just mean no more climbing, the route tilts upward again. Around the **8.7**-mile mark, the trail noodles forward, then drops to a small meadow. But the descent is short-lived as the trail inches towards 7,000 feet, gaining elevation in fits and starts, through small fir and mountain hemlock.

At **10.4** miles, crest a false summit. Reach a fork at **10.7** miles and go left From here, it's a fun descent to an open rocky creek crossing at **11.2** miles.

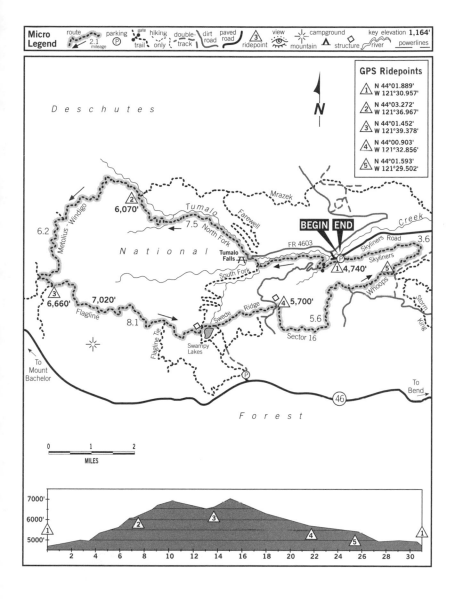

Then it's up again, and back into the shade of the trees. Ignore a hiker-only trail on the left at **11.3** miles. Following a long stretch of trail that skirts a big meadow, the trail, somewhat ragged here, descends to a fork at **13.1** miles—bear left. Reach another fork at **13.2** miles and again go left, climbing now. When the trail splits at **13.7** miles (ridepoint 3), take another left toward Tumalo Falls trailhead. Thus begins Flagline Trail.

Flagline climbs eastward, then cuts south, heading straight at Tumalo Mountain, a huge cylindrical cone immediately northeast of Mount Bachelor. *WOOF!* At **15.2** miles, you finally pass over the top of the loop. From here, it's downhill, and you'll like it. During the descent you'll find lots of ramps, ladders and the occasional jump. At **18** miles, reach a fork and bear left, following the signs toward Swampy Shelter. At **19.2** miles, hit a T and turn left. When you reach a fork at the shelter at **19.4** miles, go right. When the trail forks again at **19.9** miles, stay to the left. From here, the trail climbs at a gentle rate before romping down Swede Ridge. At **21.8** miles (ridepoint 4), arrive at a dirt road. Across the road, take Sector 16 Trail.

Sector 16 Trail, narrow, schizophrenic, and serpentine, marks quite a change from the wide, romping descent down Flagline and Swede Ridge. After countless ups and downs, arounds, and needle-threads, cross a dirt road at **25** miles (from here, it's 9.2 miles to Phil's trailhead; 6 miles to Skyliners trailhead). Cross a doubletrack near a shelter at **25.3** miles, then cross another dirt road a short time later. At **25.8** miles, the trail crosses a dirt road at Junction 30 and becomes Upper Whoops Trail, an intermediate version of a downhill course. It's fun, though the trail is loose in places. *WHOA!* At **27.4** miles (ridepoint 5), reach a confusing intersection: Bear right on the doubletrack then immediately left on a singletrack (Skyliners Trail) toward Skyliners trailhead.

Skyliners, zippy and fast in sections, slower and methodical in others, heads east before wrapping around the sharp base of the ridge. From here, through darker forest, the route aims westward. It's a fun, middle-chainring trail. Around **30.5** miles, stay on the main trail, which descends quickly. Reach Skyliners trailhead at **31** miles.

Gazetteer
Nearby camping: Tumalo State Park
Nearest food, drink, services: Bend

Distance	14-mile lollipop
Route	Singletrack with some doubletrack
Climbs	Some steep climbing; high point: 5,980 ft, gain: 1,180 ft
Duration	Fitness rider: 2 hours; scenery rider: 3 to 4 hours
Travel	Bend—12 miles; Eugene—141 miles
Skill	Intermediate
Season	Summer, fall
Map	U.S. Forest Service: Bend Ranger District
Rules	National Forest Recreation Pass required
Manager	Deschutes National Forest, Bend–Fort Rock District, 541-383-4000
Web	www.fs.fed.us/r6/centraloregon/recreation/trails/trail-district-bend

Who Will Like This Ride
You've got a different definition of Happy Hour.

The Scoop

A series of very ridable switchbacks ascend from pine forest into stands of fir and hemlock. But because of a persistent snowpack, which can refuse to melt until sometime late in the summer, this ride can be tricky. We once got lost near Swampy Lakes and wandered through the snow with our bikes on our shoulders. The GPS, map, compass, altimeter, and Snickers bar saved us from our wandering. And, after figuring out the twists and turns of a trail under several feet of snow, we rocketed back down the ridge to Tumalo Creek, jonesing to explore the cornucopia of trails that branch out from Tumalo Falls and Swampy Lakes Shelter. It's some of the best riding anywhere.

Driving Directions

From the junction of US Highway 97 and Northwest Franklin Avenue in Bend, set your odometer to zero and head west on Franklin (which becomes Northwest Riverside Boulevard). At 1.2 miles, turn right onto Northwest Tumalo Avenue. Continue straight ahead as Tumalo becomes Northwest Galveston Avenue and then Skyliners Road. At 4.5 miles, pass Forest Road

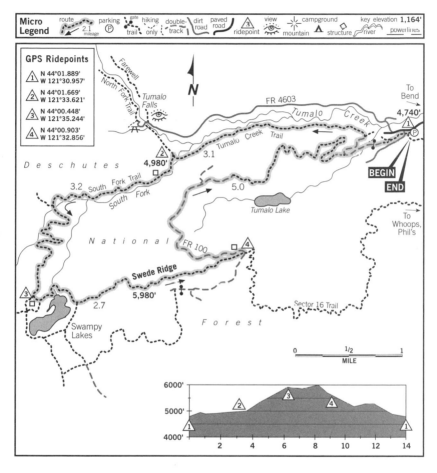

Micro Legend — route 2.1 mileage, parking Ⓟ, gate hiking trail only, double-track, dirt road, paved road, △3 ridepoint, view, campground, mountain, structure, river, key elevation **1,164'**, powerlines

GPS Ridepoints

△1 N 44°01.889'
W 121°30.957'

△2 N 44°01.669'
W 121°33.621'

△3 N 44°00.448'
W 121°35.244'

△4 N 44°00.903'
W 121°32.856'

North Fork Trail · *Farewell* · *Tumalo Falls*

FR 4603 · *Tumalo Creek* · To Bend · **4,740'** · △1

Deschutes · △2 **4,980'** · 3.1 *Tumalo Creek Trail*

BEGIN **END**

3.2 *South Fork Trail* · *South Fork* · 5.0 · *Tumalo Lake*

To Whoops, Phil's

National · FR 100 · △4

Swede Ridge · **5,980'** · *Sector 16 Trail*

△3 · 2.7 · *Swampy Lakes* · *Forest*

0 1/2 1 MILE

Elevation profile: 6000' — 5000' — 4000', markers △1 △2 △3 △4, horizontal axis 2, 4, 6, 8, 10, 12, 14

4604 (to Phil's trailhead) on the left. At 11.9 miles, bear left into the wide, gravel parking lot for Skyliners trailhead and Sno-Park.

The Ride

From the parking area, take Tumalo Creek Trail, which begins just to the right of the bathrooms. Almost immediately, ignore a trail that cuts back on the left. Cross a dirt road and reach a fork—go left, paralleling the dirt road. From here, the trail, climbing slightly, winds through second-growth forest. At **0.6** mile, pass around an old green gate and climb what used to be FR

434. When you reach a fork at **0.7** mile, take a hard right, continue up for a short way, then descend. At **1.1** miles, reach a fork and bear left, heading toward Tumalo Falls. From here, the trail gradually ascends in quick ups and downs, along the south bank of Tumalo Creek. Scattered pines and thick manzanita line the trail, with views of the bare hillside north of Tumalo Creek. At **2.1** miles, stay to the left at a fork.

Cross over a small creek at **3** miles. At **3.1** miles (ridepoint 2), reach a fork and take a sharp left (you can bear right and ride less than one-half mile up to Tumalo Falls, then turn around and ride back to this fork). The trail follows the South Fork of Tumalo Creek, climbing. Pass a camping shelter on the right at **3.3** miles. Reach a fork at **4.5** miles and turn left, immediately crossing a bridge. From here, the trail leaves the creek and switchbacks up the hillside, through a shaded forest of various pines, firs, and mountain hemlock. Just after passing a shallow lake on the right, reach an unmarked fork at **6.3** miles (ridepoint 3)—turn left. At Swampy Lakes Shelter, **6.4** miles, the trail divides again—bear left.

Pass by the large meadow at Swampy Lakes, then cross a small creek. The trail bends to the right here. A short distance farther, the trail veers back to the left and climbs gently to the ride's high point around **8** miles. A fun descent down Swede Ridge follows. At **9** miles (ridepoint 4), the trail dumps out at FR 100—turn left toward Swede Ridge Shelter. (Note: Sector 16 Trail is just across FR 100, see map for ride 28.) Pass by the shelter and descend quickly on FR 100, a doubletrack. At **10.6** miles, stay to the right, ignoring a faint doubletrack on the left. At **10.7** miles, the doubletrack narrows, finally becoming singletrack at **10.9** miles. The trail, loose and rocky in sections, weaves across the top of the flat ridge before switchbacking down a steep manzanita-covered slope. Reach a fork at **13.3** miles and bear right. Pass around the old green gate and bear left on the trail. After numerous twists and turns, cross a dirt road and then reach the trailhead parking area at **14** miles to complete the ride.

Gazetteer

Nearby camping: Tumalo State Park
Nearest food, drink, services: Bend

Distance	18.8-mile lollipop
Route	Glorious singletrack
Climbs	Gentle, no long ascents; high point: 4680 ft, gain: 820 ft
Duration	Fitness rider: 2 hours; scenery rider: 3 to 4 hours
Travel	Bend—3 miles; Eugene—132 miles
Skill	Intermediate
Season	Summer, fall
Map	U.S. Forest Service: Bend Ranger District
Rules	None
Manager	Deschutes National Forest, Bend–Fort Rock District, 541-383-4000
Web	www.fs.fed.us/r6/centraloregon/recreation/trails/trail-district-bend

Who Will Like This Ride

Whether all-mountain, single speed or cross-country, it's all good. Peace.

The Scoop

Along with its older cousin, Phil's Trail, which sits immediately to the north, C.O.D. epitomizes mountain biking close to Bend. It's a user-built trail that whips, winds, and whorls through a sparse pine forest. Sometimes the tread is swoopy and butter smooth, sometimes it spits you through rocky chokepoints onto raggedy off-camber chutes. Since it's built for speed and there's not much elevation gain here, it's the kind of trail where you can throw down 18 miles in a hurry, and smile the entire way. C.O.D. teeters between three and four wheels. It's longer than the 18-mile limit for three-wheel rides and there are some advanced sections of trail, but the elevation gain is gentle and much of the riding is fast and easy. Given its close proximity to town, most Bend locals ride to and from this trail.

Driving Directions

From the junction of US Highway 97 and Northwest Franklin Avenue in Bend, set your odometer to zero and head west on Franklin. Franklin becomes Northwest Riverside Boulevard. At 1.2 miles, turn right onto

Northwest Tumalo Avenue. Continue straight ahead as Tumalo becomes Northwest Galveston Avenue. At 1.6 miles, turn left onto Northwest 14th Street; this soon becomes Century Drive. ***WHOA!*** At 4.8 miles, find a small (five cars max), nondescript trailhead parking area on the right.

The Ride

From the parking area, the trail climbs straight up the sage-covered embankment, and the first few hundred yards may be a push. The top of the bluff is reached quickly, however, and the steepest climb of the day is done. At **0.1** mile, reach a fork and bear left. After taking you pinwheeling around sage and flowing over small rocks, the trail enters a sparse pine forest. At **1.2** miles, ride straight through a four-way. Between **1.4** miles and **1.9** miles, the route becomes quite narrow in places, rocky, and technical. Ride straight through a four-way at **2.4** miles (ridepoint 2). After a few more pedal rotations, reach a fork and bear left (right is the trail E.L.V.) Over the next mile you'll cross at least three doubletracks as you focus on keeping up with the riders in front of you.

At **3.6** miles, cross over a small ridge, then descend. When you reach a T at **4** miles (Junction 21), go right. From here, the route climbs on an occasionally rough trail. Stay on the main trail, which crosses several more doubletracks over the next two miles. At **6.1** miles, cross a gravel road (FR 4610). As you continue, you'll cross numerous doubletracks as you drop, spin, and climb your way toward Storm King. Several sections feel as though you're riding a giant slalom, only upward.

When you reach a T at **8.5** miles (ridepoint 3) (Junction 32), you've arrived at the King—go

Playing on a C.O.D. tetter

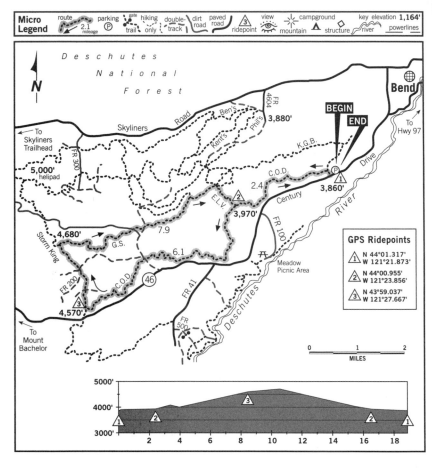

route 2.1 mileage · parking ℗ · gate · hiking trail · double-track · dirt road · paved road · ③ ridepoint · view · mountain · campground · structure · river · key elevation 1,164' · powerlines

Deschutes
National
Forest

N

To Skyliners Trailhead

Skyliners Road

Ben's
Phil's
Kent's

FR 4604
3,880'

K.G.B.

BEGIN
END

Bend

To Hwy 97

5,000' helipad

FR 300

Century Drive

River

C.O.D.

℗ ① 3,860'

2.4

② 3,970'
E.L.V.

4,680'
G.S.

Storm King

7.9

6.1

FR 100

FR 41

46

C.O.D.

FR 200

③ 4,570'

To Mount Bachelor

FR 500

Meadow Picnic Area

Deschutes

GPS Ridepoints

① N 44°01.317'
W 121°21.873'

② N 44°00.955'
W 121°23.856'

③ N 43°59.037'
W 121°27.667'

0   1   2
MILES

5000'
4000'
3000'

① ② ③ ② ①

2   4   6   8   10   12   14   16   18

right and continue up. At **9.7** miles, the trail seems to end at a dirt road—turn right. When the road forks a few pedal strokes farther, find the singletrack that starts up again from the crotch of the fork. The trail divides again at **10.4** miles—turn right onto G.S. (left climbs toward Phil's Helipad, see ride 33). **WHOA!** Last I was there, this was an unmarked intersection. From here, the route is sometimes rough, faint, and uncertain. Stay on the main trail.

The trail drops to a 5-way intersection of dirt roads and trails at **11.4** miles. Angle to the left to stay on singletrack. The trail joyfully rockets down the

Caravanning near the beginning of C.O.D.

hillside. Cross a dirt road at **12.7** miles. Cross another road at **13.1** miles—make sure to bear left to stay on the singletrack here. When the trail divides at **14.6** miles, turn right (left is Voodoo). The trail braids apart at **14.8** miles—go right for a challenge or left for a smoother cruise. At **15.4** miles, reach a four-way and turn right onto E.L.V. (left to Phil's Trail).

At **16.4** miles (ridepoint 2), arrive at a T and turn left. You're now back on C.O.D., heading east towards the trailhead. Almost immediately you'll ride straight through a four-way. Pedal straight through another four-way at **17.6** miles. At **18.2** miles, leave the forest, and it's back out onto the sage lands. After a few tight pinwheels, the trail forks at **18.7** miles—go right. Drop to the trailhead along Century Drive, **18.8** miles.

Gazetteer

Nearby camping: Tumalo State Park
Nearest food, drink, services: Bend

Distance	8.8-mile loop
Route	Silky and sinewy singletrack
Climbs	Some ups, but none strenuous; high point: 4,510 ft, gain: 630 ft
Duration	Fitness rider: less than 1 hour; scenery rider: 1 to 2 hours
Travel	Bend—5 miles; Eugene—134 miles
Skill	Intermediate
Season	Late spring, summer, fall
Map	U.S. Forest Service: Bend Ranger District
Rules	None
Manager	Deschutes National Forest, Bend–Fort Rock District, 541-383-4000
Web	www.fs.fed.us/r6/centraloregon/recreation/trails/1042-phils

Who Will Like This Ride

Just want to get your Phil's bearings, but you aspire to Whoop de Doos, Storm King, and Ben's.

The Scoop

Whether after work, between shifts, or just before beer-thirty, many locals begin a ride on Phil's Trail right from town. It's an easy, five-mile spin up Skyliners Road or the various trails that depart from west Bend. The added benefit, of course, is that you don't need a Trail Park Pass if you don't park at the trailhead. Ahhh! The area that's known as Phil's Trail is actually a maze of trails, several days' worth of riding. And it's good riding, the epitome of Bend mountain biking, with zippy, smooth, hard-packed trails that wend through open pine forest and manzanita. This loop, the shortest of two loops that begin from Phil's trailhead, provides a good introduction to the area.

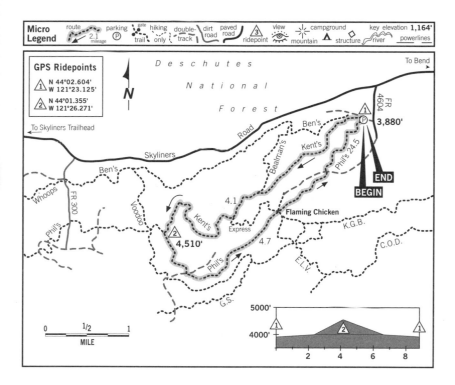

Driving Directions

From the junction of US Highway 97 and Northwest Franklin Avenue in Bend, set your odometer to zero and head west on Franklin. Franklin becomes Northwest Riverside Boulevard. At 1.2 miles, turn right onto Northwest Tumalo Avenue. Continue straight ahead as Tumalo becomes Northwest Galveston Avenue and then Skyliners Road. At 4.5 miles, turn left on Forest Road 4604 . At 4.9 miles, you'll find the parking area for Phil's trailhead on the right.

The Ride

From Phil's trailhead, take Kent's Trail 24.5, which winds and twists through an open pine forest. At **1.9** miles, reach a fork and bear left. When the trail forks again at **2.3** miles, stay to the left on Kent's Trail. The route angles up from here and you'll have to gear down. At a fork at **2.4** miles, bear left again. Ignore a trail back on the right at **2.5** miles. Reach Junction 14 at **2.6** miles, and go right.

The Flaming Chicken points the way home

The route levels somewhat after **2.8** miles. Reach a fork at **4.1** miles (ridepoint 2) (Junction 18) and go left. You are now officially on Phil's Trail. The trail, smooth and hard-packed, through ponderosa pine, zips in and around low manzanita. During the second half of the summer the trail can be somewhat dusty but remains solid and fast. Cross a dirt road at **4.8** miles. Your frolicking descent begins here, zippy, winding and fast. Unfortunately, it's over all too soon.

Reach a 5-way roundabout, referred to as the Flaming Chicken by locals, (Junctions 7 & 8) at **6.7** miles. Go counterclockwise around the chicken and take the second right toward Phil's trailhead. At **7.2** miles, the trail braids apart but reconnects after a few rotations. Cross a gravel road at **7.8** miles. Arrive at Phil's trailhead at **8.8** miles.

Gazetteer

Nearby camping: Tumalo State Park
Nearest food, drink, services: Bend

Distance	4.2-mile out-and-back
Route	Smooth, winding singletrack
Climbs	Almost level; high point: 4,010 ft, gain: 130 ft
Duration	Fitness rider: 20 minutes; scenery rider: 1 hour
Travel	Bend—5 miles; Eugene—134 miles
Skill	Intermediate
Season	Summer, fall
Map	U.S. Forest Service: Bend Ranger District
Rules	None
Manager	Deschutes National Forest, Bend–Fort Rock District, 541-383-4000
Web	www.fs.fed.us/r6/centraloregon/recreation/trails/1042-phils

Who Will Like This Ride
Families and singletrack virgins.

The Scoop

You have arrived at one of the easiest trails in the book. The cool thing is that it's all singletrack. Bring your kids on this ride and they'll love you. Just make sure they look out for other cyclists on the trail. There may be no better introduction to the beauty of sweet singletrack.

Driving Directions

From the junction of US Highway 97 and Northwest Franklin Avenue in Bend, set your odometer to zero and head west on Franklin. Franklin becomes Northwest Riverside Boulevard. At 1.2 miles, turn right onto Northwest Tumalo Avenue. Continue straight ahead as Tumalo becomes Northwest Galveston Avenue and then Skyliners Road. At 4.5 miles, turn left on Forest Road 4604. At 4.9 miles, you'll find the parking area for Phil's trailhead on the right.

The Ride

Three trails begin from Phil's trailhead. Take Phil's Trail. Almost immediately, you'll ride straight through a four-way. The smooth trail, never too narrow or sharp, winds through an open pine forest. In midsummer the tread

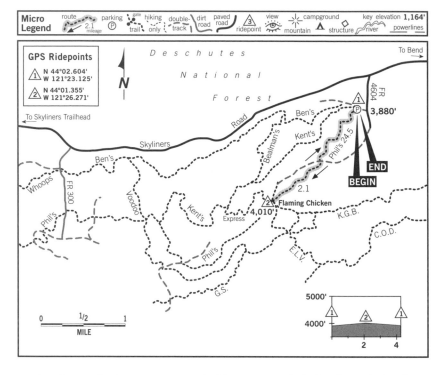

GPS Ridepoints
① N 44°02.604' W 121°23.125'
② N 44°01.355' W 121°26.271'

To Skyliners Trailhead

Deschutes

National

Forest

To Bend

N

Skyliners Road

Ben's

Kent's

Ben's

Whoops

FR 300

Voodoo

Kent's

Express

Phil's

Bealman's

Phil's 24.5

FR 4604

ⓟ **3,880'**

END

BEGIN

2.1

Flaming Chicken **4,010'**

K.G.B.

C.O.D.

E.L.V.

G.S.

0   1/2   1
MILE

5000'

4000'

2   4

---

can be dusty, which means you probably want to ride behind your kids. The trail can be fast, too, but only as fast as you want it to be. At **1** mile, cross a gravel road. At **1.6** miles, the trail splits, but it reconnects a short distance farther. Reach a 5-way roundabout at **2.1** miles (ridepoint 2). In the center of the roundabout you'll find the Flaming Chicken, so called by locals in snarky homage to a very similar piece of art at a street roundabout in Bend. Turn around at the chicken and ride back to Phil's trailhead, **4.2** miles.

Choices, choices

Gazetteer

Nearby camping: Tumalo State Park
Nearest food, drink, services: Bend

Distance	20.1-mile loop
Route	Superfun singletrack
Climbs	Several tough climbs; high point: 5,420 ft, gain: 1,540 ft
Duration	Fitness rider: 2 hours; scenery rider: 3 to 4 hours
Travel	Bend—5 miles; Eugene—134 miles
Skill	Advanced
Season	Summer, fall
Map	U.S. Forest Service: Bend Ranger District
Rules	None
Manager	Deschutes National Forest, Bend–Fort Rock District, 541-383-4000
Web	www.fs.fed.us/r6/centraloregon/recreation/trails/1042-phils

Who Will Like This Ride
Perhaps not quite a "best of" Phil's, but close enough.

The Scoop
This is kid-in-a-candy-store stuff. It all happens on a big chunk of land between Skyliners Road to the north, State Highway 46 (Century Drive) to the south, and Bend and Tumalo Falls to the east and west—more than twenty square miles—a terabyte worth of whorling singletrack, switchbacking grunts, and high-speed smiles. Ride on!

Driving Directions
From the junction of US Highway 97 and Northwest Franklin Avenue in Bend, set your odometer to zero and head west on Franklin. Franklin becomes Northwest Riverside Boulevard. At 1.2 miles, turn right onto Northwest Tumalo Avenue. Continue straight ahead as Tumalo becomes Northwest Galveston Avenue and then Skyliners Road. At 4.5 miles, turn left on Forest Road 4604. At 4.9 miles, you'll find the parking area for Phil's trailhead on the right.

The Ride
From the trailhead, take Phil's Trail. After riding straight through a four-way, the fun kicks in as you swoop and wind along a fast, smooth,

Having fun at Phil's

occasionally dusty tread. The sparse pine forest afford good sight lines. Cross a gravel road at **1** mile. At **1.6** miles, the trail braids apart for a rock drop then quickly reconnects. At **2.1** miles, reach a 5-way junction, referred to as the Flaming Chicken roundabout. Essentially you need to ride straight through this intersection, which means taking the second left if you're riding clockwise around the chicken. From here the trail climbs at a gentle, and then not-quite-as-gentle, rate. The grade levels out before you cross a dirt road at **4.0** miles.

At **4.7** miles (ridepoint 2), reach a fork at Junction 18—go left. Ride straight through a four-way at **5** miles. Cross a doubletrack. When you reach FR 300 at **6.1** miles, turn left onto the road and then almost immediately right onto singletrack again. From here, it's a steep climb to Phil's Helipad. Though often smooth, through manzanita and sparse pines, the tread is loose and rocky in sections, with a few technical step-ups and tightly wound switchbacks. *WOOF!* At **7.8** miles, reach the so-called helipad, a weird collection of small rocks in a flat open circle surrounded by tall manzanita.

From the trippy helipad top, the way descends gradually then quickly. At **8** miles, reach a fork and bear right. At **8.4** miles, the trail hits a dirt road at

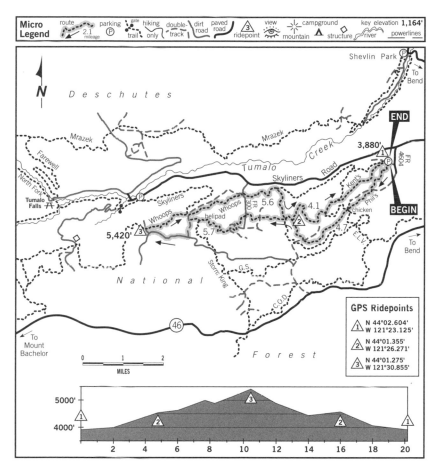

a T—turn left. You're now climbing on FR 310. At **9** miles, reach a T and turn right on FR 4615. Climb steadily up the main road, ignoring lesser spurs, into a mixed forest that includes grand fir and, farther up, noble fir. Pass a doubletrack on the right, then, at **10.3** miles, reach a four-way and turn right on FR 300 (don't confuse this road with the FR 300 near Junction 24 later in the ride). Just up the hill, **10.4** miles (ridepoint 3), a singletrack crosses the dirt road. This is Junction 30 and the ride's high point. Turn right onto this trail. This is Upper Whoops, sometimes referred to as Upper Whoop de Doos. Say the word "contact" out loud before starting down the trail.

From the top at FR 300, the trail romps down the hillside, slaloming in and out of the grand firs. **WHOA!** The trail here is often dusty, and the bumps will throw you if you're not paying attention. At **12** miles, the trail dumps out onto a doubletrack—bear right. Almost immediately the doubletrack ends at a T at FR 310. Whoops starts up again on the opposite side of FR 310. The trail winds and rolls up the hillside through ponderosa pine forest. Cross a doubletrack. At **13.7** miles, bear right on a dirt road. Immediately reach a T with FR 300. This is Junction 24. Across FR 300, Ben's Trail starts up—take it. The trail rips across the open forest, crossing several doubletracks along the way. At **15** miles, reach a fork and bear right onto Voodoo Trail. The trail dips, then climbs.

At **15.7** miles, reach a four-way and turn left. At **16** miles (ridepoint 2), reach a T at Junction 18 (you passed this way at 4.7 miles). If you turn right, you'll retrace your tracks to the trailhead via Phil's Trail. Instead, turn left onto Kent's Trail. Cross several dirt roads. At **17.5** miles (Junction 14), reach a fork and bear left. From here, it's a fast cruise back to Phil's trailhead. Just stay to the right when the trail divides at **17.6**, **17.7**, **17.8** and **18.2** miles. Arrive back at the trailhead at **20.1** miles.

Gazetteer
Nearby camping: Tumalo State Park
Nearest food, drink, services: Bend

Distance	16.6-mile out-and-back
Route	Sometimes confusing, riverside singletrack
Climbs	Rolling, no long ascents; high point: 4,180, ft, gain: 360 ft
Duration	Fitness rider: 1 to 2 hours, scenery rider: 3 to 4 hours
Travel	Bend—7 miles; Eugene—136 miles
Skill	Intermediate
Season	Late spring, summer, fall
Map	U.S. Forest Service: Bend Ranger District
Rules	National Forest Recreation Pass required
Manager	Deschutes National Forest, Bend–Fort Rock District, 541-383-4000
Web	www.fs.fed.us/r6/centraloregon/recreation/trails/1002a-deschutesriver

Who Will Like This Ride
Out-of-towners looking for beauty and a buff singletrack.

The Scoop

The Deschutes River Trail may be the most heavily used trail in the Bend area. And for good reason—it's a beautiful riverside trail close to town with no long climbs. In late spring and then again in the fall, when there's less daylight and fewer nonresidents to crowd the trail, Bend locals ride here, often riding to the trailhead from town (which adds about 15 miles). During the summer, though, especially on weekends when this trail is abuzz with walkers, bicyclists, and equestrians, locals hide out on the high, remote trails west of town.

Though rated three wheels, there's a hitch: The Deschutes River Trail is actually a pretty confusing system of three parallel trails—a hiking trail, a biking trail (Trail 2.3), and an equestrian trail—each of which join together in places and split apart in others. Pile on the spur trails, both signed and unsigned, and the whole thing can make following a specific route—this one, for instance—extremely frustrating. Because of this, the trail requires a fair amount of routefinding Zen. Just continue on along the river and you'll be fine. But for those of you who need to know exactly where you are at all times, this may not be the trail for you. Bikes are allowed on most of the hiking trail, and this description details that route. It's the most winding as well as the most scenic of the three trails. (Just don't run anybody down or it will surely be closed to bikes.)

Driving Directions

From the junction of US Highway 97 and Northwest Franklin Avenue in Bend, set your odometer to zero and head west on Franklin. Franklin becomes Northwest Riverside Boulevard. At 1.2 miles, turn right onto Northwest Tumalo Avenue. Continue straight ahead as Tumalo becomes Northwest Galveston Avenue. At 1.6 miles, turn left onto Northwest 14th Street; this soon becomes Century Drive (State Highway 46). At 6.4 miles, turn left at the Meadow Picnic Area sign onto Forest Road 100, which is dirt. At 7.8 miles, reach the trailhead and the end of the road at Meadow Picnic Area.

Deschutes River Trail

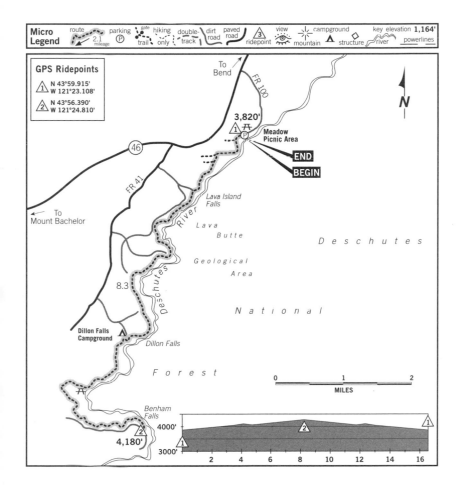

The Ride

The Deschutes River Trail, wide and hard-packed, heads away from the turnaround at Meadow Picnic Area, running just above the bank of the river. Tall ponderosa pines shade the trail. At **0.5** mile, reach a fork and turn left, riding along a sometimes muddy trail that bisects two ponds. From here, turn on your Zen and stay on the main trail, ignoring numerous lesser spurs on the right. At **0.7** mile, continue on the trail across the gravel turnaround. At **0.8** mile, ignore a steep trenchy trail on the left. At **1.3** miles, pass through a gravel turnaround at the Lava Island boat launch.

Across the river you'll see the sharp, jagged, char-black formations of Lava Butte Geological Area. Continuing on from the Lava Island boat launch, the trail, rolling and tricky in sections, kisses the equestrian trail several times— stay to the left. Around the **2**-mile mark, the route follows a dirt road. Stay to the left and regain the trail after a short distance. At **2.2** miles, reach a fork in the trail and bear right, following the bike sign. Reach a four-way at **2.4** miles and proceed straight ahead. At **3.4** miles, pass by the Big Eddy boat launch—stay on the trail on the left.

Reach a fork at **3.9** miles—turn right and climb a short hill. When the trail forks again at **4.1** miles, bear left. At **4.4** miles, ignore the trail back on the left. At **4.8** miles, reach Dillon Falls Campground. Stay to the left on the campground road. At **4.9** miles, turn left on a narrow trail that passes through a gap in the fence and crosses a wide meadow along the river. Reenter the pine forest at **5.3** miles and wind along the buff trail. When the trail forks at **6.3** miles, bear right. At **6.6** miles, the trail passes through another picnic area next to a flat-water section of the river.

Ride the slight ups and downs as the trail follows the river. At **7.4** miles, ignore a trail on the right. Reach a T at **7.9** miles and turn left. Benham Falls—a rush of water through a narrow rock canyon—appears on the left. The trail, quite wide now, switchbacks up the bank next to the falls. Continue up to the parking area above Benham Falls, **8.3** miles (ridepoint 2). After you're done checking out the falls, turn around and follow the trail back to Meadow Picnic Area, **16.6** miles.

Gazetteer

Nearby camping: Tumalo State Park
Nearest food, drink, services: Bend

Distance	30-mile loop
Route	Singletrack and paved roads
Climbs	One strenuous climb; high point: 5,000 ft, gain: 1,410 ft
Duration	Fitness rider: 3 hours; scenery rider: 4 to 6 hours
Travel	Bend—0 miles; Eugene—129 miles
Skill	Advanced
Season	Summer, fall
Map	U.S. Forest Service: Bend Ranger District
Rules	None
Manager	Deschutes National Forest, Bend—Fort Rock District, 541-383-4000
Web	www.fs.fed.us/r6/centraloregon/recreation/trails/trail-district-bend

Who Will Like This Ride
Driving to the trailhead gives you hives.

The Scoop
In the first edition of KTTO, Storm King was new, hardly raked out, half secret, and definitely not official. But trail status changes more quickly in Bend than most places in the trail universe. Today, recognized by the Forest Service, Storm King feels like one of the old guard Bend trails, which is to say good. The trail builders did it right. Storm King's original breakthrough was that it connected the Phil's Trail system (rides 31, 32, 33) with the Deschutes River Trail (ride 34). And when you add in the help of Skyliners Trail (see rides 27 and 28), you can now ride singletrack between the Deschutes River Trail and Mrazek (rides 24 and 27), something only the biggest bong hit could have conjured up before the millennium rolled over. And the audacious ambition that precipitated Storm King definitely helped make the way for C.O.D. (ride 30) and others. Just as it was originally written, this ride still begins from town as a reminder that you don't always have to drive to the trailhead, as well as an homage to Bend's awesome trail advocates, planners, and builders.

Note: Though the start and finish of this ride are routed on roads, there are many newer paved and soft-surface trails that connect west Bend with the trailheads at Phil's and C.O.D., which are two of the trailheads used in this loop.

Driving Directions

From the junction of US Highway 97 and Northwest Franklin Avenue in Bend, set your odometer to zero and head west on Franklin. Franklin becomes Northwest Riverside Boulevard. At 1.2 miles, turn right onto Northwest Tumalo Avenue. Continue straight ahead as Tumalo becomes Northwest Galveston Avenue. At 1.6 miles, park near the intersection of Galveston and Northwest 14th Street.

The Ride

From the intersection of Galveston and Northwest 14th Street, pedal east on Galveston, which soon becomes Skyliners Road. At **2.9** miles, turn left on Forest Road 4604. At **3.3** miles, arrive at Phil's trailhead on the right. Three official trails begin here: Take Phil's Trail 24.5. Almost immediately you'll ride straight through a four-way. From here, the smooth trail winds through the pine forest. Cross a gravel road at **4.3** mile. At **4.9** miles, the trail braids apart then quickly reconnects.

Reach the locally infamous "Flaming Chicken" roundabout, a 5-way junction, at **5.4** miles. Essentially you need to ride straight through this intersection, which means taking the second left if you're riding clockwise

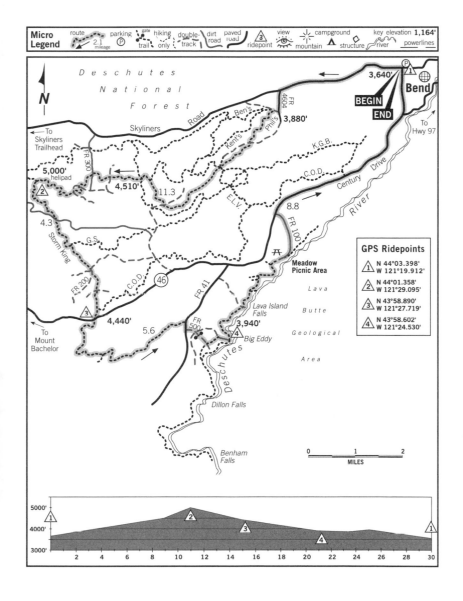

Micro Legend
route — 2.1 mileage | parking ⓟ | gate — hiking trail | hiking only | double-track | dirt road | paved road | ③ ridepoint | view 👁 | mountain | campground | ▲ structure | river | key elevation **1,164'** powerlines

Deschutes National Forest

N

To Skyliners Trailhead

Skyliners Road

Ben's

Kents

Phil's

FR 4604

3,880'

K.G.B.

C.O.D.

Century Drive

River

3,640'

BEGIN

END

Bend

To Hwy 97

5,000' helipad

4,510'

11.3

E.L.V.

8.8

FR 100

2

4.3

Storm King

G.S.

C.O.D.

FR 200

FR 300

46

FR 41

Meadow Picnic Area

GPS Ridepoints

△1 N 44°03.398'
W 121°19.912'

△2 N 44°01.358'
W 121°29.095'

△3 N 43°58.890'
W 121°27.719'

△4 N 43°58.602'
W 121°24.530'

Lava

Butte

Geological

Area

3

4,440'

5.6

To Mount Bachelor

FR 500

4

3,940'

Lava Island Falls

Big Eddy

Deschutes

Dillon Falls

Benham Falls

0   1   2
MILES

5000'
4000'
3000'
2   4   6   8   10   12   14   16   18   20   22   24   26   28   30

around the chicken. From here, the trail climbs steadily, though it's never too steep. The grade levels out before you cross a dirt road at **7.3** miles.

At **8** miles, reach a fork at Junction 18—go left. Ride straight through a four-way at **8.3** miles. Cross a doubletrack. When you reach FR 300 at **9.4** miles, turn left onto the road and then almost immediately right onto singletrack again. From here, it's a steep, grinding climb to Phil's Helipad. Though often smooth, through manzanita and pine, the tread is loose and rocky in sections, with a few technical step-ups and high blood pressure switchbacks. **WOOF!** At **11.1** miles, reach the helipad, a collection of small rocks in a flat open circle surrounded by tall manzanita.

Ride across the flat top, then gradually descend. **WHOA!** Before you get going too fast, reach a fork and bear left, **11.3** miles (ridepoint 2). This is Storm King. The trail begins with a few whoops, then snakes through the woods on a gradual decline, crossing several dirt roads and doubletracks. At **13.5** miles, reach a fork and bear right (left is G.S., see ride 30).

At **14.2** miles, when the trail dumps out at a three-way intersection of dirt roads, take a soft right on FR 200. At **14.3** miles, find a singletrack on the left and take it. From here, the trail rises and falls through pine and scattered manzanita. Cross a dirt road. At **15.4** miles, reach a fork at Junction 32 and bear right (left is C.O.D., ride 30). Drop to State Highway 46 at **15.6** miles (ridepoint 3). **WHOA!** Be careful crossing the highway to the trail opposite.

From the south side of Hwy 46, the trail drifts across the rolls and swells of the land, waiting patiently for the wave it will surf most of the way down to the Deschutes River. When the descent begins, you'll understand it was worth the short wait as you corkscrew down one hillside after another and funnel around banked corners. You'll cross a number of old doubletracks that are being decommissioned, meaning eliminated and returned to the forest.

At **17.4** miles, ignore a track back on the right. After crossing a couple more doubletracks, the excellent descent continues. At **19.1** miles, you'll have to gear down for a short climb up to the terrace of an old roadbed. Cross a doubletrack and then a dirt road. At **19.9** miles, the trail ends at a paved road (FR 41). This is Junction 31. Turn right onto FR 41 and climb a short hill.

At **20.1** miles, turn left onto FR 500 toward Big Eddy. When you reach a four-way at **20.3** miles, go straight, riding around a gate. Stay on the

Reading the Storm King tea leaves

doubletrack as it crosses a trail at **20.5** miles. At **20.9** miles, reach a four-way and turn left off the doubletrack and onto a trail. From here, the trail cruises along, smooth and fast. At **21.2** miles (ridepoint 4), reach a dirt road, turn right, and ride fifty yards to the parking area at Big Eddy, where you'll find the Deschutes River Trail on the left. Follow the bike signs. Note: Spur trails and alternate routes make the next three plus miles a bit confusing, and you'll have to use a little Zen to make it through.

At **22.5** miles, pass through the boat launch area at Lava Island. Stay to the right to continue along the trail. From here, stay on the main trail. Cross a gravel turnaround. At **23** miles, bear left at the fork. At **23.1** miles, stay on the main trail. At **23.2** miles, turn right and then right again to take the sometimes muddy trail that cuts between two ponds. Reach a T at **23.3** miles and turn right. The trail ends at Meadow Picnic Area, **23.8** miles.

From the trailhead at Meadow Picnic Area, ride along the dirt road, bearing left and climbing to the paved road, Century Drive (Hwy 46), at **25.2** miles. (Note: The Deschutes River Trail continues northeast from Meadow trailhead and connects with Century Drive closer to town near the small trailhead for C.O.D., but I've found that route overly confusing.) Turn right on Century Drive and ride the highway into Bend. When the road divides closer to town, bear left and Century Drive becomes Northwest 14th Street. Ride to the intersection of Northwest 14th Street and Northwest Galveston Avenue to complete the loop, **30** miles.

Gazetteer
Nearby camping: Tumalo State Park
Nearest food, drink, services: Bend

Distance	8.2-mile loop
Route	Singletrack and dirt roads
Climbs	Moderate climbs and descents; high point: 5,980 ft, gain: 180 ft
Duration	Fitness rider: 30 minutes; scenery rider: 1 to 2 hours
Travel	Bend—16 miles; Eugene—145 miles
Skill	Intermediate
Season	Summer, fall
Map	U.S. Forest Service: Bend Ranger District
Rules	None
Manager	Deschutes National Forest, Bend–Fort Rock District, 541-383-4000
Web	www.fs.fed.us/r6/centraloregon/recreation/trails/trail-district-bend

Who Will Like This Ride
You feel like eight miles is plenty, especially at nearly 6,000 feet.

The Scoop
   Swampy Lakes is a ditty of a ride, perfect for intermediate riders who want to push themselves a little but don't want to be out too long. It's also an excellent introduction to some of the trails that branch out from the Swampy Lakes trailhead. Advanced riders will likely want to head off and explore—north toward Tumalo Falls (ride 26) and Mrazek (ride 24), west toward Flagline (see ride 28) and Metolius-Windigo, and east toward Sector 16 and the entire Phil's system (rides 31, 32, 33). Clearly this trailhead can be the start of many a fine ride. But while some of you are fit explorers itching for epics, many of you aspire to 8-mile rides like this one, which can be more than enough at 6,000-feet elevation.

Driving Directions
   From the junction of US Highway 97 and Northwest Franklin Avenue in Bend, set your odometer to zero and head west on Franklin. Franklin becomes Northwest Riverside Boulevard. At 1.2 miles, turn right onto Northwest Tumalo Avenue. Continue straight ahead as Tumalo becomes Northwest Galveston Avenue. At 1.6 miles, turn left onto Northwest 14th

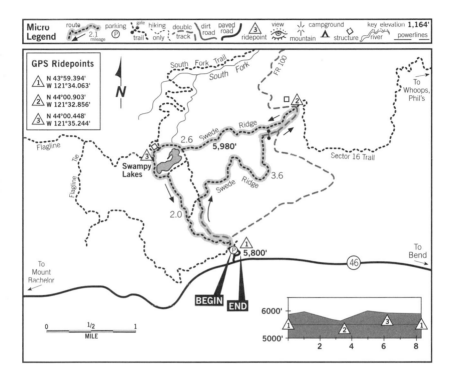

Street; this soon becomes Century Drive (State Highway 46). Proceed west on Century Drive, and at 16.5 miles turn right toward Swampy Lakes Sno-Park. At 16.6 miles, park near the bathrooms.

The Ride

Facing the two trails at the parking area, take the one on the left. From there, take a right, a left, and another right in quick succession. At **0.1** mile, reach three dirt roads—go left. The road climbs gently, as it gradually becomes doubletrack and then, around **0.8** mile, singletrack. Soon after the route becomes singletrack, reach a four-way and turn right, riding now toward Swede Ridge Shelter. It's a smooth, fun downward cruise, winding back and forth and back again. After a short climb, reach a T at a doubletrack at **2.8** miles and turn right, passing around a gate. At **2.9** miles, reach another T and turn left, continuing toward Swede Shelter.

Heading towards Swede Ridge

The trail drops and then climbs. When you crest a hill, **3.6** miles (ridepoint 2), find a singletrack on the left and take it. This is Swede Ridge Trail. From here, the trail climbs toward the west. It gets quite steep around the **4.7**-mile mark. Pass over a high knoll at **5** miles. At **5.5** miles, reach a T and turn right, following the sign toward Swampy Shelter. When you arrive at the shelter, **6.1** miles, turn left. At **6.2** miles (ridepoint 3), reach a fork and bear left again, heading south now, back toward the sno-park. Though you'll hit a few sand bogs, most of the trail is zippy and fast as it descends to Hwy 46.

When the trail divides at **7.3** miles, stay to the right. At **7.5** miles, reach a fork and bear left, continuing the descent. Arrive at a T at **8.1** miles and turn right. The trail leaves the pine forest and pops out into the trailhead parking area at **8.2** miles.

Gazetteer

Nearby camping: Elk Lake, Soda Creek (primitive)
Nearest food, drink, services: Bend, Sunriver

Distance	24.5-mile loop
Route	Gradual but zippy singletrack descent, paved road climb
Climbs	Moderate; high point: 5,500 ft, gain: 720 ft; views
Duration	Fitness rider: 2 to 3 hours; scenery rider: 3 to 5 hours
Travel	Bend—27 miles; Eugene—156 miles
Skill	Intermediate
Season	Summer, fall
Map	U.S. Forest Service: Bend Ranger District
Rules	None
Manager	Deschutes National Forest, Bend–Fort Rock District, 541-383-4000
Web	www.fs.fed.us/r6/centraloregon/recreation/trails/trail-district-bend

Who Will Like This Ride
You like rides with cool names and zippy pumice treads.

The Scoop
Lava Lake is big and deep blue—a great swim on those dry, 90-degree summer days around Bend. From the trailhead near Sparks Lake, the pumice-treaded singletrack weaves south toward Lava Lake. After some gentle climbing over the first two miles, the trail rolls in places, zips in others,

Fall morning on Sparks Lake Trail

The Metolius-Windigo Trail hits the northeast shore of Lava Lake

as it winds downward through low pines. Sporadically located water bars and embedded rocks make the trail interesting for intermediate riders but all-out fun if you have your advanced degree. The only negative here is that from the south end of the loop, it's a long paved-road ride to complete the route. Can you say "out and back"? Better yet, if you have all day, construct the epic loop around Mount Bachelor by turning left on Trail 31 at the south end of Lava Lake and then stitching together a series of roads on the east side of the mountain. Check out the USFS map.

Driving Directions

From the junction of US Highway 97 and Northwest Franklin Avenue in Bend, set your odometer to zero and head west on Franklin. Franklin becomes Northwest Riverside Boulevard. At 1.2 miles, turn right onto Northwest Tumalo Avenue. Continue straight ahead as Tumalo becomes Northwest Galveston Avenue. At 1.6 miles, turn left onto Northwest 14th Street; this soon becomes Century Drive. Proceed west on Century Drive (State Highway 46) past Mount Bachelor. At 27.3 miles, turn left toward Sparks Lake and Soda Creek Campground on graveled Forest Road 400. Immediately bear left at the fork and park on the left next to the trailhead, 27.5 miles.

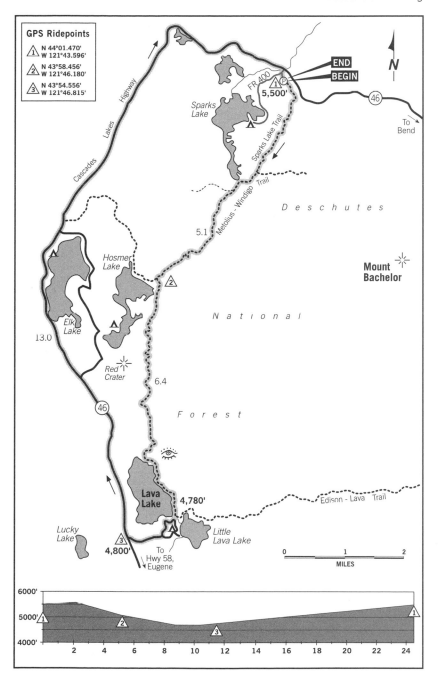

GPS Ridepoints

1. N 44°01.470'
   W 121°43.596'
2. N 43°58.456'
   W 121°46.180'
3. N 43°54.556'
   W 121°46.815'

Cascades Lakes Highway

FR 400

Sparks Lake

END
BEGIN

1 5,500'

P

46

To Bend

Sparks Lake Trail

Metolius - Windigo Trail

D e s c h u t e s

5.1

Hosmer Lake

2

Mount Bachelor

Elk Lake

13.0

Red Crater

N a t i o n a l

3

6.4

46

F o r e s t

Lava Lake

4,780'

Edison - Lava Trail

Lucky Lake

3
4,800'

To Hwy 58, Eugene

Little Lava Lake

0   1   2
MILES

6000'
5000'
4000'

2   4   6   8   10   12   14   16   18   20   22   24

The Ride

From the trailhead, take the singletrack toward South Sparks Lake. Cruise through the pine forest on a pumice-gray, rolling singletrack. After numerous twists and turns, short climbs and descents, reach a fork at **2.1** miles and bear right, heading toward Quinn Meadow. At **2.5** miles, the trail divides again: Go left. From here the trail noodles for a distance before descending toward Hosmer Lake. At **5.1** miles (ridepoint 2), reach a fork and turn left, toward Lava Lake. The trail descends quickly from the fork, then noodles again as it skirts to the east of Red Crater. Just past the **7**-mile mark, check out views of Lava Lake to the south.

From here, the trail rips downhill, slaloming through the pines. At **8.9** miles, reach the northeast corner of Lava Lake. Follow the trail, at times root-strewn, as it hugs the eastern shore of the lake. At **10.4** miles, reach a fork and turn right. Immediately cross a small creek to

Near Hosmer Lake

the boat launch at Lava Lake Campground. Check out the picturesque views across the lake of South Sister and Mount Bachelor. From the launch, take the main campground road to Hwy 46. At **11.5** miles (ridepoint 3), turn right on Hwy 46. The paved road climbs gradually to the north toward South Sister. **WHOA!** Watch the traffic, which travels fast. At **14.4** miles, pass by the road to Hosmer Lake on the right. Just over a mile farther, the highway wraps around the west side of Elk Lake. Pass the turnoff to Elk Lake on the right at **17** miles. At **24.3** miles, turn right on the dirt road toward Sparks Lake. Bear left at the fork and arrive at the trailhead, **24.5** miles.

Gazetteer

Nearby camping: Elk Lake, Soda Creek (primitive)
Nearest food, drink, services: Bend, Sunriver

38 PAULINA CREEK

Distance	17.3-mile loop (11.2-mile option)
Route	Singletrack up, bomber doubletrack down; views
Climbs	Moderate to tough; high point: 6,380 ft, gain: 2,080 ft
Duration	Fitness rider: 2 to 3 hours; scenery rider: 3 to 4 hours
Travel	Bend—28 miles; Eugene—117 miles
Skill	Intermediate
Season	Summer, fall
Map	U.S. Forest Service: Fort Rock Ranger District
Rules	Trail is uphill-only for bikes; National Forest Recreation Pass required
Manager	Newberry National Volcanic Monument, 541-593-2421
Web	www.fs.fed.us/r6/centraloregon/newberrynvm/index.shtml

Who Will Like This Ride
Singletrack climbing freaks who like waterfalls and probably still use bar ends.

The Scoop
When I reached the top of this loop at Paulina Lake, I was surprised to realize I'd climbed more than 2,000 feet. That's because the ascent up Paulina Creek, along the Peter Skene Ogden Trail, is so well graded. Since it's also well traveled by hikers and equestrians, the trail is open to bicycles only for uphill riding. Not to fret: The steadiness of the grade and the smooth, hard-packed tread mitigate the pain, and the breakneck double-track descent is a nice consolation, despite the restriction. Cut it short with the option, or combine this ride with the loop around Newberry Caldera (ride 39) for an outstanding, five-wheel epic.

Driving Directions
From Bend, drive about 24 miles south on US Highway 97 and turn left on Paulina East Lake Road (Forest Road 21), following the sign for Newberry Crater. Zero out your odometer here. At 2.9 miles, turn left toward Ogden Group Camp. At 3 miles, bear right toward the trailhead. At 3.2 miles, reach the gravel parking area at the trailhead.

Paulina Falls

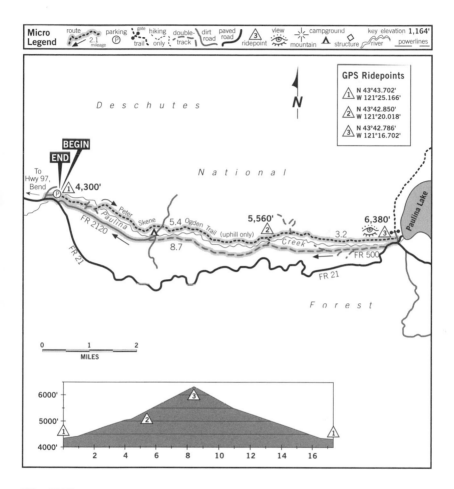

The Ride

From the parking area, immediately cross the creek and ride up Peter Skene Ogden Trail toward Paulina Lake. The trail braids apart at **0.3** mile, reconnects, then crosses a doubletrack. Reach a T at **0.8** mile: Turn right, then immediately left on a doubletrack. A few pedal rotations farther, reach a fork and bear left. At **1** mile, the trail crosses Paulina Creek, narrows to singletrack, and climbs, paralleling the creek through a pine forest. After passing a small waterfall on the right, the trail bends away from the creek, cutting around the outside of the McKay Crossing Campground. At **2.8** miles, cross a dirt road and continue up on Peter Skene Ogden Trail.

The trail, which never drifts too far from the river, climbs at an even rate. Around **3.5** miles, the trail passes through an old burn. After passing another falls at **4.4** miles, the trail ascends more steeply. At **5.4** miles (ridepoint 2), reach a fork and bear left (right is a bailout; see the Option, below). At **6.1** miles, ride through a small campsite; follow the trail as it jogs to the left here and continues the steady climb. At **8.3** miles, pass Paulina Falls. It's a surprising and stunning piece of nature's work. *WOOF!* After burning several large Toblerones' worth of calories, reach the upper trailhead at **8.6** miles (ridepoint 3). Bear right to reach the paved road, then turn right and ride over Paulina Creek as it flows out of Paulina Lake.

At the T, turn right on FR 21, which is paved. From here, burn ass downhill. At **8.9** miles, bear right into a parking area. Under powerlines at the far side of the lot, find a rough doubletrack, FR 500, and take it. The bomber descent continues, with the old, scooped-out doubletrack nearly forming a half pipe in places. Reach a fork at **9.6** miles and stay to the right, following the powerlines. At **9.8** miles, bear right, again mimicking the powerlines. At **10.1** miles, stay to the left. At **11.7** miles, pass the short tie trail on the right that crosses the creek and connects with Peter Skene Ogden Trail (across the bridge, you'd find ridepoint 2).

From the tie trail, continue the fast descent. When you pass through the burn around the **12.7**-mile point, follow the main road beneath the powerlines. Ride straight through a four-way at **14.3** miles. When FR 500 merges with a wide gravel road, FR 2120, at **14.6** miles, bear left. Stay on FR 2120. At **16.8** miles, turn right on FR 21. Ride a short distance down this paved road and then turn right, heading toward Ogden Group Camp. Bear right at the fork, reaching the trailhead to complete the loop at **17.3** miles.

Option

For riders with less time or an insufficient supply of calories, turn right at the fork at **5.4** miles. From there, the trail drops to a bridge over Paulina Creek, then climbs to meet FR 500 at **5.6** miles (the 11.7-mile point above). Turn right on FR 500 and descend to the trailhead, **11.2** miles.

Gazetteer

Nearby camping: Paulina Lake, McKay Crossing (primitive)
Nearest food, drink, services: La Pine, Sunriver, Bend

Distance	22.4-mile loop (39.7-mile epic option)
Route	Dirt-road climb, then dirt and pumice singletrack; views
Climbs	Grinding then painful; high point: 7,900 ft, gain: 2,880 ft
Duration	Fitness rider: 2.5 to 4 hours; scenery rider: 4 to 6 hours
Travel	Bend—38 miles; Eugene—127 miles
Skill	Intermediate
Season	Late summer, early fall
Map	U.S. Forest Service: Fort Rock Ranger District
Rules	National Forest Recreation Pass required
Manager	Newberry National Volcanic Monument, 541-593-2421
Web	www.fs.fed.us/r6/centraloregon/newberrynvm/index.shtml

Who Will Like This Ride

This is a must-ride for everyone who considers themselves a mountain biker, but do the necessary training before heading there.

The Scoop

About 20 miles due south of Bend, the Paulina Mountains rise modestly out of the gently rolling central Oregon desert, and you might not think twice about driving right past the sign pointing toward Newberry Crater. That would be a big mistake. Newberry Crater, actually a true caldera, born at the junction of three fault zones, may be less spectacular than its Crater Lake buddy to the south, but it is more interesting, especially if there's a mountain bike on top of your car. And of course there is! The Newberry National Volcanic Monument, established in 1990, sports views, remarkable geographic features, and a wonderful rim trail, making this one of the most outstanding rides I've ever done. Top ten, for sure. The loop begins with a strenuous dirt-road climb up Paulina Peak. To the west, across the wide Deschutes River valley, the Cascade Range juts up from the hot plain; to the east the hazy swells of eastern Oregon seem to go on forever (and in fact they do). It's a challenging trail, with lots of heady views, and a great descent at the end.

Paulina Lake and part of the caldera as seen from Paulina Peak

Driving Directions

From Bend, drive about 24 miles south on US Highway 97 and turn left on Paulina East Lake Road (Forest Road 21), following the sign for Newberry Crater. Zero out your odometer here. At 13 miles, turn left into the parking area opposite the visitors center.

The Ride

Turn left out of the visitors center parking (across from the building) and ride out FR 21 toward East Lake. At **0.2** mile, turn right on FR 500 toward Paulina Peak. The road becomes gravel at **0.7** mile, and the long, grinding climb up Paulina Peak, Newberry's high point at nearly 8,000 feet, begins. Stay on the main road as you climb. Pass Trail 57 on the left at **0.9** mile and then again, on both the right and left, at **3.3** miles (ridepoint 2). (Note: you will take Trail 57, but only after climbing to the summit and returning to this point.) If you're coming from sea level, hallucinations begin shortly. **WOOF!** After a grueling set of short switchbacks, reach the parking area at the top of Paulina Peak, **4.3** miles (ridepoint 3). From the top, on the southern edge, trace with a finger your counterclockwise route around the outer rim of the caldera. Inside the forested caldera, your eyes will feast on a bouillabaisse of lakes, lava flows, obsidian glints, and stubby pumice cones. And, if you are lucky to see them, bears!

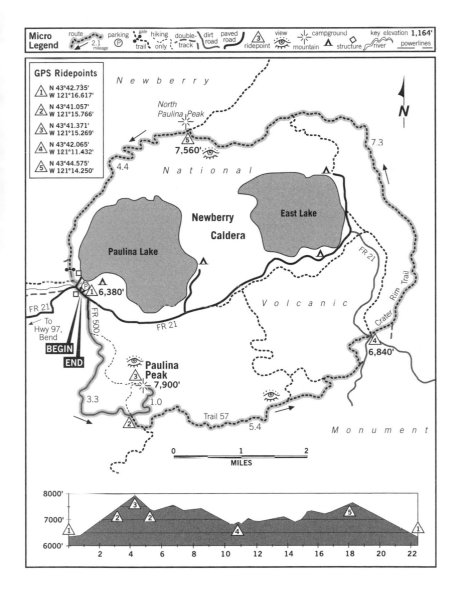

Micro Legend — route, 2.1 mileage; parking P; gate, hiking trail only; double-track; dirt road; paved road; ridepoint; view, mountain; campground; structure; river; key elevation 1,164', powerlines

GPS Ridepoints

1. N 43°42.735' W 121°16.617'
2. N 43°41.057' W 121°15.766'
3. N 43°41.371' W 121°15.269'
4. N 43°42.065' W 121°11.432'
5. N 43°44.575' W 121°14.250'

N e w b e r r y

North Paulina Peak

7,560'

4.4

7.3

N a t i o n a l

Newberry Caldera

East Lake

Paulina Lake

6,380'

FR 21

To Hwy 97, Bend

FR 500

FR 21

V o l c a n i c

Crater Rim Trail

6,840'

BEGIN
END

Paulina Peak
7,900'

3.3

1.0

Trail 57

5.4

M o n u m e n t

0   1   2
MILES

8000'
7000'
6000'

2 4 6 8 10 12 14 16 18 20 22

Spinning along the pumice trail on the east side of the caldera

When you're done catching the view—and your breath—ride back down the dirt road (the trail from the top is closed to bikes). At **5.3** miles (ridepoint 2), turn left on Trail 57, rocky and loose at the start. When the trail forks at **5.4** miles, bear left. Ride along a pine-needled trail through a stand of grand fir for a distance before entering a longer section of low pines located on the top edge of the pumice rim, which affords views of the lakes and the obsidian flows in the crater below. At **7.8** miles, go right at the fork, staying on Crater Rim Trail. After several more swells and a short noodle through stunted pine, the trail switchbacks through loose pumice down the outside lip of the caldera. At times it's a pum surf.

After a fast descent, reach a fork at **9.7** miles and bear left. At **10.7** miles (ridepoint 4), the trail crosses FR 21, which is dirt. After crossing the road, the trail immediately forks—go right on Crater Rim Trail, heading north now. At **11.3** miles, bear left on a wide trail. From here, the oversize trail climbs, then drops (fast and straight!), then climbs some more, inching toward the north rim's high point—North Paulina Peak. Some of the pitches are very steep and inching may well describe your progress. Pass the red cinder viewpoint at **15.3** miles. Ignore a ski trail on the right at **15.5** miles. At **16.4** miles, reach a fork and bear right, climbing through pine and mountain hemlock.

When the trail forks again, at **18** miles (ridepoint 5), bear left and follow the sign to Paulina Lake (you don't want to go to Swampwells, which is far down the mountain in the wrong direction). The trail noodles across the southern toe of North Paulina Peak, then descends. Pass a wonderful viewpoint on the left at **18.6** miles. Check your brakes here because the trail launches down the west side of the caldera's rim, aiming south now. At **22** miles, stay left at the fork. At **22.3** miles, pass Paulina Creek Trail on the right and bear left, passing around a green gate to a paved road. Turn right on the road, immediately crossing Paulina Creek, then reach a T at a stop sign and turn left. A few pedal rotations farther, reach the visitors center parking lot, **22.4** miles, to complete the ride.

Newberry Epic Option

Add the Paulina Creek loop (ride 38) to this ride to create a five-wheel epic. Ride up Paulina Creek, grind to the top of Paulina Peak, spin counterclockwise around the rim, and then bomb down FR 500 to complete the madness. It's a 39.4-mile trip, with a 3,600-foot gain—***WOOF!***—but for those who aren't intimidated, this is one of the best rides anywhere.

Gazetteer

Nearby camping: Paulina Lake, McKay Crossing (primitive)
Nearest food, drink, services: La Pine, Sunriver, Bend

Descending from North Paulina Peak

40 CULTUS LAKE

Distance	15.4-mile loop
Route	Singletrack and dirt roads; views
Climbs	Up and down but no major climbs; high point: 4,920 ft, gain: 400 ft
Duration	Fitness rider: 1.5 to 2 hours; scenery rider: 3 to 4 hours
Travel	Bend—42 miles; Eugene—100 miles
Skill	Intermediate
Season	Late summer, fall
Map	U.S. Forest Service: Bend Ranger District
Rules	None
Manager	Deschutes National Forest, Bend–Fort Rock District, 541-383-4000
Web	www.fs.fed.us/r6/centraloregon/recreation/trails/1006-deerlake

Who Will Like This Ride
You like to eat ice cream bars half-way through your rides. And who doesn't?

The Scoop
We scouted the ride around Cultus Lake twice. The first time, in June, the snowpack had barely melted out and we were swarmed by mosquitoes and forced to steeplechase the blowdown. Not the best time. In late August, though, with the trail bare and dry and the mosquito population kept at bay by a nighttime freeze, we enjoyed the jaunt. The trail wraps around the north side of Little Cultus Lake, swings past Deer Lake, then rounds the expanse of Cultus Lake. From the small resort on the east end of Cultus Lake, the route uses forest roads to finish the loop. The trail rolls and heaves in spots, but there are no monster climbs to worry about.

Driving Directions
From Bend, drive south on US Highway 97. After about 15 miles, turn right on Forest Road 40. After traveling 22 miles farther, turn left onto State Highway 46 and set your odometer to zero. At 1.3 miles, turn right on FR 4635. At 2 miles, turn left on FR 4630 toward Little Cultus Lake. FR 4630 becomes FR 4636. At 3.9 miles, bear left on FR 4636, then bear right toward Little Cultus Lake Campground. Keep the campground on your

right and proceed to the day-use parking area next to the second boat launch, 5.2 miles.

The Ride

From the parking area at the second boat launch, turn left on FR 4636 and ride back through the campground. At **0.6** mile, bear left toward Deer Lake Trail, staying on FR 4636. At **1** mile, right at a campsite, you'll find the start of Deer Lake Trail on the left. The trail follows the contour of the north side of Little Cultus Lake. At **2.5** miles, cross an intermittent creek. At **2.8** miles, pass a campsite on the shore of Deer Lake. Over the next half-mile, ignore several blocked-off spur trails. Cross a bridge at **3.4** miles (ridepoint 2) and immediately take a right at the fork, following the bike route sign toward Cultus Lake.

Little Cultus Lake

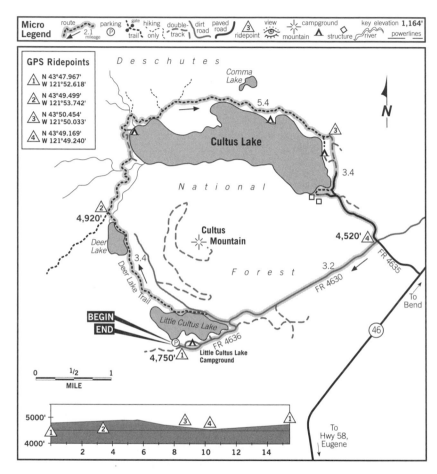

Micro Legend — route 2.1 mileage, parking ℗, gate, hiking trail only, double-track, dirt road, paved road, 3 ridepoint, view, mountain, campground, structure, river, key elevation **1,164'**, powerlines

GPS Ridepoints

1. N 43°47.967'
   W 121°52.618'
2. N 43°49.499'
   W 121°53.742'
3. N 43°50.454'
   W 121°50.033'
4. N 43°49.169'
   W 121°49.240'

D e s c h u t e s

Comma Lake

5.4

Cultus Lake

N a t i o n a l

3.4

4,920' 2

Deer Lake

Cultus Mountain

4,520' 4

3.4

F o r e s t

3.2

FR 4630

FR 4635

To Bend

Deer Lake Trail

BEGIN
END

Little Cultus Lake

FR 4636

46

4,750' 1

Little Cultus Lake Campground

N

0   1/2   1
MILE

5000'

4000'

2   4   6   8   10   12   14

To Hwy 58, Eugene

At **4.6** miles, reach a T at a doubletrack and turn left. The doubletrack affords the first through-the-trees views of Cultus Lake. Pass West Cultus Lake Campground on the right. Stay on the doubletrack, ignoring trails down into the campground. **WHOA!** At **4.9** miles, just as the doubletrack drops down to the campground, bear left onto the singletrack. At **5.4** miles, cross a log bridge and reach a T—turn right. From here, stay to the right, bypassing trails on the left that head into Three Sisters Wilderness. Ride straight through a three-way at **6.9** miles. Stay on the main trail as you pass through another campground. At **8.7** miles, reach a fork and turn left, following the sign to the trailhead.

At **8.8** miles (ridepoint 3), reach the trailhead and bear right on the dirt road. Ignore a spur road on the left. At **9** miles, continue straight when you reach an improved gravel road, bypassing the campground entrance. The road becomes paved at **9.4** miles. When you reach a kiosk on the right at **9.7** miles, bear right and ride down toward the lake. Follow the trail that hugs the lakeshore. Cross a bridge after leaving the campground, then turn right, continuing along the lake. At **9.9** miles, arrive at Cultus Lake Resort and turn left onto a gravel road. Turn left again on the paved road. At **10.3** miles, reach a T and turn right onto FR 4635. At **12.2** miles (ridepoint 4), turn right onto gravel FR 4630, which is washboard in spots. Continue straight at **13.9** miles toward Little Cultus Lake as the road becomes FR 4636. At **14.7** miles, turn left at the fork. Bear right, then ride past the campground to the day-use area at the second boat launch, ending the ride at **15.4** miles.

Gazetteer

Nearby camping: Little Cultus Lake
Nearest food, drink, services: Sunriver, Bend

Distance	13-mile lollipop (18.6-mile option)
Route	Singletrack loop with short doubletrack access; views
Climbs	A few short, tough ascents; high point: 5,590 ft, gain: 840 ft
Duration	Fitness rider: 1 to 1.5 hours; scenery rider: 2 to 3 hours
Travel	Bend—42 miles; Eugene—100 miles
Skill	Advanced
Season	Late summer, fall
Map	U.S. Forest Service: Bend Ranger District
Rules	None
Manager	Deschutes National Forest, Bend–Fort Rock District, 541-383-4000
Web	www.fs.fed.us/r6/centraloregon/recreation/trails/1019b-lemishlake

Who Will Like This Ride
You like to get away from it all and explore.

The Scoop
Like most of the other high lakes southwest of Bend—Todd, Sparks, Hosmer, Lava, Cultus, and Waldo, to name a few of mountain-bike interest—the trails around Lemish Lake can be a mosquito war zone in July and August. This is not to say don't go—it's a fine ride that passes a nice mountain lake—only to say that a long soak in the DEET tub wouldn't be a bad idea. For fewer bugs, try riding it after the first nighttime freeze, usually around mid-August. Aside from the terror of mosquitoes, this is one of the more solitary rides in this section, with lots of opportunity to explore. Also note: This trail is often not cleared of blowdown until August, another great reason to wait until late season.

Driving Directions
From Bend, drive about 15 miles south on US Highway 97 and then turn right on Forest Road 40. After traveling 22 miles farther, turn left onto State Highway 46 and set your odometer to zero. At 1.3 miles, turn right on FR 4635. At 2 miles, turn left on FR 4630 toward Little Cultus Lake. FR 4630

becomes FR 4636. At 3.9 miles, bear left on FR 4636, then bear right toward Little Cultus Lake Campground. Keep the campground on your right and proceed to the day-use parking area next to the second boat ramp, 5.2 miles.

Lemish Lake

The Ride

From the parking area at the second boat ramp, pedal back to FR 4636 and turn right, riding away from the campground. At **0.2** mile, bear right at the fork. When the doubletrack divides again at **0.3** mile, stay left on FR 4636, heading toward Lemish Lake Trail. Stay on the main road, gradually ascending through a fir and pine forest. At **2** miles, turn left into a small trailhead parking area and head out Lemish Lake Trail. Although the trail is wide leaving the trailhead, it soon narrows and climbs steadily around the broad, oblong west flank of Lemish Butte. At **2.5** miles (ridepoint 2), the trail divides as it reaches

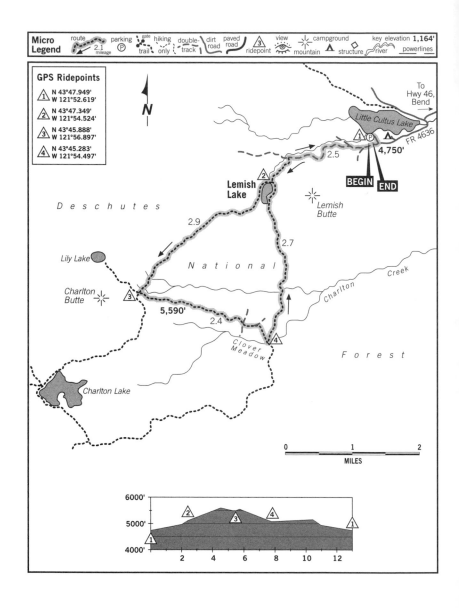

GPS Ridepoints

△1 N 43°47.949'
W 121°52.619'

△2 N 43°47.349'
W 121°54.524'

△3 N 43°45.888'
W 121°56.897'

△4 N 43°45.283'
W 121°54.497'

N

To
Hwy 46,
Bend

Little Cultus Lake

FR 4636

△1 ℗ ▲

2.5

4,750'

BEGIN END

D e s c h u t e s

Lemish
Lake

△2

Lemish
Butte

2.9

2.7

Lily Lake

N a t i o n a l

Charlton
Butte

△3

Charlton Creek

Creek

5,590'

2.4

△4

Clover
Meadow

F o r e s t

Charlton Lake

0   1   2
MILES

6000'

5000'

4000'

△2
△3
△4
△1

△1

2   4   6   8   10   12

Lemish Lake—turn right. After traversing the west shoreline, the trail becomes faint as it climbs through a rocky meadow.

Away from the lake, the trail ascends, steep and then level, steep and then level. After rolling over several high points around the **5**-mile mark, the trail drops to a sump at the eastern base of Charlton Butte and crosses a low bridge over the meadow. At **5.4** miles (ridepoint 3), reach a four-way and turn left, toward Clover Meadow (for a longer ride, see the Option below). Through a dark forest, mixed with fir and pine, the trail quickly climbs to the ride's high point at **5.6** miles. From here, the trail races eastward, traversing down a ridge away from the butte.

Around **6.8** miles, ride into a bright, open stand of lodgepole pine. At **7.2** miles, cross a doubletrack. The trail widens to doubletrack and forks at **7.4** miles—take the right prong. **WHOA!** This turn is easy to miss. At **7.8** miles (ridepoint 4), reach a T at Clover Meadow and turn left, heading back toward Lemish Lake. Somewhat sandy, the trail weaves through young pines. At **8.6** miles, cross a fork of Charlton Creek. Back in the mixed forest now, the trail rolls north. Lemish Lake is visible again around **10** miles. At **10.5** miles (ridepoint 2), reach a fork to complete the lollipop. Turn right and descend to the trailhead at **11** miles. Turn right on the road and glide back to the boat ramp at Little Cultus Lake, **13** miles.

Option

From the four-way intersection at the **5.4**-mile point, continue straight toward Charlton Lake. The trail climbs for about two miles and then drops to the lake. Ride along the westside of the lake counterclockwise, then at the south end climb steeply away from the lake. After the climb, stay to the left, rolling and then descending. Reach Clover Meadow at about **13.4** miles (the 7.8-mile mark above). This option adds **5.6** miles and several tough climbs on a sometimes technical trail. (Pull out the maps and you'll see you can combine this loop with Waldo Lake, ride 61, for an all-day epic.)

Gazetteer

Nearby camping: Little Cultus Lake
Nearest food, drink, services: Sunriver, Bend

If the blue lights don't waylay you along Highway 58 southeast of Eugene, you'll blow right through Oakridge. But for all its blink-and-you'll-miss-it, Oakridge has as much mountain-bike cred as Bend. And it's an easy day trip from Eugene or weekend from Portland. The rides are mostly either riverside traverses or steep mountain climbs followed by wild singletrack descents, and the trails vary from beginner to expert. The forests are darker and wilder than Bend, too, with Douglas fir, hemlock, and cedar—and poison oak to keep things interesting.

But let's start with Oregon's most famous ride: the McKenzie River Trail (rides 45 and 46), which isn't near Oakridge but on Highway 126 east of Eugene. The McKenzie definitely lives up to its billing. The waterfalls, the Blue Pool, the technical lava rock sections, and the zippy, big-tree slaloms make this all the ride you could ever want.

Moving from famous to infamous, the North Umpqua Trail (rides 65 and 66) is new to this second edition. Another classic, but one that is feared as much for its epic proportions as its logistical challenges. I've tried to make some sense of it, but wrapping your head around 80 miles of singletrack isn't easy. Nonetheless, it's a trail every mountain biker should endure, or at least sample.

Back to Oakridge: Alpine Epic (ride 56) is also new to this edition. Add the Tire Mountain Option and you'll clock in nearly 50 miles. Either option follows the classic cross-country format of a dirt road climb followed by a singletrack descent (well, kind of). Ten other rides in this section follow the same format, and each one will put a smile on your face. Olallie Mountain (ride 47), King Castle (ride 48), Aubrey Mountain (ride 53), Dead Mountain (ride 54), and Larison Rock (ride 57) are on the short side but are all thrilling. Hardesty Mountain (ride 50), Alpine (ride 55), Larison Creek (ride 58), Moon Point (ride 60), and Windy Lakes (ride 62) are longer and more difficult. Moon Point might be the best—faster and more baby-bottom smooth than the others.

Waldo Lake (ride 61) doesn't fit into either a riverside or mountain-climb category, but as one of the top trails in Oregon it deserves some ink. This 21-mile singletrack is spectacular and challenging.

Kudos to the Middle Fork Ranger District for keeping their non–wilderness area trails open to bikes. But don't abuse the Goodman Creek/Hardesty Mountain trails. If it's wet, ride elsewhere or the forest service may close it. Kudos as well to the Disciples of Dirt. They lead rides, work on trails, and help keep trails open. If you like riding here, become a member.

42 CUMMINS CREEK

Distance	10.4-mile loop
Route	Paved road climb, fast singletrack descent; views
Climbs	Long, relentless; high point: 1,520 ft, gain: 1,440 ft
Duration	Fitness rider: 1 hour; scenery rider: 2 to 3 hours
Travel	Eugene—84 miles; Portland—163 miles
Skill	Intermediate
Season	Year-round
Map	Cummins Creek Wilderness map
Rules	National Forest Recreation Pass required
Manager	Siuslaw National Forest, Waldport District, 541-563-3211
Web	www.fs.fed.us/r6/siuslaw/recreation/tripplanning/newpflor/list

Who Will Like This Ride
Cross-country riders who actually like to smile on descents and aren't too picky about riding on pavement.

Heceta Head lighthouse

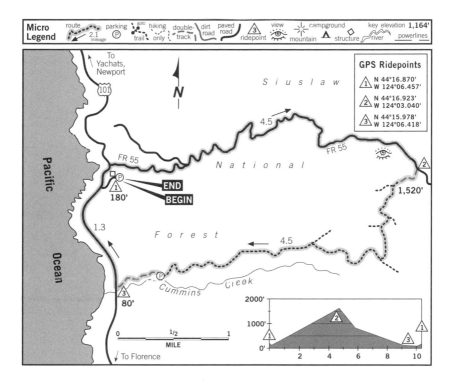

| Micro Legend | route 2.1 mileage | parking P | goto hiking trail only | double-track | dirt road | paved road | ⚠3 ridepoint | view 👁 mountain 🔆 | campground ⛺ structure ◇ river | key elevation **1,164'** powerlines |

GPS Ridepoints

⚠1 N 44°16.870' W 124°06.457'

⚠2 N 44°16.923' W 124°03.040'

⚠3 N 44°15.978' W 124°06.418'

The Scoop

This is one of just two rides in this book close to the Pacific Ocean, and whenever you can be close to the ocean, that's a good thing. Unfortunately, nearly half this ride follows a paved road. Sure it's isolated and rough and gravel in sections, and I saw a bear once on it, but it's paved. But there are excellent views and a side-splitting descent to mediate the overdose of asphalt. The paved climb is actually kind of nice, as it takes some of the bite out of the 1,500-foot climb to the trailhead. And despite the proximity to US Highway 101, it does feel remote out there. From the top, the trail follows the edge of Cummins Creek Wilderness Area to drop through old-growth stands toward the Pacific Ocean. After a steep, technical drop, the descent follows what used to be an old road—it's fast and fun. Although most of the trails around Cape Perpetua are closed to bicycles, the Forest Service deserves credit for keeping this one open. This ride begins in the parking area of the Cape Perpetua Visitors Center (541-547-3289).

Driving Directions

From Eugene, drive west on State Highway 126. When Hwy 126 ends at the Pacific Ocean in Florence, turn right and drive north on US Highway 101. Proceed 23 miles north, then turn right and follow the sign for Cape Perpetua Visitors Center. Park in the visitors center parking lot.

The Ride

From the visitors center, ride down the entrance road to US 101 and turn right, **0.2** mile. Northbound on US 101, take the first right turn, **0.4** mile,

An old road reverts to a fast trail

onto Forest Road 55. Thus the long climb begins. Pass the turnoff to Cape Perpetua Campground on the right. At **1.2** miles, bear right onto FR 55 (marked 5500 in places), which is the lesser road. (The left fork, FR 5553, heads up to Cape Perpetua Overlook, a side trip that adds 2 miles and 400 feet of climbing.) FR 55 continues its steady, winding ascent. From about **2.0** miles on, the road alternates between pavement and gravel. At **4.1** miles, reach a fork—stay to the right on the main road. **WOOF!** At **4.5** miles (ridepoint 2), find a gravel parking area on the right. This is the Cooks Ridge trailhead.

From the trailhead, pedal out the wide trail to a fork at **4.7** miles—bear left on Cummins Creek Trail and climb to the crest of the ridge. (Note: Don't take either Gywnn Creek Trail or Cooks Ridge Trail, as they are hiker-only.) At **5.0** miles, reach another fork and keep right, staying on the main trail. At **5.2** miles, reach a fork and bear left. For the next one-half mile, the trail descends precipitously on a loose, rocky tread, so parts may have to be walked. Stay on the main trail, ignoring a trail on the left to a viewpoint and one on the right that's shorter but more challenging. On a long bend to the right, the trail widens and levels out as it meets the terrace of an old road, **5.9** miles. This is Cummins Creek Loop Trail.

Decommissioned for many years, the road is now a wide trail, with a sweet downhill grade and long sweeping turns that follow Cummins Creek along the edge of the wilderness area. At **7.4** miles, pass a trail on the right. At **8.8** miles, the trail ends at a dirt road. At **9.0** miles, pass by the Coast Trail on the right. Follow the road down to US 101 at **9.1** miles (ridepoint 3). Turn right onto the highway and ride north to the visitors center entrance road on the right, **10.2** miles. Pedal up the hill to the parking lot to complete the ride, **10.4** miles.

Gazetteer
Nearby camping: Cape Perpetua, Carl Washburne State Park
Nearest food, drink, services: Yachats, Florence

43 SILTCOOS LAKE

Distance	4-mile lollipop
Route	Rolling singletrack
Climbs	Short climbs, some steep; high point: 340 ft, gain: 300 ft
Duration	Fitness rider: 30 minutes; scenery rider: 1 hour
Travel	Florence—8 miles; Eugene—69 miles
Skill	Intermediate
Season	Spring, summer, fall
Map	No helpful supplementary map available
Rules	National Forest Recreation Pass required
Manager	Oregon Dunes National Recreation Area, 541-271-6019
Web	www.fs.fed.us/r6/siuslaw/recreation/tripplanning/florcoos/list

Who Will Like This Ride
You like mountain bike picnicking with your family, but let's make it singletrack.

The Scoop
Located south of Florence on the Oregon coast, lovely Siltcoos Lake, part of the Siuslaw National Forest, sits a couple of miles inland from the ocean, just across the highway from some the state's vast coastal sand dunes. The singletrack winds and rolls through a dark forest down to a number of primitive campsites along the lake—a good place for mountain-bike camping. This is a short, easy ride, a great place to introduce beginners to singletrack. Or for families. One note, however, while the hills are short, they are steep in some sections, a challenge perhaps for the very youngest riders. For experienced cyclists touring down the coast, this trail would present little problem, even with panniers and slicks.

Driving Directions
From Eugene, drive west on State Highway 126. When Hwy 126 ends at the Pacific Ocean in Florence, set your odometer to zero, turn left, and drive south on US Highway 101. At 8 miles, turn left onto the paved road that leads to Siltcoos Lake trailhead, less than 100 yards up the hill.

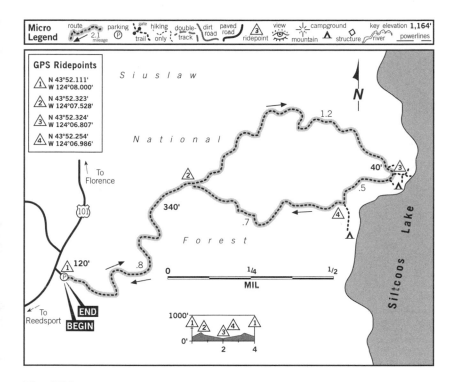

Micro Legend: route — 2.1 mileage; parking P; gate; hiking trail; double-track; dirt road; paved road; ridepoint; view; mountain; campground; structure; river; key elevation 1,164'; powerlines

GPS Ridepoints
1. N 43°52.111' W 124°08.000'
2. N 43°52.323' W 124°07.528'
3. N 43°52.324' W 124°06.807'
4. N 43°52.254' W 124°06.986'

Siuslaw National Forest

To Florence

To Reedsport

Siltcoos Lake

The Ride

From the parking area, take the wide, smooth dirt trail. Lined with fern, salal, and Oregon grape, the trail ascends into a dark, often fog-draped forest. It's a moderate climb, though it may be a challenge for first-timers. After topping out, the trail drops to a fork at **0.8** mile (ridepoint 2). Bear left on North Route Trail. The trail surfs the landscape's waves, through cedar and spruce, toward Siltcoos Lake. Ignore a lesser trail on the left, then immediately reach a fork at **1.9** miles. Turn left, riding past primitive camp-sites on the left and right, to the lake shore, **2** miles (ridepoint 3).

To return, ride back to the fork you first reached at **1.9** miles, now **2.1** miles, and bear left on South Route Trail toward US 101. Stay on the main trail. At **2.5** miles (ridepoint 4), reach a fork and turn right (a left leads to more primitive sites at South Camp). Walk up a short set of stairs, then grind up a winding climb. When you arrive at a fork, **3.2** miles (ridepoint 2), turn

Finding some bliss near the Siltcoos Lake trailhead

left and continue the ascent. Cross over the high point at **3.5** miles, and then glide down to the trailhead to complete the ride, **4** miles.

Gazetteer

Nearby camping: Carter Lake, Siltcoos Lake (primitive)
Nearest food, drink, services: Florence

Distance	8.2-mile out-and-back
Route	Wide and narrow trails, numerous intersections
Climbs	Some tough grinding; high point: 1,600 ft, gain: 980 ft
Duration	Fitness rider: 1 hour; scenery rider: 1 to 2.5 hours
Travel	Portland—80 miles; Salem—35 miles
Skill	Intermediate
Season	Spring, summer, fall
Map	McDonald Dunn Multiple-Use Road and Trail Map
Rules	Closed November through mid-April
Manager	McDonald Dunn Research Forest, 541-737-4452
Web	www.cof.orst.edu/cf/recreation/trails.php

Who Will Like This Ride

Grad students who are either too busy or serious to drive out to Oakridge.

The Scoop

McDonald Dunn Research Forest, owned by Oregon State University and managed by its forestry department, spreads north from the paved edges of Corvallis. Being so close to town, the forest's trail system is usually busy with runners, walkers, equestrians, picnickers, and mountain bikers, many of whom start out right from home. Despite the maze of trails and roads—making the area ripe for exploration—the system is often crowded, so ride carefully. This route, an out-and-back to the top of Dimple Hill, features a healthy singletrack climb followed by a rocking descent. It'll get your adrenaline flowing. The lower section of this trail is closed in the winter, but the upper segment of Dan's Trail stays open year-round. One more thing: Don't ride off-trail because sensitive research projects can be damaged, costing lots of money, screwing up important data, and possibly wrecking someone's Ph.D. chances.

Driving Directions

From Portland or Salem, drive south on Interstate 5 to exit 234B (about 65 miles south of Portland and 20 south of Salem). Zero out your odometer as the end of the interstate ramp becomes Pacific Boulevard Southeast. At 1 mile, Pacific Boulevard becomes US Highway 20 westbound toward Corvallis. At 2.1 miles, exit to the right, following US 20. At 10.8 miles, turn right on Conifer Boulevard. At 12.2 miles, turn left on State Highway 99 West (Pacific Highway West). At 12.5 miles, turn right on Walnut Boulevard. At 13.6 miles, turn right on Northwest Highland Drive. At 14.5 miles, turn left on Lester Avenue. At 15.4 miles, reach the trailhead at the end of the road.

The Ride

Several trails exit from the parking area at the end of the road—take the one on the right beyond the yellow gate. The trail, a narrow old road, immediately forks: Bear right and begin climbing. Pass by a singletrack on the left and then

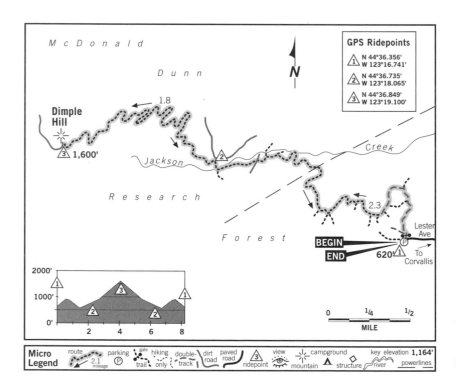

on the right as you ascend. At **0.5** mile, the wide trail levels somewhat and climbs more gently. Ignore two faint trails on the left. The way bends to the right, bypassing two more faint trails on the left, and affords views of Corvallis. Continue up and around to the right on the main trail. Just past a bench on the right at **0.8** mile, reach a fork and bear right onto a narrow trail.

The singletrack descends quickly. Reach a four-way at **1** mile and turn right. After a few spins of the pedals, reach a fork and bear right on Dan's Trail. Ignore a trail back to the left at **1.1** miles. At **1.2** miles, as you pass under a set of powerlines, ignore another trail on the left. From here, the trail, covered with roots but still fast, descends vigorously, corkscrewing down the hillside. At **1.6** miles, ignore a faint trail back on the right. A couple pedal strokes farther, reach a fork and bear left toward Dimple Hill. Cross a gravel road and continue along Dan's Trail. At **2.1** miles, ignore a lesser trail on the left and then drop to a bridge. At **2.3** miles (ridepoint 2), the trail kisses a dirt road— bear left on the single-track and stick it into a low gear.

Fast descent from Dimple Hill

At **2.8** miles, pass straight through a four-way. The hard-packed trail switch-backs up the hillside through fir, bigleaf maple, and oak. It's a tough climb without much of a break, but it's all ridable. **WOOF!** At **4.1** miles (ridepoint 3), reach the top of Dimple Hill. The trail ends here at a gravel road. Turn around and retrace your route. The first segment—a rocket down the south slope of Dimple Hill—is fun, but remember to watch for walkers, runners, and other cyclists on the trail. Return to the parking area at **8.2** miles.

Gazetteer

Nearby camping: Mary's Peak, Blackberry
Nearest food, drink, services: Corvallis

Distance	26.9-mile one-way shuttle
Route	Riverside singletrack—zippy, technical, endless; views
Climbs	Steep but not too long; high point: 3,160 ft, loss: 1,770 ft
Duration	Fitness rider: 3 to 4 hours; scenery rider: 5 to 8 hours
Travel	Eugene—75 miles; Bend—75 miles; Portland—185 miles
Skill	Advanced
Season	Summer, fall
Map	Green Trails: McKenzie Bridge, Echo Mountain
Rules	None
Manager	Willamette National Forest, McKenzie District, 541-822-3381
Web	www.fs.fed.us/r6/willamette/recreation/tripplanning/list_mk

Who Will Like This Ride

Unless you're a die-hard recumbent rider, this should be on your ride list every year.

The Scoop

The McKenzie River National Recreation Trail is one of the best rides anywhere, and that's not limited to Oregon. The spectacular scenery—

waterfalls and blue pools, blooming rhododendrons, humongous cedars, and 600-year-old Douglas firs—seems perfectly balanced with the ride's challenging singletrack and all-day distance. Put off taking this incredible one-way trip, though, until you've put in enough training miles to enjoy the entire length and organized the two-car shuttle.

Hans Rey could ride it

Because riding this as a partial out-and-back is not going to put as many stories in your head or as big a smile on your face. Ride a good story!

Driving Directions

From Eugene, drive just over 51 miles east on State Highway 126. Before reaching milepost 52, find the McKenzie River trailhead on the left alongside the highway. Leave a car here. Set your odometer to zero and continue east on Hwy 126. At 3.3 miles, bear left to remain on Hwy 126. At 22.2 miles, turn right on a dirt road, following the sign to the McKenzie River trailhead.

The Ride

Two trails exit from the south end of the trailhead parking area—take the one on the right that immediately crosses the creek. At **0.2** mile, cross a dirt road. At **0.9** mile, reach a fork and bear right. (Note that a left turn here will route you around the south side of Clear Lake, adding a technical ride over lots of lava.) The trail, fast and hard-packed with some roots, bends around Clear Lake to the right. At **2.3** miles, reach a T at a gravelly road at Clear Lake Resort. Bear left, riding down the road and past a parking area. At **2.5** miles, bear left to regain the McKenzie River Trail 3507.

After crossing a couple of bridges as you ride to the west of Clear Lake, reach a T at **3.6** miles and turn right toward Sahalie Falls. The trail is narrower and more technical here, a taste of what's to come. At **4.1** miles (ridepoint 2), cross a paved road and then carefully cross Hwy 126. After following the river for a short distance, bear right at a wide gravel pullout

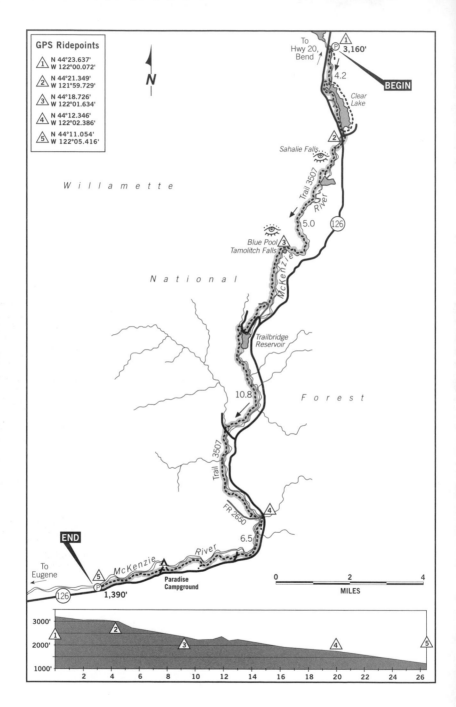

and cross over the McKenzie River. From here, the trail follows the west bank of the river, descending. At **4.8** miles, pass Sahalie Falls. It's spectacular, especially during early summer melt-off.

When the trail divides at **5.5** miles, turn right, continuing down McKenzie River Trail toward Tamolitch Falls. The trail becomes gradually more technical, with roots and rocks and tight corners, as it meanders through a deep forest, highlighted by huge Douglas firs and cedars. It's suddenly quiet, the roar of the river gone; freakishly, most of the McKenzie River flows underground at this point. At **9.2** miles (ridepoint 3), the river's back as it pours into the Blue Pool at Tamolitch Falls. It's an awesome and wonderful sight, and though it's short of the halfway mark, this is the lunch spot.

McKenzie River emerges again at Tamolitch Falls and the Blue Pool

Below the Blue Pool, the trail becomes quite a bit more technical—expert-level, really—zagging through corridors of sharp pumice, up and down. But the actual trials-riding doesn't last long as you drop alongside the river. The trail upsurges and crosses two forest roads. At **12.4** miles, after a short cannonball, reach a paved road and turn right. After a few pedal strokes, the McKenzie River Trail begins again on the left and immediately begins climbing. At **13.2** miles, the trail kisses a gravel road at a yellow gate.

A few miles downriver, the riding is idyllic, winding next to the river through bunches of fern and Oregon grape, rhododendron, and salal. Moss is everywhere, and the old-growth cedar and Douglas fir are just awesome. At **16.3** miles, cross over a bridge and then a paved road. From here, the trail climbs unexpectedly for a short distance, but then drops and crosses a series of bridges. Creepy-looking vine maples are part of the riverside flora now; the forest is dense with undergrowth.

At **18.3** miles, reach a gravelly doubletrack and bear left, continuing downriver. Pass through a gate at **18.6** miles, and immediately turn right to regain the singletrack. Just after a bridge crossing, **19.8** miles, bear left at the fork. At **19.9** miles, reach a T and turn left onto Forest Road 2650. Cross to the east side of McKenzie River to find the trail. A few spins of the pedals farther, reach Hwy 126 (ridepoint 4). The McKenzie River Trail starts up again here on the right, now paralleling the highway for a short distance. When the trail forks at **20.2** miles, bear right, following the trail sign. Reach a T at a dirt road, **20.9** miles, and turn left. Follow the trail signs. At **21.4** miles, reach a fork and bear left. At **21.5** miles, again bear left at the fork, pedal down the narrow dirt trail, and cross a paved road near Belknap Hot Spring.

The singletrack continues downriver. When the trail divides at **22.5** miles, stay to the right to continue down McKenzie River Trail. Pass through a grove of giant cedars. Cross a dirt road at **23.1** miles. The trail forks at **24** miles: Bear right. A short distance farther, cross the paved entrance road to Paradise Campground. The hard-packed trail zips along here, winding through the salal and Oregon grape. Stay to the left. At **25.1** miles, cross a dirt road. From here, the trail noodles the flats between the river and the highway. At **25.8** miles, stay to the right. Reach the lower McKenzie River trailhead at **26.9** miles to complete the ride (ridepoint 5).

Gazetteer

Nearby camping: Paradise
Nearest food, drink, services: McKenzie Bridge, Eugene

46 McKENZIE RIVER SHORT

Distance	5.4-mile out-and-back
Route	Winding singletrack along river
Climbs	Essentially flat; high point: 1,560 ft, gain: 170 ft
Duration	Fitness rider: 30 minutes; scenery rider: 1 hour
Travel	Eugene—52 miles; Bend—75 miles; Portland—160 miles
Skill	Intermediate
Season	Late spring, summer, fall
Map	Green Trails: McKenzie Bridge
Rules	None
Manager	Willamette National Forest, McKenzie District, 541-822-3381
Web	www.fs.fed.us/r6/willamette/recreation/tripplanning/list_mk

Who Will Like This Ride
You want a taste of the McKenzie.

The Scoop
The McKenzie River Trail is one of the most talked-about trails in the West, and it should be: The river is beautiful, the trail is buff, and the old

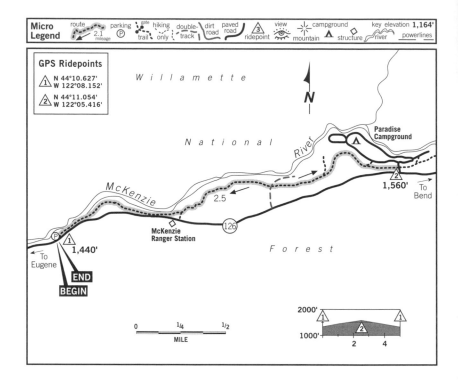

Micro Legend: route · 2.1 mileage · parking ℗ · gate · hiking trail · double-track · dirt road · paved road · 3 ridepoint · view · mountain · campground · structure · river · key elevation **1,164'** · powerlines

GPS Ridepoints

⚠ 1 N 44°10.627'
W 122°08.152'

⚠ 2 N 44°11.054'
W 122°05.416'

W i l l a m e t t e

N

N a t i o n a l

Paradise Campground

River

McKenzie

2.5

2

1,560' To Bend

126

McKenzie Ranger Station

F o r e s t

℗ 1 **1,440'**

To Eugene

END
BEGIN

0   1/4   1/2
MILE

2000'
1000'
2   4

---

growth is magic. This is the ultrashort version for beginners and families. Well, maybe not absolute beginners, as the singletrack bounces out to the precipitous riverbank in numerous places. From the turnaround point at Paradise Campground, 2.7 miles into the ride, the trail continues 24 more miles upriver, and depending on your fitness you may want to continue up. Go explore, but you don't really reach any obvious turnaround point until the Blue Pool at Tamolitch Falls, 17 tough miles upriver.

Driving Directions

From Eugene, drive just over 51 miles east on State Highway 126. Before reaching milepost 52, find the McKenzie River trailhead on the left alongside the highway. Park here.

....

The Ride

From the trailhead, pedal east (upriver) on McKenzie River Trail 3507. The trail, wide and hard-packed, noodles through the fir and cedar flats between the highway and the river. For a couple hundred yards near the beginning the trail runs right along the highway, but mostly it follows the forested bank of the river, past an understory of fern, moss, Oregon grape and salal. At **1.1** miles, reach a fork and stay left (right heads toward the highway and ranger station). At **1.8** miles, cross a dirt road. From here, the trails bears away from the river. Reach a fork at **2.1** miles and go right. Stay right again when the trail divides at **2.5** miles. At **2.7** miles (ridepoint 2), reach the paved entrance road to Paradise Campground. Across the entrance road you can see the McKenzie River Trail continuing upriver. For this easy beginner ride, turn around here and pedal back to the lower trailhead, **5.4** miles.

Gazetteer

Nearby camping: Paradise
Nearest food, drink, services: McKenzie Bridge, Eugene

Distance	9.5-mile loop
Route	Paved and dirt-road climb, sweet singletrack descent; views
Climbs	Long but bearable; high point: 4,830 ft, gain: 2,280 ft
Duration	Fitness rider: 1 to 2 hours; scenery rider: 2 to 3 hours
Travel	Eugene—55 miles; Bend—80 miles; Portland—165 miles
Skill	Advanced
Season	Summer, fall
Map	Green Trails: McKenzie Bridge
Rules	None
Manager	Willamette National Forest, McKenzie District, 541-822-3381
Web	www.fs.fed.us/r6/willamette/recreation/tripplanning/list_mk

Who Will Like This Ride

You like all things in moderation, except your climbs.

The Scoop

Olallie Mountain is a standard forest-road climb with a gee-whiz singletrack descent. It's fun and not too long, though the fat elevation gain gives the ride a serious side. For most of the ascent you're on a narrow, winding paved road that's never too steep. The first dirt-road pitch, however, is straight up, but that's it for the hard climbing. As a distraction during the climb, you can check out views of the central Oregon Cascades, including Hood, Jefferson, Washington, and Three Sisters. The singletrack zips down the north slope of O'Leary Mountain on Olallie Trail. However, the trail's namesake, Olallie Mountain (olallie

Trail 3529 at the big rock

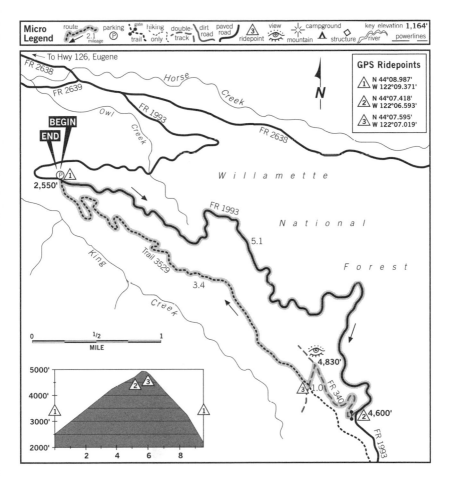

| Micro Legend | route 2.1 mileage | parking ℗ | gate hiking trail only | double-track | dirt road | paved road | 3 ridepoint | view | campground mountain | ▲ structure | ◇ river | key elevation **1,164'** powerlines |

To Hwy 126, Eugene

FR 2638
FR 2639
Horse Creek
FR 1993
Owl Creek
FR 2638

GPS Ridepoints

⚠1 N 44°08.987' W 122°09.371'
⚠2 N 44°07.418' W 122°06.593'
⚠3 N 44°07.595' W 122°07.019'

N

BEGIN
END

℗ 1
2,550'

W i l l a m e t t e

FR 1993

N a t i o n a l

5.1

King

Trail 3529

3.4

Creek

F o r e s t

0   1/2   1
MILE

4,830'
3 1.0
FR 340
2 4,600'
FR 1993

5000'
4000'
3000'
2000'
2   4   6   8

is the Chinook word for "berries"), is actually located many miles to the south of this loop. Adventurous riders may want to attempt both Olallie Mountain and King Castle (ride 48)—a 24-mile, 5,000-foot-gain day.

Driving Directions

From Eugene, drive about 50 miles east on State Highway 126. Just past the tiny town of McKenzie Bridge, turn right on Horse Creek Road (Forest Road 2638), and set your odometer to zero. Pass by FR 2639 on the right,

then at 1.8 miles turn right onto FR 1993. At 4.7 miles, stop at the small trailhead parking pullout on the left.

The Ride

From the pullout on FR 1993, ride up the paved road. It's narrow, winding, and steep, and it seems to go on forever. At **3.7** miles, cross over a sharp ridge that runs northeast. On clear days, Mount Washington and Three Sisters come into view as you crest the ridge. The climb continues. At **5.1** miles (ridepoint 2), turn right onto FR 340, passing around a big green gate. The gravel road climbs steeply at first, but then the grade eases and traverses.

After a short, sweeping descent, reach a fork in the road at **5.9** miles. There's a pullout on the right that affords excellent views of Mount Hood, Mount Jefferson, Mount Washington, and Three Sisters. When you are done soaking it in, take the left fork. Ignore a road back to the right. *WHOA!* At **6.1** miles (ridepoint 3), turn right on an unmarked and easily missed single-track. The trail, Olallie Trail 3529, descends quickly. It's a fast drop down a ridge that extends north from O'Leary Mountain. At **8.5** miles, pass an enormous rock wall on the left. In late spring and early summer, rhododen-drons bloom across the hillside. At **9.5** miles, the trail dumps out onto FR 1993 at the parking area.

Gazetteer

Nearby camping: Paradise

Nearest food, drink, services: McKenzie Bridge, Eugene

Distance	14.5-mile loop (12.5-mile option)
Route	Dirt road and singletrack climb, singletrack descent; views
Climbs	Brutal; high point: 3,810 ft, gain: 2,370 ft
Duration	Fitness rider: 2 hours; scenery rider: 3 to 5 hours
Travel	Eugene—55 miles; Bend—80 miles; Portland—165 miles
Skill	Advanced
Season	Summer, fall
Map	Green Trails: McKenzie Bridge
Rules	None
Manager	Willamette National Forest, McKenzie District, 541-822-3381
Web	www.fs.fed.us/r6/willamette/recreation/tripplanning/list_mk

Who Will Like This Ride
You stick by your motto—no pain, no gain.

The McKenzie River Valley from the north cliffs of Castle Rock

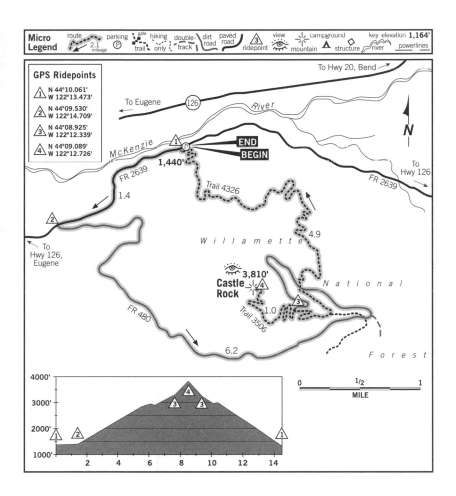

Micro Legend

route — 2.1 mileage · parking ℗ · gate · hiking trail · double-track · dirt road · paved road · △3 ridepoint · view · mountain · campground · △ structure · river · key elevation **1,164'** powerlines

GPS Ridepoints

△1 N 44°10.061' W 122°13.473'
△2 N 44°09.530' W 122°14.709'
△3 N 44°08.925' W 122°12.339'
△4 N 44°09.089' W 122°12.726'

To Hwy 20, Bend

To Eugene 126 River

McKenzie

△1 ℗ **END** **BEGIN**

1,440'

FR 2639

Trail 4326

1.4

△2

To Hwy 126, Eugene

W i l l a m e t t e

4.9

👁 **3,810'**
Castle Rock △4

N a t i o n a l

FR 480

Trail 3506 △3 1.0

6.2

F o r e s t

To Hwy 126

FR 2639

0 1/2 1
MILE

N

The Scoop

This ride is tougher than Olallie Mountain (ride 47), with a longer climb on a gravelly road and a taxing singletrack ascent to the very top. And for sure the views are terrific, but the real reason for this ride's existence is the descent. It's sick. From the tight, steep switchbacks near the summit to the no-brakes forest traverses farther down, the descent from Castle Rock is nearly perfect. Hardcores may want to attempt King Castle and Olallie

Working those Castle Rock switchbacks

Mountain on the same day—a 24-mile, 5,000-foot-gain feat. If you do, be certain to get a photo of you and your bike at the top with Deathball Rock in the distance. Yeah, Deathball Rock, that's cool. Note that some prefer this as an out-and-back, grinding up the singletrack rather than the gravel road.

Driving Directions

From Eugene, drive about 50 miles east on State Highway 126. Just past the tiny town of McKenzie Bridge, turn right on Horse Creek Road (Forest Road 2638), and set your odometer to zero. At 1.4 miles, turn right onto King Road East (FR 2639). At 5.4 miles, turn left into King Castle trailhead and park.

The Ride

From the trailhead, ride back to FR 2639, which is paved, and turn left. At **1.4** miles (ridepoint 2), turn left onto a dirt road (FR 480) and begin the serious climb. Stay on the main road as you ascend. After a couple miles, the road, gravelly in sections, spirals counterclockwise around Castle Rock, climbing in fits and starts. At **7.6** miles (ridepoint 3), the main road ends at a trailhead. The trail, Castle Rock Trail 3506, immediately splits—go right on Castle Rock Trail and climb toward the top of the mountain. Steep, tight switchbacks mount the southwest face of Castle Rock. **WOOF!** Reach the rocky summit at **8.6** miles (ridepoint 4) and—before passing out—check out the terrific views in every direction.

When you're done communing with the edge of the cliffs, ride the tight switchies back toward the trailhead. At **9.6** miles (ridepoint 3), just before returning to the trailhead, reach a fork and take a hard right toward King Castle Trail and continue the fast descent. At **10.1** miles, reach a fork and bear left on King Castle Trail 4326. The trail climbs for a short distance and then resumes the frolicking descent. At **10.7** miles, reach a T at a dirt road and turn right. Immediately turn left onto a doubletrack to continue down King Castle Trail. The doubletrack quickly narrows to a fast, hard-packed singletrack, and slingshots you around the lower north slope of Castle Rock. It's a sweet descent through a thick forest. At **14.5** miles, reach the trailhead parking to complete the loop.

Option

From the **7.6**-mile point, turn left at the fork. This eliminates the one-mile climb to the top of Castle Rock (and the subsequent one-mile descent). Follow the directions from the **9.6**-mile mark.

Gazetteer

Nearby camping: Paradise

Nearest food, drink, services: McKenzie Bridge, Eugene

49 ELIJAH BRISTOW STATE PARK ⚙⚙

Distance	1 to 12 miles
Route	Wide, easy, dirt trails, some paved
Climbs	Flat; high point: 670 ft, gain: none
Duration	All riders: 1 to 2 hours
Travel	Eugene—15 miles
Skill	Beginner
Season	Spring, summer, fall
Map	Elijah Bristow State Park Trail Guide
Rules	None
Manager	Oregon State Parks, 800-551-6949
Web	www.oregonstateparks.org/park_83.php

Who Will Like This Ride
Families and first-timers

The Scoop

Elijah Bristow State Park, named after one of Lane County's first pioneers, has about 12 miles of multi-use trails, as well as grassy fields and picnic areas. And it's all ridable. Some of the trails at the park are rocky and more technical, especially the trails along the Middle Fork of the Willamette River. The short Turtle and Oak Nature trails are closed to bikes. Additionally, the park is heavily used by equestrians, so ride with care. Remember, when you meet horses on the trail, stop and talk to the horse and rider as they pass. Since there are numerous trails and intersections in the park, following a  turn-by-turn description is more difficult than just exploring the trails and turning around when you feel done. So there's no detailed route description included here, just driving directions and a thought about the start of a ride. Have fun.

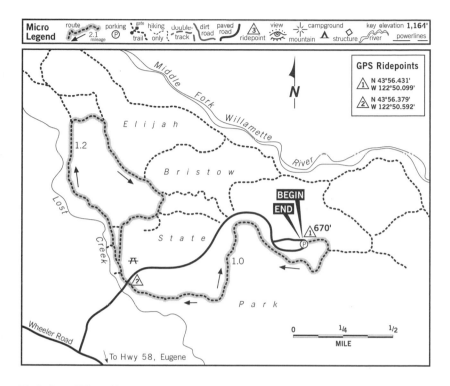

GPS Ridepoints

⚠1 N 43°56.431'
W 122°50.099'

⚠2 N 43°56.379'
W 122°50.592'

Driving Directions

From Eugene, drive south on Interstate 5. Take exit 188A and head east on State Highway 58. Drive about 10 miles east on Hwy 58, and turn left on Wheeler Road, setting your odometer to zero and following the signs for Elijah Bristow State Park. At 0.3 mile, turn right into the park. Proceed to the paved parking area at the end of the road, 1.1 miles.

Starting the Ride

Adjacent to the paved parking area and next to the bathrooms, there's a grassy dirt area for overflow parking. From the overflow parking area, take the wide dirt trail that begins near the wooden hitching post and exits into the trees. Just beyond, reach a T and turn right.

Gazetteer

Nearby camping: Black Canyon
Nearest food, drink, services: Eugene

Distance	19.5-mile loop
Route	Dirt road and singletrack climbs, zowie singletrack descent
Climbs	Tough then numbing; high point: 4,260 ft, gain: 3,240 ft
Duration	Fitness rider: 3 hours; scenery rider: 4 to 6 hours
Travel	Eugene—27 miles; Bend—115 miles
Skill	Advanced
Season	Summer, fall
Map	Middle Fork Ranger District map
Rules	None
Manager	Willamette National Forest, Middle Fork District, 541-782-2283
Web	www.fs.fed.us/r6/willamette/recreation/tripplanning/list_mf

Who Will Like This Ride
You like it wild, wholly, and whorling.

The Scoop
The trail system that originates from the Goodman Creek /Hardesty Mountain trailhead gets a lot of use. The big parking area fills up on sunny

Fern corridor on South Willamette Trail

Saturdays and Sundays with cyclists itching to head out onto Hardesty, Goodman, South Fork Willamette, and Eula Ridge trails, and beyond. It's a great area that expands as the map unfolds, full of intermediate and advanced riding, steep climbs, and space-voyager descents. If "climb high and descend fast" is your motto, you'll love this area. However, all this trail love can lead to a trail that's overused. If you've got time, check out the great rides farther east near Oakridge. Avoid this area altogether during wet weather when riding can damage the trails. And hey, don't skid. If this area continues to get overridden, the Forest Service may close it to bikes. Note: This is a tough loop, as the trail gains and loses a lot of elevation over the first five miles before you ever even begin the 3,240-foot grunt. Pack your food and water accordingly. And watch out for poison oak.

Driving Directions

From Eugene, drive south on Interstate 5. Take exit 188A and head east on State Highway 58. Drive about 22 miles east on Hwy 58, and turn right into a big dirt parking area. This is the Goodman Creek/Hardesty Mountain trailhead.

The Ride

From the trailhead, ride out Hardesty Trail, a buff dirt singletrack, toward South Willamette Trail. At **0.2** mile, reach a fork—bear left and begin climbing. Ignore a lesser trail on the left at **0.3** mile. The singletrack is nice, but the climb is steep. At **0.6** mile (ridepoint 2), reach a fork and bear left on South Willamette Trail 3465. The trail begins by traversing the hillside, then quickly descends. A short climb follows the descent. At **2** miles, reach a gravel road and turn left, following the trail sign. A short distance farther, turn right on singletrack again. After noodling through a rich forest, the trail becomes gravel, veers to the right, and starts climbing. Cross a doubletrack and continue up. Segments of the South Willamette Trail may be overgrown, just put your head down and hog through the underbrush.

After a long climb, the trail descends quickly to a creek crossing at **4.4** miles. From here, the trail mounts a sharp ridge, and parts of the next quarter mile may have to be walked. Drop to another creek, North Creek, at **5.3** miles. After a short push out of the ravine, reach an unmarked fork and bear left. Cross South Creek a short distance farther. The trail ends at Eula Ridge trailhead, **5.7** miles, on Hwy 58. Turn right and pedal along the highway.

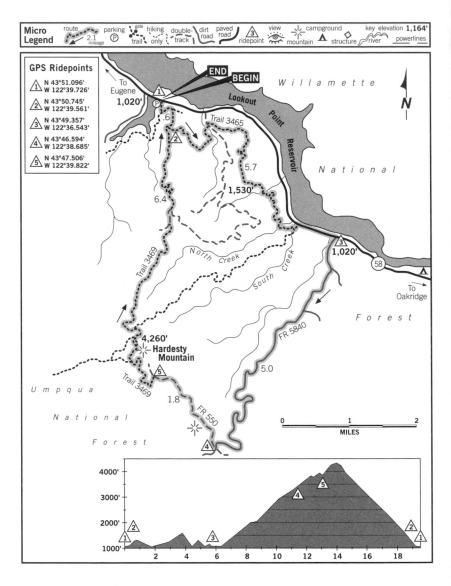

Micro Legend

route — 2.1 mileage | parking ℗ | gate, hiking trail, only | double-track | dirt road | paved road | 3 ridepoint | view, mountain | campground, structure | key elevation 1,164', river, powerlines

GPS Ridepoints

1. N 43°51.096' W 122°39.726'
2. N 43°50.745' W 122°39.561'
3. N 43°49.357' W 122°36.543'
4. N 43°46.594' W 122°38.685'
5. N 43°47.506' W 122°39.822'

WHOA! The traffic comes fast along the highway, so ride with care. At **6.3** miles (ridepoint 3), turn right on Patterson Mountain Road (FR 5840). The paved road immediately becomes gravel and starts climbing. Stay on the main road as you climb. At **6.8** miles, reach a fork and bear right. At **7.7** miles, bear right and continue up the main road. The ascent is steep and relentless.

At **11.3** miles (ridepoint 4), reach a four-way at Patterson Saddle. Take a hard right turn onto FR 550 and continue the climb up toward Hardesty Mountain. At **13.1** miles (ride-point 5), take Trail 3469 on the left. The trail climbs, then traverses to a fork at **13.7** miles—take a sharp right, continuing the climb on Hardesty Trail 3469. ***WOOF!*** Finally the trail crests the western shoulder of Hardesty Mountain. It's downhill from here; the trail is narrow and, in spots, technical, and the hillside is nearly straight down. At **14** miles, reach an unmarked fork and bear left. A

Nearing the top of Hardesty Mountain

few pedal strokes farther, ignore a trail on the right. At **14.1** miles, reach a fork and turn left (to the right are the concrete footings that used to be the old Hardesty Mountain lookout). Around the corner, **14.2** miles, reach a fork and stay right.

From here the trail frolics down the north slope of the mountain. Steep switchbacks and fast traverses are spiced with technical sections that force short, hair-ball maneuvers. When the trail divides at **14.5** miles, go left to continue on Trail 3469. At **17.1** miles, hit a doubletrack and bear right. The singletrack begins again on the left at **17.2** miles. Switchie practice begins in earnest. Cross a doubletrack at **18.4** miles. At **18.9** miles (ridepoint 2), reach a fork and bear left. At **19.2** miles, pass by Goodman Trail on the left. Reach the trailhead at **19.5** miles to complete the loop.

Gazetteer

Nearby camping: Black Canyon
Nearest food, drink, services: Oakridge

Distance	7.5-mile loop
Route	Singletrack loop, sometimes technical
Climbs	A few short rises; high point: 1,440 ft, gain: 160 ft
Duration	Fitness rider: 1 hour; scenery rider: 2 hours
Travel	Eugene—42 miles; Bend—100 miles
Skill	Intermediate
Season	Spring, summer, fall
Map	Middle Fork Ranger District map
Rules	None
Manager	Willamette National Forest, Middle Fork District, 541-782-2283
Web	www.fs.fed.us/r6/willamette/

Who Will Like This Ride

You're a morning person who wants to get in a short ride before the slackers wake up.

The Scoop

The first half of this loop, up the north side of Salmon Creek (see ride 52), is heavily used by walkers and runners. Numerous interconnecting trails, most of which are wide and easy, crisscross the north side of the creek, making it a fun, if sometimes confusing, route. Once you cross the bridge over the creek at the halfway point, though, the trail becomes narrower, more technical, and less traveled, but the route is easier to follow. Be sure to check out the view of Salmon Creek from the bridge at the top of the loop—water running across green rock slabs though a fir and vine maple forest. It's extraordinary.

Driving Directions

From Eugene, drive south on Interstate 5. Take exit 188A and head east on State Highway 58. Drive about 36 miles east on Hwy 58 to Oakridge. At the stoplight at Crestview Street in Oakridge, set your odometer to zero and continue east on Hwy 58. At 1.7 miles, turn left on Fish Hatchery Road. At 3

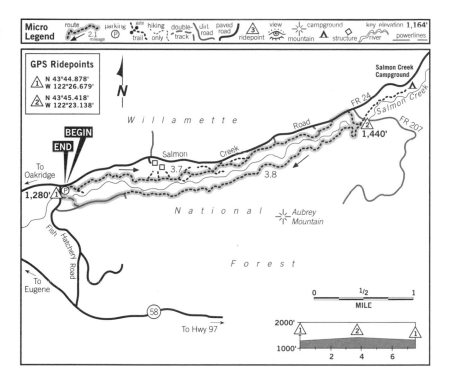

miles, cross Salmon Creek, then immediately—before crossing the railroad tracks and before reaching Forest Road 24 (Salmon Creek Road)—park in the dirt parking area on the right.

The Ride

From the dirt parking area, head out Salmon Creek Trail 4365. You immediately drop to cross a small bridge. ***WHOA!*** Stay on the main trail, ignoring spurs down to the creek. The trail is wide, rolling, and hard-packed. At **0.9** mile, pass under a railroad trestle. From **1** mile to **1.2** miles, ignore three trails on the left that lead to the former ranger station. At **1.3** miles, reach a fork and bear right. Ignore a spur on the right, then, at **1.5** miles, bear right at the fork. At the **2**-mile mark, ride straight through a four-way. At **2.1** miles, stay to the right, passing two trails on the left. At **2.4** miles, ignore a trail back to the left. The way narrows here. A short distance farther, pass by

Salmon Creek

a doubletrack spur on the left that leads to Salmon Creek Road. Remain on the singletrack along the creek. Then reach a doubletrack and bear right.

At **2.6** miles, ignore a spur to a camp spot on the right. At **2.9** miles, stay on the main doubletrack, ignoring a spur on the left to Salmon Creek Road. At **3.2** miles, bear left on a dirt road (a camp spot is straight ahead). *WHOA!* Immediately turn right on an easily missed singletrack—Salmon Creek Trail 4365. After a short climb through the woods, the trail parallels Salmon Creek Road. At the **3.5**-mile mark, Trail 4365 bears right and heads into the woods, away from the road. Stay on the main trail as it crosses a doubletrack. At **3.7** miles (ridepoint 2), reach a fork and take a hard right, now heading downriver. Cross the elaborately constructed wood bridge over Salmon Creek. The creek is beautiful here, a good place to linger.

From the bridge, the trail is ragged and root-strewn as it follows the creek, and some riders may be forced to walk short sections. At **6.4** miles, the trail routes around the rocky base of a railroad trestle. Shoulder your bike and climb underneath the trestle to the trail beyond. At **6.5** miles, cross over a tiny diversion dam and then bear left on the doubletrack. At **6.8** miles, cross a bridge and veer right on the dirt road. *WHOA!* Reach a fork in the road at **7.1** miles, turn right on the lesser doubletrack, and head toward the creek. The doubletrack follows the creek and then ends at Fish Hatchery Road. Turn right on this paved road. Cross over Salmon Creek to reach the parking area at **7.5** miles.

Gazetteer
Nearby camping: Salmon Creek Falls, Packard Creek
Nearest food, drink, services: Oakridge

Distance	5.2-mile out-and-back
Route	Wide singletrack
Climbs	Nearly flat; high point: 1,420 ft, gain: 140 ft
Duration	Fitness rider: 30 minutes; scenery rider: 1 hour
Travel	Eugene—42 miles; Bend—100 miles
Skill	Beginner
Season	Spring, summer, fall
Map	Middle Fork Ranger District map
Rules	None
Manager	Willamette National Forest, Middle Fork District, 541-782-2283
Web	www.fs.fed.us/r6/willamette/

Who Will Like This Ride

Beginners, families, and five-year-old future racers.

The Scoop

Salmon Creek Trail, also known as Warrior Cross-Country Trail because of the local high school cross-country runners who train here, is heavily used by runners, walkers, and cyclists. For the most part the wide trail has good sight lines and accommodates users well. That doesn't mean, however, that you shouldn't ride with caution. If you want to hammer, this isn't the best trail. It is a good trail, however, easily-negotiated and flat, for beginners and families, as it winds along Salmon Creek through a pretty forest.

Driving Directions

From Eugene, drive south on Interstate 5. Take exit 188A and head east on State Highway 58. Drive about 36 miles east on Hwy 58 to Oakridge. At the stoplight at Crestview Street in Oakridge, set your odometer to zero and continue east on Hwy 58. At 1.7 miles, turn left on Fish Hatchery Road. At 3 miles, cross Salmon Creek, then immediately—before crossing the railroad tracks and before reaching Forest Road 24 (Salmon Creek Road)—park in the dirt parking area on the right.

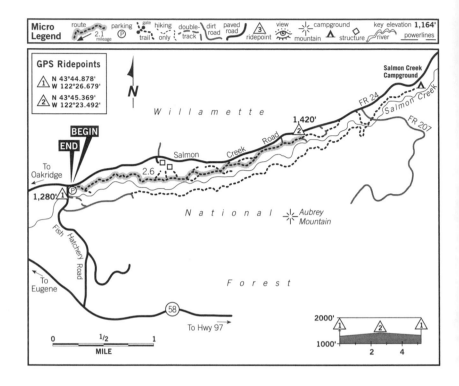

The Ride

From the dirt parking area, head out Salmon Creek Trail 4365. It immediately descends then crosses a bridge. From here, stay on the main trail, ignoring spurs on the right which head down to the creek. The trail is wide, rolling, and hard-packed. At **0.9** mile, pass under a railroad trestle. From **1** mile to **1.2** miles, ignore three trails on the left that lead to the former ranger station. At **1.3** miles, reach a fork and bear right. Ignore a spur on the right, then at **1.5** miles, bear right at the fork. At the **2**-mile mark, ride straight through a four-way.

At **2.1** miles, stay to the right, passing two trails on the left. At **2.4** miles, ignore a trail back to the left. The way narrows here. A short distance farther, pass by a doubletrack spur on the left that leads to Salmon Creek Road. Stay on the singletrack along the creek, then when you reach a doubletrack, bear right. At **2.6** miles (ridepoint 2), you'll find a camp spot on the right

Salmon Creek Trail kisses its namesake

and a doubletrack on the left. Turn around here and return to the parking area at **5.2** miles.

Gazetteer
Nearby camping: Salmon Creek Falls, Packard Creek
Nearest food, drink, services: Oakridge

Distance	11.4-mile loop
Route	Dirt-road ascent, nice singletrack descent, paved connector
Climbs	Wicked; high point: 2,500 ft, gain: 1,220 ft
Duration	Fitness rider: 1 hour; scenery rider: 2 to 3 hours
Travel	Eugene—42 miles; Bend—100 miles
Skill	Intermediate
Season	Late spring, summer, fall
Map	Middle Fork Ranger District map
Rules	None
Manager	Willamette National Forest, Middle Fork District, 541-782-2283
Web	www.fs.fed.us/r6/willamette/

Who Will Like This Ride

You want a short fitness ride with an emphasis on climbing.

The Scoop

The ride begins with a playful pedal along Salmon Creek Trail. After the four-mile warm-up, a dirt road heads up Aubrey Mountain at an insane clip—one of the steepest climbs in this book. Some call it The Wall. A friend

Salmon Creek

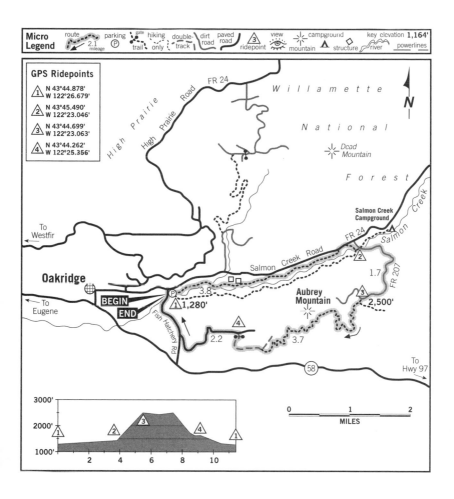

said he preferred Aubrey as a night ride so, while he rode, he wouldn't have to look at the incline ahead of him. Okay, but how hard can a one-and-a-half mile climb really be? Go find out. The traversing then switchbacking descent may change your face of pain to a smile, though it's over all too quickly. The south slope of Aubrey Mountain affords great views of the Middle Fork of the Willamette River valley. Unless you're riding at night. Note: Watch for poison oak!

Driving Directions

From Eugene, drive south on Interstate 5. Take exit 188A and head east on State Highway 58. Drive about 36 miles east on Hwy 58 to Oakridge. At the stoplight at Crestview Street in Oakridge, set your odometer to zero and continue east on Hwy 58. At 1.7 miles, turn left on Fish Hatchery Road. At 3 miles, cross Salmon Creek, then immediately—before crossing the railroad tracks and reaching Forest Road 24 (Salmon Creek Road)—park in the dirt area on the right.

The Ride

From the parking area, head out Salmon Creek Trail 4365. Watch out for other trail users. (In fact, if you want to hammer, you might consider riding up FR 24 to FR 207 near the 3.5-mile mark.) Stay on the main trail, ignoring spurs down to the creek. The trail is wide, rolling, and hard-packed. At **0.9** mile, pass under a railroad trestle. From **1** mile to **1.2** miles, ignore three trails on the left that lead to the former ranger station. At **1.3** miles, reach a fork and bear right. Ignore a spur on the right, then at **1.5** miles bear right at the fork. At the 2-mile mark, ride straight through a four-way. At **2.1** miles, stay to the right, passing two trails on the left. At **2.4** miles, ignore a trail back to the left. The way narrows here. A short distance farther, pass by a doubletrack spur on the left that leads to Salmon Creek Road. Stay on the singletrack along the creek, then reach a doubletrack and bear right.

At **2.6** miles, ignore a spur to a camp spot on the right. At **2.9** miles, stay on the main doubletrack, ignoring another spur on the left to Salmon Creek Road. At **3.2** miles, bear left on a dirt road (a camp spot is straight ahead). **WHOA!** Immediately, turn right on an easily missed singletrack—Salmon Creek Trail 4365. After a short climb through the woods, the trail parallels Salmon Creek Road. At the **3.5**-mile mark, the track heads into the woods again, veering away from the road to the right. Stay on the main trail as it crosses a doubletrack. At **3.7** miles, reach a fork and bear left. Ignore another trail on the left. Then at **3.8** miles (ridepoint 2), reach FR 207 and turn right.

FR 207 crosses over Salmon Creek and becomes gravel. At **4.1** miles, the road bends to the right and heads steeply up the eastern shoulder of Aubrey Mountain, affectionately known as The Wall. What this means is that from here the road gains elevation in huge, grueling, and unrelenting

Looking west from the south slope of Aubrey Mountain

chunks. Though it's short, at over 700 feet per mile it's one of the steepest climbs in this book. At **5.2** miles, pass an unmarked singletrack on the left. At **5.5** miles (ridepoint 3), turn left onto Eugene to Crest Trail 3559. The trail immediately divides—bear right. This is a fun section, traversing in and out of the steep side-sloped folds of Aubrey Mountain on a gradual descent. At **7.5** miles, you pop out of the fir forest into an open hillside of low oaks with views of the valley.

At **7.6** miles, the trail reenters the fir forest and immediately begins a furious, switchbacking descent. When the trail ends at a doubletrack, FR 022, at **8.5** miles, turn left and descend. The dirt road winds and rolls. At **9.2** miles, pass through a gate and reach a paved road. Turn left and cruise down this fast, winding descent (too bad it's pavement). Cross a set of railroad tracks at **10.2** miles. The road ends at a T at **10.5** miles—turn right. This is Fish Hatchery Road. At **11.4** miles, cross over Salmon Creek and reach the dirt parking area on the right to complete the loop.

Gazetteer
Nearby camping: Salmon Creek Falls, Packard Creek
Nearest food, drink, services: Oakridge

Distance	12.4-mile loop
Route	Paved and dirt-road ascent, short but fast singletrack descent
Climbs	Healthy but no killer; high point: 3,040 ft, gain: 1,760 ft
Duration	Fitness rider: 1 hour; scenery rider: 2 to 3 hours
Travel	Eugene—42 miles; Bend—100 miles
Skill	Intermediate
Season	Late spring, summer, fall
Map	Middle Fork Ranger District map
Rules	None
Manager	Willamette National Forest, Middle Fork District, 541-782-2283
Web	www.fs.fed.us/r6/willamette/

Who Will Like This Ride

Yesterday you combined nearby Alpine with Tire Mountain (see ride 56 and its option), today you plan to combine bacon, eggs, and the Sunday paper with Dead Mountain.

The Scoop

This ride is a cousin to Aubrey Mountain (ride 53): Both rides begin from the same trailhead, combine road climbs with ripping singletrack descents, and neither is overly long. Dead Mountain explores the north side of the Salmon Creek valley, Aubrey Mountain the south. If you are in shape, a reasonable day might even include both loops. Dead Mountain begins with a long, paved-road climb through Oakridge and up and across High Prairie, followed by a shorter dirt-road ascent. From the top, the singletrack flies down the southwestern edge of the mountain. Like Aubrey, though, the ratio of singletrack to road isn't so good, with just 2.5 miles of trail. If you're hungry for skinny trails, you might want to pick out a different ride.

Driving Directions

From Eugene, drive south on Interstate 5. Take exit 188A and head east on State Highway 58. Drive about 36 miles east on Hwy 58 to Oakridge. At the stoplight at Crestview Street in Oakridge, set your odometer to zero

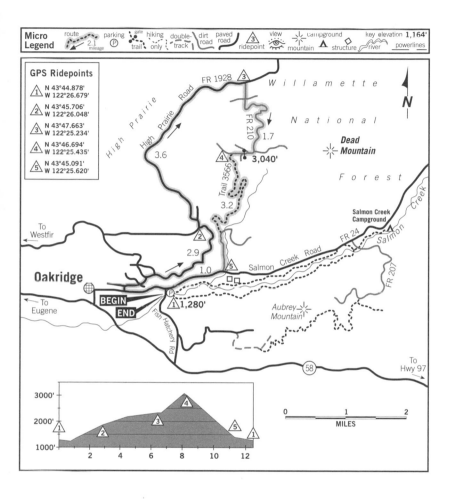

Micro Legend route parking gate hiking double- dirt paved view campground key elevation **1,164'**
2.1 mileage P trail only track road road ridepoint mountain structure river powerlines

GPS Ridepoints

1. N 43°44.878'
   W 122°26.679'
2. N 43°45.706'
   W 122°26.048'
3. N 43°47.663'
   W 122°25.234'
4. N 43°46.694'
   W 122°25.435'
5. N 43°45.091'
   W 122°25.620'

and continue east on Hwy 58. At 1.7 miles, turn left on Fish Hatchery Road. At 3 miles, cross Salmon Creek, then immediately—before crossing the railroad tracks and before reaching Forest Road 24 (Salmon Creek Road)— park in the dirt area on the right.

The Ride

From the parking area, cross the railroad tracks to Salmon Creek Road (FR 24) and turn left toward Oakridge. As you enter Oakridge, heading west, the road becomes East First Street. At **0.7** mile, turn right on Oak Street. Proceed one block up the hill and turn right on East Second Street, still climbing. A few pedal strokes farther, bear left on Westoak Road. At **1.2** miles, bear right on High Prairie Road, climbing and still on pavement. At **2.9** miles (ridepoint 2), reach a fork and bear right. Bear left a short distance farther, continuing north on High Prairie Road (FR 1928). After another mile of steady climbing, follow the road's northwest bend, past farms and through scattered oak, across the rolling plain of High Prairie.

At **6.5** miles (ridepoint 3), turn right on Dead Mountain Road (FR 210), which begins as gravel but quickly changes to dirt. At **6.7** miles, bear left and gear down. From here, the road winds steeply up the northwest flank of Dead Mountain, through a fir forest. The climb is relentless, though not too long. Stay on the main road. At **8.1** miles, reach a T and turn right on FR 190. It's

Wildlife along High Prairie Road

here that you cross over the western ridge of Dead Mountain. At **8.2** miles, when the road divides again, bear left and ride around the gate. The road almost immediately divides again—stay to the right. **WHOA!** Just as you might think about gaining some speed, turn left onto Flat Creek Trail 3566 (ridepoint 4).

The sweet, smooth, fern-lined singletrack slaloms down the hillside. The forest is somewhat open and light, and the trail is fast. At **10.3** miles, ignore an unmarked trail on the right. At **10.7** miles, cross a creek and climb to FR 2404. Turn right on this gravel road and descend. At **11.4** miles (ridepoint 5), FR 2404 ends at a T with Salmon Creek Road (FR 24). Turn right on Salmon Creek Road. Pass by the former ranger station on the left. At **12.4** miles, turn left and cross the railroad tracks to the parking area to complete the loop.

Gazetteer
Nearby camping: Salmon Creek Falls, Packard Creek
Nearest food, drink, services: Oakridge

Distance	19.9-mile loop
Route	Dirt-road climb, singletrack descent
Climbs	Long and strenuous; high point: 4,080 ft, gain: 2,970 ft
Duration	Fitness rider: 2.5 to 3 hours; scenery rider: 4 to 6 hours
Travel	Eugene—38 miles; Bend—105 miles
Skill	Advanced
Season	Summer, fall
Map	Middle Fork Ranger District map
Rules	None
Manager	Willamette National Forest, Middle Fork District, 541-782-2283
Web	www.fs.fed.us/r6/willamette/recreation/tripplanning/list_mf

Who Will Like This Ride
Descending is in your blood, and you'll climb anything to get there.

The Scoop
From the town of Westfir numerous forest roads climb toward Buckhead Mountain, on toward Sourgrass Mountain, and way up to Alpine Ridge.

The covered bridge at Westfir

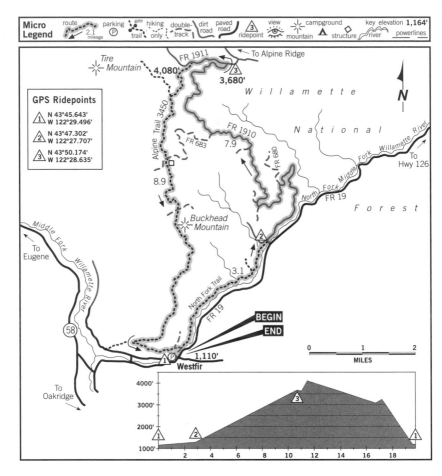

route ⋯ parking Ⓟ hiking trail only double-track dirt road paved road ③ ridepoint view mountain campground ▲ structure river key elevation **1,164'** powerlines

2.1 mileage

gate

GPS Ridepoints

△1 N 43°45.643' W 122°29.496'

△2 N 43°47.302' W 122°27.707'

△3 N 43°50.174' W 122°28.635'

Tire Mountain **4,080'**

FR 1911

To Alpine Ridge

③ **3,680'**

W i l l a m e t t e

N

N a t i o n a l

Alpine Trail 3450

FR 1910

FR 683

7.9

FR 680

8.9

North Fork Middle Fork Willamette River

To Hwy 126

FR 19

F o r e s t

Buckhead Mountain

②

Middle Fork Willamette River

To Eugene

3.1

North Fork Trail

FR 19

BEGIN

END

58

△1 Ⓟ **1,110'**

Westfir

To Oakridge

0   1   2

MILES

4000'
3000'
2000'
1000'

③

△1   △2   ②   △1

2   4   6   8   10   12   14   16   18

And if you can take the punishment, it's a big chunk of Turkish Mountain Bike Delight. After a raggity, off-camber singletrack start—with a significant amount of poison oak—the route turns up a dirt road and climbs, climbs, climbs. From the top, the singletrack dives down the ridgeline, hairball in spots, overgrown in others, but always upping the G-force ante. And the occasional singletrack ascent allows the water in your eyes to dry before the next precipitous drop. Note: You may want to ride out FR 19 and pick up this ride at FR 1910—it's a nice warm-up and avoids the ragged, poison oak-strewn North Fork Trail.

Wishing for a higher gear

Driving Directions

From Eugene, drive south on Interstate 5. Take exit 188A and head east on State Highway 58. After driving about 32 miles east on Hwy 58 toward Oakridge, turn left, following the signs to Westfir. Set your odometer to zero. Cross the Middle Fork of the Willamette River and reach a T at 0.5 mile—turn left on Westfir-Oakridge Road, continuing toward Westfir. Stay to the right on Westfir-Oakridge Road into Westfir. At 2.3 miles, reach a four-way stop. Turn left and drive through a covered bridge over the river. At 2.4 miles, find the trailhead.

The Ride

From the trailhead, proceed around the gate and up the wide gravel trail, passing under the railroad tracks. (Note: you can save a little time by taking paved FR 19 on the opposite side of the river. See the map.) At **0.1** mile, find North Fork Trail 3666 on the right and take it. At **0.6** mile, meet a doubletrack and bear right, descending. The way soon narrows to singletrack again. This riverside trail, overgrown with blackberry in places and poison oak in others, can be off-camber, rocky and uneven, so the riding isn't particularly fast or smooth. Arrive at a fork at **2.7** miles, and stay low to the right. The trail climbs then descends, then squeezes through a bit of forest between the river on one side and a dirt road on the other. At **3.1** miles, reach FR 1910, with is dirt, and turn left. The road forks immediately—bear right on the main road.

The climbing begins pronto and doesn't relent as it winds up the steep ridge between Dartmouth and Short Creeks, east of Buckhead Mountain. Stay on the main road as you climb, passing FR 680 on the right at **5.2** miles and several lesser roads on the left. At **8.6** miles, reach a fork and bear right, continuing on FR 1910 (FR 683 is to the left).

WOOF! At **11** miles, reach the top of the road section at a fork. Turn left onto FR 1911. Stay on the main road to the left. At **11.4** miles, turn left onto a singletrack, Alpine Trail 3450. The trail immediately begins a serious climb up and around a high knoll. At **11.7** miles, the way levels and traverses, crossing the ride's high point a short distance farther. Reach a fork in the trail at **12.3** miles and bear left, beginning a nearly continuous  eight-mile descent. At **14** miles, cross a dirt road, then stay to the right of a wood structure. Reach a fork at **14.5** miles and bear left. After crossing a dirt road at **16.4** miles, the trail climbs around Buckhead Mountain.

After a clearing, **16.8** miles, the trail romps and corkscrews down the ridge that extends south from Buckhead Mountain. After a couple of hair-ball sections, three road crossings and lots of excellent descending traverses, reach a fork at **18.8** miles and turn left, traversing east now. At **19.7** miles, the trail ends at a road—bear right and descend. Pass around the gate, bear right, and ride under the railroad tracks. Just around the bend you'll find the trailhead parking, **19.9** miles.

Gazetteer
Nearby camping: Salmon Creek Falls, Packard Creek
Nearest food, drink, services: Oakridge

Distance	36.7-mile figure eight (48.1-mile Option)
Route	Dirt road and singletrack climbs, singletrack descents
Climbs	WOOF!; high point: 4,960 ft, gain: 3,850 ft
Duration	Fitness rider: 4 to 5 hours; scenery rider: 6 to 10 hours
Travel	Eugene—38 miles; Bend—105 miles
Skill	Advanced
Season	Summer, fall
Map	Middle Fork Ranger District map
Rules	None
Manager	Willamette National Forest, Middle Fork District, 541-782-2283
Web	www.fs.fed.us/r6/willamette/recreation/tripplanning/list_mf

Who Will Like This Ride

Your pupils were dilated when you decided this was a good idea.

The Scoop

Site of the legendary Cascade Cream Puff 100 (as in 100 miles), the potential for suffering out Alpine is beyond mind-boggling. But it's also beautiful, challenging, and adventurous. Load up on calories and bring it on. Note: You may want to ride out FR 19 and pick up this ride at FR 1910—it's a nice warm-up and avoids the ragged, poison oak-strewn North Fork Trail. In fact, watch out for poison oak on any trail below about 4,000 ft in the Middle Fork Ranger District.

Driving Directions

From Eugene, drive south on Interstate 5. Take exit 188A and head east on State Highway 58. After driving about 32 miles east on Hwy 58 toward Oakridge, turn left, following the signs to Westfir. Set your odometer to zero. Cross the Middle Fork of the Willamette River and reach a T at 0.5 mile—turn left on Westfir-Oakridge Road, continuing toward Westfir. Stay to the right on Westfir-Oakridge Road into Westfir. At 2.3 miles, reach a four-way stop. Turn left and drive through a covered bridge over the river. At 2.4 miles, find the trailhead.

The Ride

From the trailhead, proceed around the gate and up the wide gravel trail, passing under the railroad tracks. (Note: you can save a little time by taking paved FR 19 on the opposite side of the river. See the map.) At **0.1** mile, find North Fork Trail 3666 on the right and take it. At **0.6** mile, meet a double-track and bear right, descending. The way soon narrows to singletrack again. This riverside trail, overgrown with blackberry in places, can be off-camber, rocky and uneven, so the riding isn't particularly fast or smooth. Arrive at a fork at **2.7** miles, and stay low to the right. The trail climbs then descends, then squeezes through a bit of forest between the river on one side and a dirt road on the other. At **3.1** miles (ridepoint 2), reach FR 1910, with is dirt, and turn left. The road forks immediately—bear right on the main road.

The climbing begins pronto and doesn't relent as it winds up the steep ridge between Dartmouth and Short creeks, east of Buckhead Mountain. Stay on the main road as you climb, passing FR 680 on the right at **5.2** miles and several lesser roads on the left. At **8.6** miles, reach a fork and bear right, continuing on FR 1910 (FR 683 is to the left).

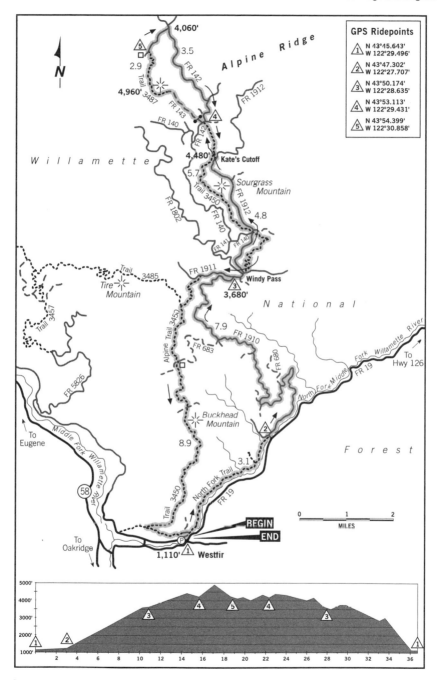

GPS Ridepoints

△1 N 43°45.643'
W 122°29.496'

△2 N 43°47.302'
W 122°27.707'

△3 N 43°50.174'
W 122°28.635'

△4 N 43°53.113'
W 122°29.431'

△5 N 43°54.399'
W 122°30.858'

4,060'

3.5

Alpine Ridge

FR 142

2.9

△5

Trail 3487

4,960'

FR 143

FR 1912

FR 140

△4

FR 142

4,480'

Kate's Cutoff

5.7

Trail 3450

Sourgrass Mountain

FR 140

FR 1912

4.8

FR 141   FR 140

W i l l a m e t t e

FR 1802

Trail 3485

Tire Mountain

Trail 3457

FR 5826

FR 1911

Windy Pass

△3

3,680'

N a t i o n a l

Alpine Trail 3450

7.9

FR 1910

FR 683

FR 680

North Fork Middle Fork Willamette River

To Hwy 126

FR 19

8.9

Buckhead Mountain

△2

3.1

F o r e s t

Trail 3450

North Fork Trail

FR 19

To Eugene

Middle Fork Willamette River

58

BEGIN
END

0   1   2
MILES

To Oakridge

P

1,110' △1 **Westfir**

5000'
4000'
3000'
2000'
1000'

△1   △2   △3   △4   △5   △4   △3   △1

2   4   6   8   10   12   14   16   18   20   22   24   26   28   30   32   34   36

Kicking it on Alpine

WOOF! At **11** miles (ridepoint 3), reach the top of the road section at a fork. Bear right, continuing up FR 1910. At **11.2** miles, arrive at Windy Pass, a junction of dirt roads and Upper Alpine Trail 3450. From the junction at Windy Pass, take the center route, bearing left, on FR 1912. The dirt and gravel road climbs and descends, but mostly climbs, though at a much more moderate rate than the first seven miles.

Note: From Windy Pass there are two ways to get to the **15.8**-mile mark (ridepoint 4). One is to take FR 140 and FR 142 around the west side of Sourgrass Mountain. This way requires no scrambling or guesswork, but it's all on dirt road. Still, it's probably the way you should go if you don't have an odometer. The second route, which I've written up below, routes via Kate's Cutoff. It's somewhat more dicey, but hey, you're riding the Alpine Epic so no whining, eh?

Around the **12**-mile mark, ride straight through a four-way (to the left you'll see FR 140). Continue out FR 1912. **WHOA!** At **14.6** miles, look to the left for an opening in the forest. It's called Kate's Cutoff, but the turn is not marked and it's not even a trail! Still you need to take it, lest you end up way out at Sardine Butte (and you don't want to go there). At this opening in the forest on the left, before the road bends too far to the right, put your bike on your shoulder and scramble up the hillside. **WHOA!** two. Don't get lost. Within a couple hundred yards, soon after you enter the forest, you should hit Upper Alpine Trail. When you do, turn right. The trail undulates through the forest, then drops to a dirt road at **15.8** miles.

From here, the loop around Saddleblanket Mountain begins. Go left on the road, then immediately turn right onto a gated dirt road, FR 143, which is signed closed. The road, a doubletrack really, climbs toward Saddleblanket Mountain. At **16.8** miles, reach a fork and go left on Saddleblanket Trail 3487. The singletrack climb is steep and painful. *WOOF!* Push over the high point, past a fire lookout, at **17.3** miles. From here, the trail descends to a road, **18.7** miles (ridepoint 5), and you'll see Little Blanket Shelter to the left. Turn right on the road, FR 144. When the road divides at **19.4** miles, go right on FR 142 and immediately crank up a short hill. The way levels, then rides the topographic waves along the northeast flank of Saddleblanket Mountain.

At **21.6** miles, the road forks—bear right to remain on FR 142. Reach a four-way that should be familiar (remember 15.8 miles?) at **22.2** miles (ridepoint 4) to complete the Saddleblanket loop at the top of Upper Alpine. Immediately before the gated dirt road on the right, turn left on Alpine Trail, which is unmarked. The trail is up and down, twisting the turning. Pass by Kate's Cutoff, on your left, at **23.3** miles. Less than a mile farther, cross through an open grassy meadow. And around the **23.5**-mile mark you'll pedal along the sharp edge of a ridge. The trail crosses a dirt road near a four-way in the road at **26.1** miles. Look for the signed trail opposite to continue on singletrack. From the road crossing, there's a wondrous stretch of trail back to Windy Pass, through a beautiful stand of old growth, sometimes referred to as the Jedi Section.

Arrive back at Windy Pass at **27.7** miles. When the trail dumps out to the road, go left then immediately right onto FR 1910, which is the road you climbed up earlier. The road divides at **27.9** miles (ridepoint 3)—bear right on FR 1911. *WHOA!* At **28.2** miles, find the singletrack on the left. Thus begins the lower section of Alpine Trail 3450.

Training for the Cream Puff 100

Immediately the trail heads up a short but serious climb around a high knoll. At **28.5** miles, the way levels and traverses, crossing a high point a short distance farther. When you reach a fork at **29.1** miles, bear left and begin a nearly continuous eight-mile descent. (To extend this ride out beyond Tire Mountain, see Option, below.) At **30.8** miles, cross a dirt road, then stay to the right of a wood structure. Reach a fork at **31.3** miles and bear left. After crossing a dirt road at **33.2** miles, the trail climbs around Buckhead Mountain.

After a clearing, **33.6** miles, the trail romps and corkscrews down the ridge that extends south from Buckhead Mountain. After a couple of hair-ball sections, three road crossings and lots of excellent descending traverses, reach a fork at **35.6** miles and turn left, traversing east now. At **36.5** miles, the trail ends at a road—bear right and descend. Pass around the gate, bear right, and ride under the railroad tracks. Just around the bend you'll find the trailhead parking, **36.7** miles.

Option
So you want to add on Tire Mountain? It extends the ride considerably, but most of the extra mileage ends up being dirt road riding, and descents at that. Of course you still want to do it, so here you go: At the **29.1**-mile mark, turn right on the narrow, unmarked trail. It's up and down then up, up, up. At **31.3** miles, bypass the trail to the summit of Tire Mountain on the left (it's an ultra steep trail to an uninteresting summit with no view). At **34.4** miles, reach a fork and go left on Cloverpatch Trail (a right heads toward Winberry Divide trailhead). At **35.2** miles, reach a T and go right. A few pedal strokes farther, regain the trail on the left. At **38.2** miles, reach a T at FR 5826 and go right. The singletrack's over. At **42** miles, reach a T and turn left, crossing the railroad tracks. At **44.8** miles, reach a T and turn right. Cross back and forth across the railroad tracks. At **46.6** miles, turn right on Windfrey Road. At **47** miles, turn right again. At **47.1** miles, turn left on Oakridge Road. Reach the covered bridge in Westfir at **48** miles. Turn left, ride through the covered bridge, and arrive at the trailhead, **48.1** miles.

Gazetteer
Nearby camping: Salmon Creek Falls, Packard Creek
Nearest food, drink, services: Oakridge

Distance	10.2-mile loop
Route	Paved-road climb, steep singletrack descent
Climbs	Steep and persistent; high point: 3,220 ft, gain: 2,060 ft
Duration	Fitness rider: 1 hour; scenery rider: 2 to 3 hours
Travel	Eugene—43 miles; Bend—100 miles
Skill	Intermediate
Season	Summer, fall
Map	Middle Fork Ranger District map
Rules	None
Manager	Willamette National Forest, Middle Fork District, 541-782-2283
Web	www.fs.fed.us/r6/willamette/recreation/tripplanning/list_mf

Who Will Like This Ride

You don't have much time, you don't get vertigo, and when it comes to a steep climb, bring it on.

The Scoop

A local favorite, this ride begins with a steep paved road climb and finishes with a rocket descent down the precipitous north slope of Larison Rock.

Good thing you tuned your brakes

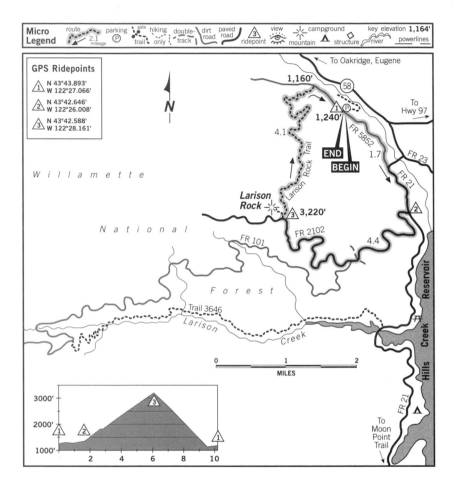

Micro Legend
route • • • • •
2.1 mileage
parking Ⓟ
gate
hiking trail
double-track
dirt road
paved road
△ ridepoint
view
mountain
campground
structure
key elevation **1,164'**
river
powerlines

GPS Ridepoints

△1 N 43°43.893'
W 122°27.066'

△2 N 43°42.646'
W 122°26.008'

△3 N 43°42.588'
W 122°28.161'

To Oakridge, Eugene

1,160'

58

To Hwy 97

1,240'

4.1

FR 5852

1.7

FR 23

△1 Ⓟ

END

BEGIN

FR 21

W i l l a m e t t e

Larison Rock Trail

Larison Rock

△3 3,220'

△2

N a t i o n a l

FR 2102

4.4

FR 101

F o r e s t

Reservoir

Trail 3646

Larison

Creek

Hills Creek

0   1   2

MILES

FR 21

To Moon Point Trail

3000'

△3

2000'

△1   △2   △1

1000'

2   4   6   8   10

The trail's signature: a 10-inch tread vanishing around one blind corner after another as it wraps around a steep (nearly sheer!) Oregon grape- and rhododendron-covered hillside. It's fun and—unless you take a flier—over all too quickly. Like many of the steep trails in the Middle Fork Ranger District, this one can get beat up during wet weather. Avoid this trail from late fall through the spring when the trail might be susceptible to damage. And watch out for hikers on those blind corners.

Driving Directions

From Eugene, drive south on Interstate 5. Take exit 188A and head east on State Highway 58. Drive about 36 miles east on Hwy 58 to Oakridge. At the stoplight at Crestview Street in Oakridge, set your odometer to zero and continue east on Hwy 58. At 1.8 miles, just past milepost 37, turn right on Kitson Springs Road (Forest Road 23) toward Hills Creek Dam. At 2.3 miles, turn right on FR 21 (Diamond Drive). At 2.6 miles, immediately after crossing the Middle Fork of the Willamette River, turn right on FR 5852. At 3.7 miles, turn right into a gravel parking area under the powerlines, which serves as a trailhead for Greenwaters Trail 4250.

The Ride

From the parking area, turn left on FR 5852 and pedal back to FR 21. Reach the T with FR 21 at **1** mile and turn right. The climbing begins gently, then ratchets up. At **1.8** miles (ridepoint 2), turn right on Larison Rock Road (FR 2102), which is paved. From here, it's a steep, four-mile climb. Stay on the main road. Just before milepost 2, pass by FR 101 on the left, **3.8** miles.

WOOF! After burning several Ben & Jerry's pints' worth of calories, turn right on Larison Rock Trail 3607 at **6.1** miles (ridepoint 3). The trail immediately forks—keep right on Trail 3607 and descend. (The left prong climbs to the top of Larison Rock.) It's an exciting descent, sweet and smooth, through an understory of salal, Oregon grape, fern, and rhododendron, as you play with the vanishing point of Larison Rock's western slope. Tight switchbacks, a narrow tread, and several ragged, hair-ball sections of trail keep it interesting. At **9.5** miles, when the trail ends at a dirt road, turn right. Reach the parking area on the left at **10.2** miles to complete the ride.

Gazetteer

Nearby camping: Packard Creek, Sand Prairie
Nearest food, drink, services: Oakridge

Distance	19.1-mile loop
Route	Paved and dirt-road up, technical singletrack down; views
Climbs	Patience required; high point: 2,920 ft, gain: 1,540 ft
Duration	Fitness rider: 2 hours; scenery rider: 3 to 6 hours
Travel	Eugene—45 miles; Bend—98 miles
Skill	Advanced
Season	Summer, fall
Map	Middle Fork Ranger District map
Rules	National Forest Recreation Pass required
Manager	Willamette National Forest, Middle Fork District, 541-782-2283
Web	www.fs.fed.us/r6/willamette/recreation/tripplanning/list_mf

Who Will Like This Ride

You like to ride with your armor, even on long cross-country routes.

The Scoop

Put on your adventurer's cap for this one. After a short paved warm-up and a steep, but also paved, climb, this loop follows a quiet dirt road that circuitously climbs to the upper reaches of Larison Creek. The upper section

Larison Creek Trail

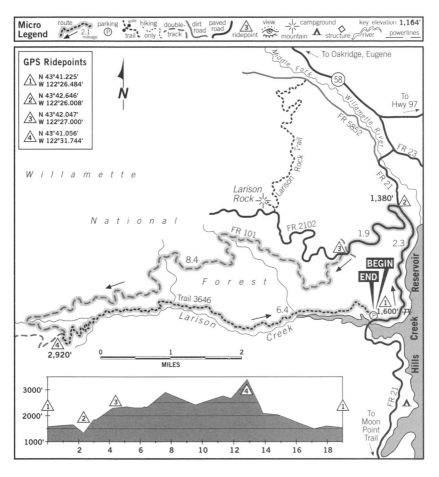

of Larison Creek Trail—technical, root-strewn, overgrown, and steep—is not well maintained. Still, advanced and expert riders may enjoy the loose, ragged trail, the sadistic blackberry vines, the stubborn manzanita branches, and the hot hillside. And it may feel as though you're one of the first to compass this route. Nineteen miles not quite enough? Consider going all-in by creating a giant figure eight out of this ride and Larison Rock (ride 57). Note: Watch for poison oak along the trail.

Driving Directions

From Eugene, drive south on Interstate 5. Take exit 188A and head east on State Highway 58. Drive about 36 miles east on Hwy 58 to Oakridge. At the stoplight at Crestview Street in Oakridge, set your odometer to zero and continue east on Hwy 58. At 1.8 miles, just past milepost 37, turn right on Kitson Springs Road (Forest Road 23) toward Hills Creek Dam. At 2.3 miles, turn right on FR 21 (Diamond Drive). Stay on FR 21. At 3.4 miles, pass by FR 2102 on the right. At 5.7 miles, turn right into a dirt parking area at the trailhead.

The Ride

From the trailhead parking area, ride back to FR 21 and turn left, heading north. The paved road follows the winding shoreline of Hills Creek Reservoir. Pass by the dam at **1.9** miles and descend. At **2.3** miles (ridepoint 2), turn left onto Larison Rock Road (FR 2102), also paved, and begin a steep climb. Stay on the main road as you ride the snaking coils upward. Just past milepost 2, reach a fork, **4.3** miles (ridepoint 3), and bear left on FR 2102-101, a.k.a. FR 101. The road may be closed to motor vehicles due to washouts, but it continues to be passable on a bike. A quiet one-laner, the road traverses high above Larison Creek and generally heads west.

After nearly five miles of rolling up and down, into creek drainages and then back out, descend quickly to a wide pullout at **9.5** miles, where views of Larison Creek valley and Diamond Peak spread out. From

Top of the Larison Creek Trail

here, continue down the road—doubletrack now—for a pitch through a diverse forest of cedar and fir, maple and oak. The doubletrack heads up again, drops to cross over Larison Creek at **12** miles, and climbs up the south side of the valley. Just after crossing over the ridge, **12.7** miles (ridepoint 4), turn left onto Larison Creek Trail 3646. The trail's top half-mile may need brushing and significant maintenance. Armor or at least long sleeves are recommended as protection against the manzanita and blackberry gantlet.

Just after the **13**-mile point, the trail slides into an older forest, and it's the technical switchbacks rather than the sadistic overgrowth that make the descent a challenge. At **13.8** miles, pass through a series of vertical, ultratight switchies into the cool grotto of Larison Creek. The next few miles are narrow, rocky, and root-strewn—technical but consistently ridable. Moss, fern, salal, and Oregon grape flourish in the shade of fir, cedar, and vine maple. Around the **17**-mile mark, the trail becomes wider and smoother. Pass through a primitive camp area at **17.5** miles. From here, the trail rolls beside a long arm of Hills Creek Reservoir. At **19.1** miles, reach the trailhead parking area to complete the loop.

Gazetteer

Nearby camping: Packard Creek, Sand Prairie
Nearest food, drink, services: Oakridge

Distance	20-mile loop
Route	Paved-road, tricky riverside singletrack
Climbs	Easy; high point: 2,050 ft, gain: 460 ft
Duration	Fitness rider: 2.5 hour; scenery rider: 3 to 5 hours
Travel	Eugene—60 miles; Bend—115 miles
Skill	Advanced
Season	Late spring, summer, fall
Map	Middle Fork Ranger District map
Rules	None
Manager	Willamette National Forest, Middle Fork District, 541-782-2283
Web	www.fs.fed.us/r6/willamette/recreation/tripplanning/list_mf

Who Will Like This Ride
You're sick of those long, grueling dirt road climbs.

The Scoop

Designated a National Recreation Trail in 2007, Middle Fork Willamette Trail runs nearly thirty miles, winding northwest from the blunt end of the Middle Fork valley near Timpanogas Lake all the way down to Sand Prairie

Crossing a tributary

Campground at Hills Creek Reservoir. A riverside trail with no long climbs, it's hard-packed and fast in some sections, ragged and rocky in others, and overgrown and difficult to follow in still others. And the ten-mile segment of trail described here is all of that. Like many riverside routes, the river periodically washes parts of the trail away, and new sections are built. This olio of old and new trails, brushy trails, and forest roads can cause confusion—be patient and take the newer trail or main route if you are unsure. A paved forest

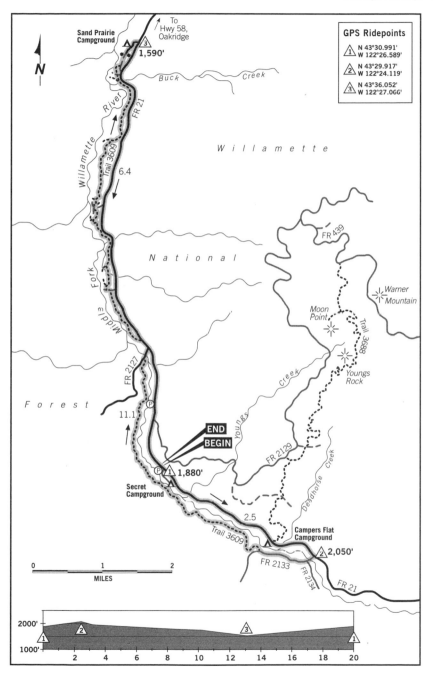

GPS Ridepoints

1 N 43°30.991'
W 122°26.589'

2 N 43°29.917'
W 122°24.119'

3 N 43°36.052'
W 122°27.066'

To Hwy 58, Oakridge

Sand Prairie Campground

1,590'

Buck Creek

Willamette River

FR 21

Trail 3609

6.4

Willamette

National

FR 439

Warner Mountain

Moon Point

Trail 3688

Middle Fork

FR 2127

Youngs Rock

Forest

11.1

P

END
BEGIN

1,880'

P 1

Secret Campground

Youngs Creek

FR 2129

Deadhorse Creek

2.5

Campers Flat Campground

Trail 3609

FR 2133

FR 2134

2 2,050'

FR 21

0   1   2
MILES

2000'
1000'

2   4   6   8   10   12   14   16   18   20

road links both ends of this Middle Fork segment to form a twenty-mile loop. Other ride formats are possible, such as an out-and-back or a two-car shuttle on this or other sections of the trail. The Middle Fork makes a good Sunday ride after a Moon Point (ride 60) Saturday. Or why not check them both off the list in one day—an epic of about 34 miles depending on how you loop it (see the Option at Moon Point, ride 60). Note: Watch for poison oak along the trail.

Driving Directions

From Eugene, drive south on Interstate 5. Take exit 188A and head east on State Highway 58. Drive about 36 miles east on Hwy 58 to Oakridge. At the stoplight at Crestview Street in Oakridge, set your odometer to zero and continue east on Hwy 58. At 1.8 miles, just past milepost 37, turn right on Kitson Springs Road (Forest Road 23) toward Hills Creek Dam. At 2.3 miles, turn right on FR 21 (Diamond Drive). Stay on FR 21. At 14.5 miles, pass Sand Prairie Campground on the right. At milepost 17, pass Youngs Flat on the right—a good place to park if you're only here for the day. At milepost 18, 21.2 miles, turn into Secret Campground on the right and park. (Note: Don't park in a camp spot if you are not camping.)

The Ride

From the dirt-road entrance to Secret Campground, turn right on FR 21. Ride up the paved forest road, climbing gradually. At **2.5** miles (ridepoint 2), turn right on FR 2134 and cross over the Middle Fork of the Willamette River. The road divides at **2.6** miles—bear right on FR 2133, which is gravel, and follow the sign for Middle Fork Trail. At **3.3** miles, turn right onto Middle Fork Trail 3609. Just after a short bridge, **3.6** miles, the trail braids apart— bear left. When the trail braids back together at **3.9** miles, stay left. The trail climbs in a few spots, but for the most part it winds and zips, following the river downward. Roots, rocks, and an off-camber side slope make the trail a challenging ride in sections.

At **7.5** miles, ignore a camp spot and a spur road on the left. At **7.7** miles, the trail seems to end at a paved road, FR 2127. Turn right and cross over the river. At **7.8** miles, reach FR 21 and turn left. A few spins of the pedals farther, turn left to return to Trail 3609, which now follows the east side of the river. At **8.8** miles, turn left at a dirt road, glide toward the river, and

Walking what could be a really cool skinny

then turn right onto the trail again. At **8.9** miles, reach a fork and bear right. At **9.4** miles, ignore a lesser trail back on the left. The trail kisses FR 21 a short distance farther, then passes through a camp spot—bear right and then left to continue on the trail.

When the trail divides at **10.2** miles, bear right on the Horse Trail. At **10.5** miles, reach a dirt road and turn right. *WHOA!* This is a confusing area without much signage for help. Pass a dirt road on the right and then immediately turn right onto an obscured and unmarked trail. Almost immediately the trail forks—bear left. At **10.7** miles, reach another fork and bear right. At **11.7** miles, ignore a trail back on the left. The trail kisses FR 21 a couple of times a short distance farther. Cross over a bridge at **12.7** miles, then reach a fork and bear right. Quickly cross a road and bear left to continue on the trail. When the trail pops out onto a gravel road at **13.1** miles, go left. Ride to the left of the gate, scooting along the river. At **13.3** miles, the trail ends at the paved road at Sand Prairie Campground. Stay to the left on the main campground road. At **13.6** miles (ridepoint 3), reach FR 21 at the entrance to the campground and turn right. Ride south on FR 21 to Secret Campground on the right, **20** miles, to complete the loop.

Gazetteer

Nearby camping: Secret (primitive), Sand Prairie
Nearest food, drink, services: Oakridge

Distance	19.1-mile loop (33.9-mile option)
Route	Dirt-road climb, epic singletrack descent; views
Climbs	Long, strenuous; high point: 5,120 ft, gain: 3,500 ft
Duration	Fitness rider: 2.5 hour; scenery rider: 3 to 6 hours
Travel	Eugene—60 miles; Bend—115 miles
Skill	Intermediate
Season	Summer, fall
Map	Middle Fork Ranger District map
Rules	None
Manager	Willamette National Forest, Middle Fork District, 541-782-2283
Web	www.fs.fed.us/r6/willamette/recreation/tripplanning/list_mf

Who Will Like This Ride

You have a philosophic aversion to using brakes.

The Scoop

Long a favorite of Eugene riders—I first circuited the loop in the early '90s—this ride around Moon Point and Youngs Rock is a classic dirt-road climb followed by singletrack descent. Scenery riders should be sure to allow for some time at Moon Point—the view is expansive and vertigo inducing. The descent is incredible, arguably the best in the Eugene and Oakridge area. It's faster and smoother (though less of a challenge) than Hardesty Mountain (ride 50), either of the Alpine routes (rides 55 and 56), or Larison Creek (ride 58); and it's longer than Olallie Mountain (ride 47), King Castle (ride 48), Aubrey or Dead Mountain (rides 53 and 54), or Larison Rock (ride 57). Sure, there are a few hairball sections, but no-brakes and ridable switchies are the rule. Once a friend went through four inner tubes on the descent. Hot rims? Tiny thorns? Sharp rocks? Defective tubes? Cheap pump? Operator error? Bad Karma? Who the hell knows. We still had a great ride.

Not many answers

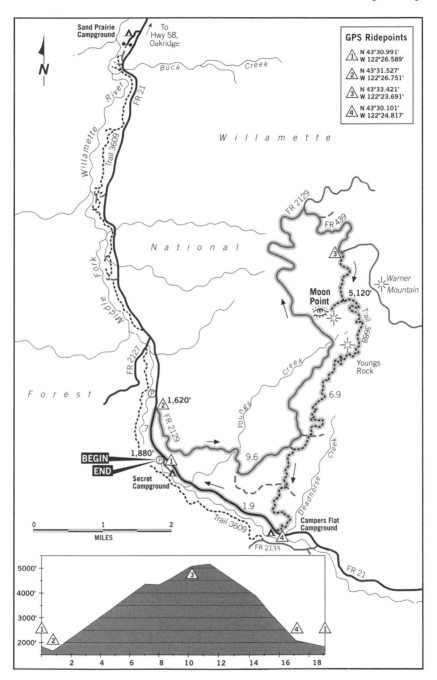

A short but zippy section near the top of Moon Point

Driving Directions

From Eugene, drive south on Interstate 5. Take exit 188A and head east on State Highway 58. Drive about 36 miles east on Hwy 58 to Oakridge. At the stoplight at Crestview Street in Oakridge, set your odometer to zero and continue east on Hwy 58. At 1.8 miles, just past milepost 37, turn right on Kitson Springs Road (Forest Road 23) toward Hills Creek Dam. At 2.3 miles, turn right on FR 21 (Diamond Drive). Stay on FR 21. At 14.5 miles, pass Sand Prairie Campground on the right. At milepost 17, pass Youngs Flat on the right—a good place to park if you're only here for the day. At milepost 18, at 21.2 miles, turn into Secret Campground on the right and park. (Note: Don't park in a camp spot if you are not camping.)

The Ride

From the entrance to Secret Campground, turn left and ride north on FR 21. At **0.7** mile (ridepoint 2), turn right on FR 2129. (If you begin from the parking area at Youngs Flat, ride south on FR 21 for just over one-quarter mile and turn left on FR 2129.) This gravelly road immediately heads straight up, winding haphazardly toward Youngs Rock and Moon Point. Stay on the main road. It's a demanding climb and, with little shade, can be quite hot. (An early start helps, as long as you didn't overdo the Secret Campground tequila shots the night before.)

The road wraps its way beneath Youngs Rock and then Moon Point, the two most prominent features of Warner Mountain, and then circles around behind Moon Point. *WOOF!* At **7** miles, the road finally flattens out. The way is easier from here, though there are still 700 feet to climb. At **8.8** miles, reach a fork and turn right on FR 439 toward Warner Mountain Lookout. At **10** miles, bear right to continue up the main road. At **10.3** miles (ridepoint 3), turn right onto Moon Point Trail 3688.The trail, narrow and overgrown in spots, ascends slightly. When the trail divides

View from Moon Point

at **11.1** miles, bear right to Moon Point. The ridable section of the trail ends at **11.5** miles. Lay your bike down and walk down to Moon Point.

When you are done checking out the spectacular views from the jagged rocks, turn around and ride back to the previous fork, now **11.9** miles, and turn right. From here, the trail takes turns switchbacking and traversing down through light forests and open ridges toward Youngs Rock. Pass around the south face of Youngs Rock on a scree slope. The fast, whorling descent continues. Cross a dirt road at **15.3** miles. At **15.6** miles, reach a fork and bear left toward Campers Flat Campground. At **16.2** miles, cross a dirt road and begin a short, no-brakes roller coaster. The trail ends at FR 21 at **17.2** miles (ridepoint 4). Turn right on the paved road and ride back to Secret Campground to complete the ride, **19.1** miles.

Moon Point Epic Option

Combine this ride with ride 59, Middle Fork Willamette, for a 33.9-mile epic. It's probably best to begin this ride from Sand Prairie Campground, about halfway through ride 59. Pedal up FR 21, turn left on FR 2129, and follow the Moon Point directions to the 17.2-mile point. From there, turn left on FR 21, pedal south about one-half mile, and turn right on FR 2134. Follow the ride description for Middle Fork Willamette beginning from the 2.5-mile point.

Gazetteer

Nearby camping: Secret (primitive), Sand Prairie
Nearest food, drink, services: Oakridge

Distance	21.4-mile loop
Route	Challenging singletrack around mountain lake; views
Climbs	Relentless up and down; high point: 5,820 ft, gain: 340 ft
Duration	Fitness rider: 2 to 3 hours; scenery rider: 4 to 6 hours
Travel	Eugene—70 miles; Bend—60 miles
Skill	Advanced
Season	Late summer, fall
Map	Middle Fork Ranger District map
Rules	National Forest Recreation Pass required
Manager	Willamette National Forest, Middle Fork District, 541-782-2283
Web	www.fs.fed.us/r6/willamette/recreation/tripplanning/list_mf

Who Will Like This Ride
You like big strong singletrack loops and dislike sissy roads.

The Scoop
Waldo Lake ranks among Oregon's best long cross-country rides, right up there with Surveyors Ridge (rides 3 and 4), Mrazek (ride 24), North Fork

to Flagline (ride 28), Newberry Caldera (ride 39), McKenzie River (rides 45 and 46), and North Umpqua (rides 65 and 66). How's that for a summer of riding? For the incredible scenery, the remoteness, and the challenge, Waldo is a must-do for every serious mountain biker. The route—entirely singletrack—circles Waldo Lake, one of the largest lakes in the central Oregon Cascades. The trail, which borders Waldo Lake Wilderness for nearly half the route, is hard-packed, zippy, and fast in spots, jagged, root-strewn, and steep in others. By the halfway point you may think that the ride will never end. But the second half of the ride is easier than the first, as long as you follow the directions below and travel clockwise. The 340-foot elevation gain belies all the ups and downs along the way—the cumulative gain is actually more than 1,500 feet. Note that mosquitoes can be worse than bad before mid-August.

Driving Directions

From Eugene, drive south on Interstate 5. Take exit 188A and head east on State Highway 58 past Oakridge. About 24 miles east of Oakridge, turn left on Forest Road 5897 and set your odometer to zero. At 7 miles, turn left on FR 5896 toward Shadow Bay Campground. Stay on the paved road. At 8.7 miles, bear left toward the boat ramp. At 9.1 miles, turn right and park in the large gravel parking area just above the lake.

From Bend, drive about 15 miles south on US Highway 97 and then turn right on FR 40. After traveling 22 miles farther, turn left onto State Highway 46. Drive about 7.5 miles south and turn right on FR 4290. This road is quite rough. Proceed 9 miles west on FR 4290, then turn left on FR 5897. Go about 4 miles south on FR 5897, turn right on FR 5896 toward Shadow Bay Campground , and set your odometer to zero. Stay on the paved road. At 1.7 miles, bear left toward the boat ramp. At 2.1 miles, turn right and park in the large gravel parking area just above the lake.

The Ride

Don't take the trail that begins from the gravel parking area. Instead, ride down to the boat ramp. From the edge of Waldo Lake at the boat ramp, take Lakeshore Trail on the left. After a few hundred yards, ignore a trail on the left. Stay on the main trail. At **0.5** mile (ridepoint 2), reach a fork and go right on Waldo Lake Trail 3590. The trail wraps clockwise around the lake.

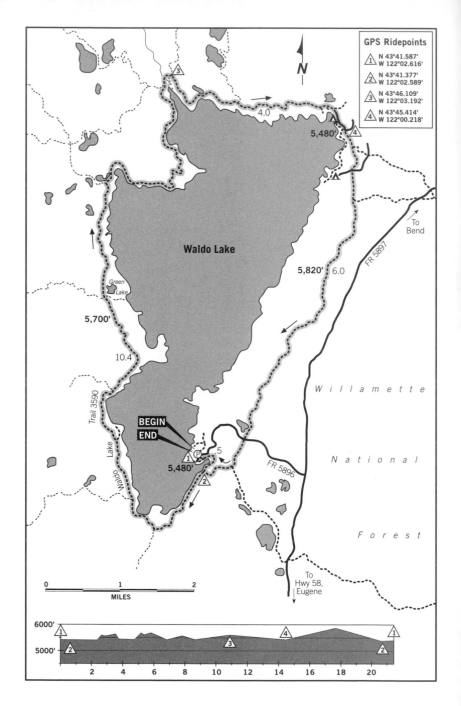

GPS Ridepoints

1	N 43°41.587' W 122°02.616'
2	N 43°41.377' W 122°02.589'
3	N 43°46.109' W 122°03.192'
4	N 43°45.414' W 122°00.218'

4.0

5,480'

To Bend

FR 5897

Waldo Lake

Green Lake

5,820'   6.0

5,700'

Willamette

10.4

Trail 3590

National

BEGIN
END

Waldo Lake

5,480'   P   5

FR 5896

Forest

0   1   2
MILES

To
Hwy 58,
Eugene

6000'

5000'

2   4   6   8   10   12   14   16   18   20

Unnamed lake along Waldo Lake Trail

Bear left to pass South Waldo Shelter, then go right at the fork at **1.7** miles. When you reach another fork at **2.3** miles, bear right again. From here, the trail becomes more technical, narrow, and steep, as it runs north along the west side of the lake.

At **3.7** miles, reach a fork and bear left. (The right prong makes an interesting side trip to Klovdahl Headgate, about one-quarter mile.) At **4.2** miles, reach a fork and bear right, following the lakeshore. The trail, which is rough in spots, rises and falls in sharp spikes, then climbs away from the lake around **4.8** miles. Ride straight through a four-way at **6.1** miles, continuing on Waldo Lake Trail. From here, the trail becomes more ridable. At **7.8** miles, bear right at the fork, following the shoreline. The trail creeps along the rocks above the lake for a distance, crosses a point, then continues along the edge of the lake.

At **10.9** miles (ridepoint 3), bear right at the fork and cross the north fork of the Middle Fork of the Willamette River. Ignore a trail on the right that leads to a picnic spot next to the lake. The trail immediately divides again—go right. After a few rolls in the terrain, enter an older catastrophic burn. The ashy gray trail is dusty but fast, and the tall, gray rampikes are quite eerie. Just after reentering the woods, reach a fork at **14.1** miles and bear left. At **14.2** miles, bear left at a second fork. When the trail divides again at **14.3** miles, go right. The trail ends at a parking area at North Waldo Campground. Pedal along the campground road, passing the boat launch on the right at **14.5** miles. Stay to the right on the paved road, ignoring several trails on the right. At **14.9** miles (ridepoint 4), just as the road veers to the left, find the continuation of Waldo Lake Trail 3590 on the right and take it. After a few pedal strokes, the trail forks—go left. When the trail divides again at **15.1** miles, bear right to stay on Trail 3590.

Cross the paved road to Islet Campground at **15.6** miles. From here, climb up the hard-packed trail toward the loop's easily gained high point at **17.7** miles. The trail traverses and then descends. Cross a paved road at **20** miles. When the trail forks at **20.4** miles, bear right. At **20.9** miles (ride-point 2), take a sharp right (unless you want to take another loop around the lake). At **21.3** miles, reach a fork and bear right. At the top of the hill, cross the road to the parking area to complete the loop, **21.4** miles.

Gazetteer

Nearby camping: Shadow Bay, Gold Lake
Nearest food, drink, services: Oakridge

Distance	21.2-mile loop (15.1-mile option)
Route	Dirt-road and singletrack ascents, singletrack descent; views
Climbs	Moderate; high point: 6,140 ft, gain: 1,300 ft
Duration	Fitness rider: 2 to 3 hours; scenery rider: 3 to 5 hours
Travel	Eugene—80 miles; Bend—70 miles
Skill	Intermediate
Season	Late summer, fall
Map	Crescent Ranger District map
Rules	None
Manager	Deschutes National Forest, Crescent Ranger District, 541-433-3200
Web	www.fs.fed.us/r6/centraloregon/recreation/trails/2050-windy

Who Will Like This Ride

You collect off-the-beaten-path rides that make your riding friends jealous.

The Scoop

The Windy Lakes loop is lousy with mosquitoes and high mountain lakes, meaning there's a lot of both. Unfortunately, there are more mosquitoes than lakes, so be prepared. Though it's a long way for most riders to travel, this is a great intermediate mountain-bike ride, and the lakes are really the highlight.

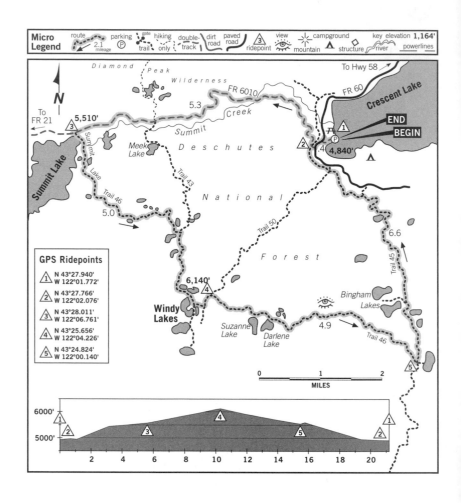

Micro Legend

route | 2.1 mileage | parking (P) | gate | hiking trail | double-track only | dirt road | paved road | 3 ridepoint | view | campground | mountain | structure | river | key elevation **1,164'** | powerlines

Diamond Peak

Wilderness

To FR 58 →

FR 6010

FR 60

Crescent Lake

To FR 21

5,510' 3

5.3

Summit Creek

END

BEGIN

Meek Lake

D e s c h u t e s

Summit Lake

Trail 43

1

2

4 **4,840'**

Summit Lake

Trail 46

5.0

N a t i o n a l

Trail 50

6.6

GPS Ridepoints

1 N 43°27.940'
W 122°01.772'

2 N 43°27.766'
W 122°02.076'

3 N 43°28.011'
W 122°06.761'

4 N 43°25.656'
W 122°04.226'

5 N 43°24.824'
W 122°00.140'

F o r e s t

Trail 45

6,140' 4

Windy Lakes

Bingham Lakes

Suzanne Lake

Darlene Lake

4.9

Trail 46

5

0   1   2
MILES

6000'

5000'

2 4 6 8 10 12 14 16 18 20

After a relatively easy dirt-road climb, a well-graded singletrack climbs and descends through the high, lake-pocked expanse between Summit and Crescent Lakes. Lots of pines grow up here, but the volcanic-gray soil reflects hot and bright in midsummer and the trail is loose and sandy in sections.

Driving Directions

From Eugene, drive south on Interstate 5. Take exit 188A and head east on State Highway 58 toward Oakridge. After about 37 miles, pass

....

through Oakridge and continue east on Hwy 58. Proceed 35 miles farther to Crescent Lake Junction and turn right on Forest Road 60. Set your odometer to zero. At 2.3 miles, turn right to remain on FR 60. At 7.4 miles, turn left on FR 290 to Tandy Bay. Park at the turnaround by the lake.

From Bend, drive south on US Highway 97 to the town of Crescent. At Crescent, turn right and take FR 61 to Hwy 58. Turn right and head north on Hwy 58. Just over 3 miles farther, reach Crescent Lake Junction and turn left onto FR 60. Zero out your odometer here. At 2.3 miles, turn right to remain on FR 60. At 7.4 miles, turn left on FR 290 to Tandy Bay on Crescent Lake. Park at the turnaround by the lake.

The Ride

From the dirt turnaround at Tandy Bay, ride FR 290 back out to FR 60 and turn left. Ride this paved road to a fork at **0.4** mile (ridepoint 2) and take a hard right onto FR 6010. This bright, almost white-colored dirt road immediately heads up. Pass Metolius-Windigo Trail on the right and left as you climb. Around **1.5** miles, check out the sporadic views of Diamond Peak (and adjacent Diamond Rockpile). The road, which winds through a pure stand of lodgepole pines, climbs in fits and starts, but it's never too steep. At **4.2** miles, bypass Meek Lake Trail on the left and Snell Lake Trail, into Diamond Peak Wilderness, on the right. Continue west on FR 6010.

At **5.7** miles (ridepoint 3), turn left into a trailhead parking area on the shore of Summit Lake. From here, take Summit Lake Trail toward Windy Lakes, heading south. The trail is easy and level here as it bends clockwise around the lake. After a short way, though, the trail veers southeast, away from the lake, and begins a steady climb into a mixed fir and pine forest. Beginning around the **7.9**-mile point, ride by a series of small lakes on the right and left. Descend for a pitch to a fork at **9** miles—turn right, continuing toward Windy Lakes. The trail, pine-needled and firm, immediately resumes the ascent. Pass more small lakes, then at **10.2** miles, reach North Windy Lake. A few spins of the pedals farther, the trail rounds the north end of East Windy Lake. Reach a T at **10.6** miles and turn left. At **10.7** miles (ridepoint 4), reach another T and again turn left, following the sign toward Oldenberg Lake. When the trail forks at **10.9** miles, bear right and begin a fast descent.

North Windy Lake

After a ripping traverse, noodle past Suzanne Lake and then Darlene Lake before cruising down the trail—no brakes—toward Oldenberg Lake. From Darlene Lake, the trail is dusty and ashy, and the forest is a pure stand of lodgepole pines. Pass Diamond Peak Viewpoint at **13.7** miles. At **15.6** miles (ridepoint 5), reach a sandy four-way and turn left (Oldenberg Lake is straight ahead). After a short climb descend to a fork at **16.6** miles. Stay to the right, following the sign toward the trailhead. The wide trail is sandy in sections, so the descent is fast in places, slower and surflike in others. Ride in control because the trail is heavily used by equestrians.

Pass a lake on the left at **18.5** miles. At **19.4** miles, reach an unmarked fork and bear left on Metolius-Windigo Horse Trail 45. At **20.1** miles, pass a trail on the right and then one on the left—continue on Metolius-Windigo Horse Trail. At **20.7** miles, reach FR 6010 and turn right. At **20.8** miles (ridepoint 2), FR 6010 ends at FR 60—turn left on this paved road. At **21.1** miles, turn right on FR 230 to Tandy Bay. Reach the picnic area at the lake at **21.2** miles to complete the loop.

Option

Feeling ready to bonk? Here's how to shave a little more than 6 miles from this loop: At the fork at **10.9** miles (just past ridepoint 4) , bear left (rather than right). The descent is a riot. When you reach the Metolius-Windigo Horse Trail, turn left and follow the directions above from the **20.1**-mile point.

Gazetteer

Nearby camping: Crescent Lake
Nearest food, drink, services: Crescent Lake Junction, La Pine

Distance	11-mile out-and-back (options up to 32 miles)
Route	Wide, paved rail-trail
Climbs	None—easy and level; high point: 950 ft, gain: 170 ft
Duration	Fitness rider: 1 hour; scenery rider: 2 hours
Travel	Eugene—21 miles; Portland—130 miles
Skill	Beginner
Season	Year-round
Map	BLM Row River Trail map
Rules	None
Manager	US Bureau of Land Management, Eugene District, 541-683-6600
Web	www.americantrails.org/nationalrecreationtrails/blm/rowriver-or

Who Will Like This Ride
A family that rides together, picnics together.

The Scoop

In 1994 the US Bureau of Land Management acquired this abandoned railroad grade set along Row River. Since then the BLM has paved nearly thirteen miles of the old grade for recreational use. The trail now has a number of trailheads and picnic areas, many right along Dorena Lake. The wide, flat, paved trail is perfect for families, from the youngest member to the oldest.

Driving Directions

From Eugene, drive about 18 miles south on Interstate 5. Take exit 174 toward Dorena Lake. At the end of the interstate ramp, set your odometer to zero and turn left on Row River Road. At 0.9 mile, turn right on Currin Conn, then quickly turn left on Mosby Creek Road. At 3.1 miles, turn left on Layng Road. Immediately turn left again into the paved parking area at Row River Trail's Mosby Creek trailhead.

The Ride

Row River Trail heads northeast from the trailhead. The trail immediately crosses Mosby Creek. At **0.7** mile, follow the trail across Layng Road.

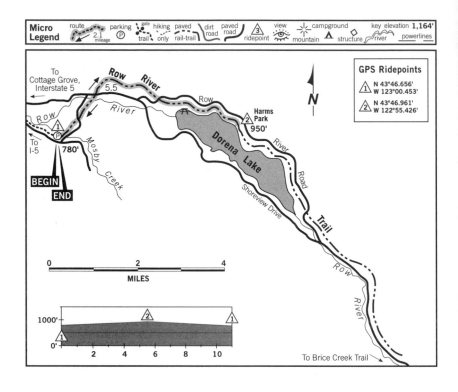

At **1.5** miles, the trail passes over Row River and then crosses Row River Road. Cross the road again at **3** miles, climbing slightly. At **3.6** miles, Dorena Lake is visible on the right. Pass Dorena Dam picnic area here. At **4.2** miles, ride by Row Point, one of the trail's seven access spots. At **5.5** miles (ridepoint 2), reach Harms Park. This Lane County park has picnic tables that overlook the lake. There are toilets here but no water, so plan your picnic accordingly. Turn around here and glide back to Mosby Creek trailhead, **11** miles.

Option

Row River Trail continues about seven and a half miles beyond Harms Park. If you start at Mosby Creek trailhead, ride to the trail's end, and return, the total trip clocks in at around 26 miles. You can also begin a Row River Trail ride way back in Forest Grove, at the start of the trail along Main Street

Row River Trail along Dorena Lake

near Highway 99. From there, it's about 3 miles to Mosby Creek trailhead and 13 more miles to the end of the trail. Thus and so, the entire trail stretches about 16 miles each way.

Gazetteer

Nearby camping: Rujada, Cedar Creek (primitive)
Nearest food, drink, services: Cottage Grove

64 BRICE CREEK

Distance	10.4-mile loop
Route	Paved-road climb, somewhat technical singletrack descent
Climbs	Gentle with a few steeps; high point: 1,830 ft, gain: 450 ft
Duration	Fitness rider: 1 hour; scenery rider: 2 to 3 hours
Travel	Eugene—41 miles; Portland—150 miles
Skill	Advanced
Season	Late spring, summer, fall
Map	USGS 7.5 minute: Rose Hill
Rules	None
Manager	Umpqua National Forest, Cottage Grove District, 541-942-5591
Web	www.fs.fed.us/r6/umpqua/recreation/biking/index

Who Will Like This Ride

You're ready at any moment to take off your clothes and take a dip in a creekside pool.

The Scoop

Here's the ride for those who just don't like those long, grinding climbs so much. The creekside trail is technical in spots and climbs in short spurts, but there's no multi-thousand-foot ascent (or subsequent attempt to cough up a lung). An easy paved-road climb leads to the upper end of the singletrack. Some riders may prefer to ride out and back on the trail rather than ride out the paved road to create a loop. Your choice. Either way, the creek, with its pools and flows and mesmerizing canyon geology, makes this a short but beautiful ride.

Driving Directions

From Eugene, drive about 18 miles south on Interstate 5. Take exit 174 toward Dorena Lake. At the end of the interstate ramp, set your odometer to zero and turn left on Row River Road. At 4.3 miles, continue straight on Shoreview Drive (Row River Road turns to the left). But at 11.3 miles, stay to the right as Shoreview merges with and becomes Row River Road. Proceed

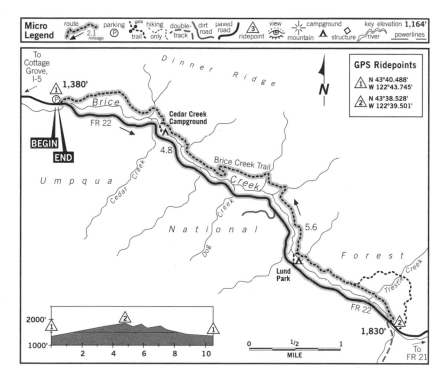

east on Row River Road. At 19.4 miles, bear right onto Brice Creek Road, which becomes Forest Road 22. At 22.8 miles, park on the left at the narrow gravel strip at Brice Creek Trail's west trailhead.

The Ride

From the west trailhead, pedal up FR 22. The paved road ascends at an easy rate as it follows the creek. Pass Cedar Creek Campground on the left at **1.2** miles. When the road forks at **2.8** miles, bear left and continue alongside Brice Creek. The deep valley and forest of cedar, fir, and maple shade the narrow road. Pass Lund Park on the left at **3.6** miles. Reach a fork at **4.8** miles—bear left and cross a bridge over Brice Creek. Immediately across the bridge, turn left on Brice Creek Trail 1403 (ridepoint 2) to head northwest on the opposite bank of Brice Creek. The singletrack traverses the bank above the creek, rising and falling with the steep folds of the

Pools and swimming holes along Brice Creek

hillside. At **5.5** miles, reach a fork and stay to the left. Climb and then descend to a fork at **6.2** miles—bear right, riding toward west trailhead. (To the left you'll find a bridge across the river to Lund Park.)

The tread is rocky in spots, root-strewn in others. Salal and Oregon grape, and various ferns and mosses, combine to form a rich understory. At **6.3** miles, ignore a trail to a camp spot on the left. From here, the trail, ragged, technical, and exposed in sections, stays close to the creek, which flows from pool to pool down the narrow, rocky canyon. It's a picturesque setting (and the swimming's good too). At **8.9** miles, reach a fork and bear right. At **10.4** miles, reach the west trailhead to complete the loop.

Gazetteer
Nearby camping: Rujada, Cedar Creek (primitive)
Nearest food, drink, services: Cottage Grove

Distance	39-mile one-way
Route	Challenging riverside singletrack
Climbs	Usually short but unrelenting; high point: 4,280 ft, loss: 2,640 ft
Duration	Fitness rider: 3 to 5 hours; scenery rider: 6 to 10 hours
Travel	Roseburg—81 miles; Eugene—152 miles
Skill	Advanced
Season	Summer, fall
Map	Umpqua National Forest map, USFS Diamond Lake District map
Rules	None
Manager	Umpqua National Forest, Diamond Lake District, 541-498-2531
Web	www.fs.fed.us/r6/umpqua/recreation/hiking/north-umpqua-trails/1414-north-umpqua-trail

Who Will Like This Ride
Hard corps adventurers.

The Scoop
North Umpqua River, a National Wild and Scenic River and one of best fly fishing streams on the planet, begins as not much more than a trickle way up in the vast north quadrant of Mount Thielsen Wilderness, not far

The Dread and Terror section begins

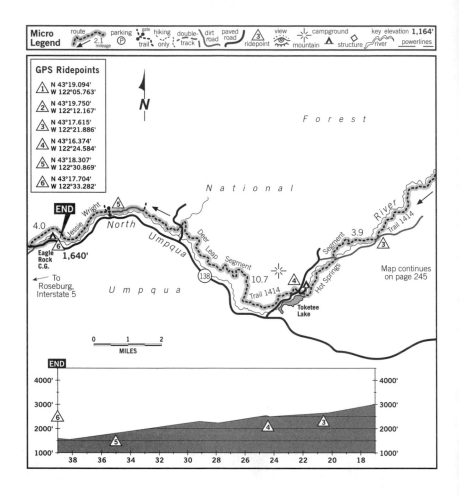

route ⌒ 2.1 mileage · parking Ⓟ · gate hiking trail only ⋮ · double-track · dirt road · paved road · △3 ridepoint · view 👁 mountain · campground structure river · key elevation **1,164'** powerlines

GPS Ridepoints

△1 N 43°19.094'
   W 122°05.763'

△2 N 43°19.750'
   W 122°12.167'

△3 N 43°17.615'
   W 122°21.886'

△4 N 43°16.374'
   W 122°24.584'

△5 N 43°18.307'
   W 122°30.869'

△6 N 43°17.704'
   W 122°33.282'

Forest

N

National

North Umpqua

Jessie Wright

END

4.0

△6

Eagle Rock C.G. **1,640'**

← To Roseburg, Interstate 5

U m p q u a

Deer Leap Segment

138

10.7

Trail 1414

△4

Toketee Lake

Hot Springs

Segment 3.9

△3

Trail 1414

River

Map continues on page 245

0   1   2
MILES

END
4000' — 4000'
3000' — 3000'
△6 2000' — 2000'
△5 1000' — 1000'
38 36 34 32 30 28 26 24 22 20 18
△4 △3

from the Pacific Crest Trail. North Umpqua Trail 1414, every bit as wild and scenic, starts up there as well, beginning an 80-mile plus trek westward. Think of it: an 80-mile riverside trail, and most of it open to mountain bikes. It's better than you can imagine—a beautiful forest, a rugged canyon, precipitous side slopes, and a sinewy, ever-changing tread. And worse, too, if you're not ready. North Umpqua is one badass trail, and if you don't watch out, it can bite. And bite hard. One section—Dread and Terror—is more remote, by a long shot, than any other trail in this book. Not the place to

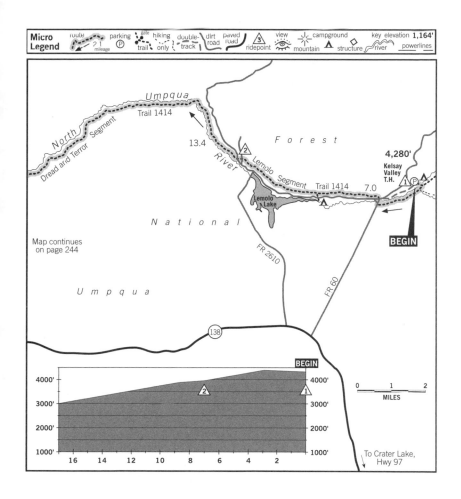

run low on calories, break a random bone, have a mechanical, or simply bonk for lack of fitness.

From top to bottom the trail descends nearly 4,000 feet, but despite the elevation loss the incessant ups and downs can put a hurt on the most trained cyclist. Beware also of the numerous trailside cliffs that drop off to the river. Less dramatic but perhaps equally punishing **WHOAS!** are the trail's many bridges, which are wet—and thus nearly frictionless—much of the year, as well as the poison oak you'll meet along the way (for

Noodling the Deer Leap segment near Slide Creek

specifics, see The Scoop for ride 66). The trail can be extremely wet and muddy, too. Small tributaries, minor waterfalls and random springs seem to be everywhere, slowing the progress. The riding times listed above assume a relatively dry August ride date. Note: For this ride more than most, you should always check the Web and call ahead to find out about current conditions.

Of the North Umpqua Trail's 11 segments, 10 are open to mountain bikes—east to west they are Lemolo, Dread and Terror, Hot Springs, Deer Leap, Jessie Wright, Marsters, Calf, Panther, Mott, and Tiogo—and they account for 70 miles of riding, almost all singletrack. So the big question is, what's the best way to get your North Umpqua ya-yas? I suggest two big epics. Camp at Eagle Rock Campground near the trail's midpoint. Ride the upper 39 miles on an August Saturday (Lemolo through Jessie Wright, this ride) and then the lower 34 miles the following day (Marsters through Tioga, ride 66). Of course, that's two difficult days in a row, and both days require a long shuttle. You can cherry pick individual segments (but then, of course, you won't have done the whole thing). There are trailheads at the beginning and end of each segment, so cherry picking is possible. Of the upper segments, Dread and Terror and Deer Leap are the longest and most memorable. Lemolo is beautiful and nice riding; the smoothie tread on the Hot Springs segment makes it perhaps the most out-and-out fun. If you stage at Toketee Lake Campground, you could ride Hot Springs and Deer Leap as out-and-backs.

What follows, however, are directions for a big ride—a one-way ass kicker—and it requires a shuttle.

Driving Directions

From Interstate 5 at Roseburg, take State Highway 138 eastbound. After about 50 miles, find Eagle Rock Campground on the left (before milepost 51). Leave a vehicle near the campground then continue eastward on Hwy 138. After about 25 more miles, turn left on Windigo Pass Road (FR 60). Zero out your odometer here. Reach a fork at 4.5 miles and turn right. Then immediately turn right again, following the signs to Kelsey Valley Horse Camp. At 5.7 miles, reach the trailhead.

Looking for another gear alongside North Umpqua River

The Ride

You'll breath crisp air as you ride through low pines away from the Kelsey Valley trailhead. At **0.1** mile, reach a fork and go right. Arrive quickly at a second fork, and again turn right, this time on North Umpqua Trail 1414. The river is not much more than a delicate little creek here, burbling and winding through sparse forest and small meadows. At **1.9** miles, the trail ends at a road—go right on the road, crossing over North Fork Umpqua. Just beyond the bridge, reach a fork at a triangle-shaped intersection. Go

A small creek floods the trail in the Dread and Terror segment

right. A few spins of the pedals farther, pick up Trail 1414 on the left. After a momentary climb, noodle, wind, and then drop through a lovely forest.

At **3.6** miles, cross a gravel road. The tread is narrow and rough in sections, but the zip quotient rises as you descend. Cross another gravel road at **6.8** miles. At **7.0** miles, the trail abruptly ends at a paved road—go straight, crossing over a bridge to a sign for the trail. Thus begins the infamous Dread and Terror segment of North Umpqua Trail. The trail, wider yet also somehow wilder, rocky and root-strewn in spots, than the Lemolo segment, immediately shows off its signature feature—the sidehill traverse high above the river, exposed and airy, an exceptional teaching moment for the rule of thumb (and limb) that goes, don't look where you don't want to go.

....

Even in August the trail can be wet due to springs and tiny tributaries that flow onto parts of the trail. And it's non-stop up and down and up. You'll switchback down to the river and cross it at **9.4** miles. From here, the trail elevators from low riverside up to high overlooks with lots of exposure and then back again. But despite its name, remoteness, airy exposure, and demand on your calories, Dread and Terror is something of an over-promise—the trail is completely ridable. The route is brushy in spots, wet, sometimes rocky, and then suddenly dry, smooth, and fast—the only thing you can count on is that it keeps going. Rhodys, vine maple, and fern crowd the bank and compete with the surrounding fir forest. The river, framed by steep canyon slopes, is extraordinarily beautiful and wild here. A river ecologist friend said to me, "It's like a river should be."

At **15.5** miles, reach a fork and bear right, continuing on North Umpqua Trail. Several miles farther, after a climb at **17.8** miles, you'll ride an airy stretch of trail, with a sheer drop down to the river followed by more ups and downs on a rocky, often wet tread. Pass Michelle Creek at **18.7** miles. At **19.1** miles, the river canyon takes an unexpectedly sharp left-hand turn. Pass Surprise Falls at **19.9** miles. When the trail climbs to a T at a gravel road, **20.4** miles and the end of Dread and Terror, go right. Immediately turn right again into the trailhead parking area for the Hot Springs segment. From the trailhead, drop to the river and cross the bridge at **20.5** miles. Note: Though passable if you are careful, this bridge has been out for several years. The Forest Service thinks it'll be rebuilt in 2008 or 2009. If it's still out and you're not comfortable crossing the log, it's an easy detour down FR 3401 to Trail 1414 just before the vehicle bridge.

After a short climb, the trail, smooth and hard-packed, whips through a big tree forest of hemlock and Douglas fir. There are a few switchbacks and steeps, but the descents outnumber the climbs, and all is good. At **22.1** miles, the trail dumps out onto a dirt road—turn left. Ride across the bridge and immediately find Trail 1414 on the right. The fun continues: whorling ups and downs on a smooth trail, with the occasional mini-bank turn. Reach a fork at **24** miles and bear right. Stay right a few rotations farther and pedal over the bridge toward Toketee Lake Campground. Reach the paved campground road at **24.1** miles and turn left. Thus ends the Hot Springs segment.

At **24.2** miles, reach a T at another paved road and turn left. Find Deer Leap Segment of North Umpqua Trail 1414 on the right at **24.3** miles. The sign reads: Soda Springs TH 9. The trail climbs steeply away from the road, but then quickly tops out. Cross a doubletrack at **24.9** miles. From here, the way descends then climbs steadily again, through sugar pine, fir, and madrone. Rising, falling and rising some more, the trail climbs around the south slope of Deer Leap Rock, a high volcanic plug, toward an unseen high point. Along many parts of the trail, you'll round steep side slopes that drop off toward the river, and some of the corners are blind. In other stretches, the trail has been etched into rocky escarpments along the canyon slope. **WHOA!** Watch out for poison oak, which begins to show up more often after the **26**-mile point.

At **29.1** miles, as the trail bears to the right, you'll reach an open knoll high above the river that affords long views out over the North Umpqua valley. Puffy rock hoodoos look like they're made from wet sand. Leaving this viewpoint, the trail rock and rolls back down toward the river, cutting a fast traversing descent across the hillside. At **31.9** miles, cross a paved road then traverse above Soda Springs Reservoir. When the trail forks at **33.5** miles, go left and down. One-tenth of a mile farther, ride under a giant water pipe then reach a T at a gravel road—turn right. Stay on this road, which soon changes from gravel to dirt.

At **35** miles, the dirt road ends at a trail. This marks the western finish of Deer Leap and the easternmost start of the Jessie Wright segment. The trail, which is still an old ragged road, climbs a short but steep hill. Pass around a gate. Just beyond, at **35.2** miles, reach a fork and bear left, descending now. The trail narrows to singletrack. Around the **36**-mile point, you'll begin a really tough set of switchbacks followed by a high traverse. When the trail divides at **37.4** miles, go left, continuing on North Umpqua Trail 1414 as you descend toward Hwy 138. At **37.8** miles, bear right on a wide, flat trail. At **38.3** miles, reach Hwy 138 at exactly milepost 50. Turn left onto the highway and ride east. The highway immediately crosses over the river. Just after the bridge, take note of FR 4770 on the right. That's the eastern starting point for the Marsters segment of the North Umpqua Trail (see North Umpqua Lower, ride 66). Pedal east on the highway. At **39** miles, arrive at Eagle Rock Campground on the left

A high point on Dread and Terror

Gazetteer

Nearby camping: Eagle Rock
Nearest food, drink, services: Roseburg

Distance	34.3-mile one-way
Route	Challenging riverside singletrack
Climbs	Usually short but unrelenting; high point: 1,640 ft, loss: 840 ft
Duration	Fitness rider: 3 to 4 hours; scenery rider: 5 to 8 hours
Travel	Roseburg—50 miles; Eugene—131 miles
Skill	Advanced
Season	Summer, fall
Map	Umpqua National Forest map, USFS North Umpqua District map
Rules	None
Manager	Umpqua National Forest, North Umpqua District, 541-496-3532; For Tioga segment: Bureau of Land Management, 541-440-4930
Web	www.fs.fed.us/r6/umpqua/recreation/hiking/north-umpqua-trails/1414-north-umpqua-trail

Who Will Like This Ride
As a kid you were ready for anything, and you still consider yourself a kid.

The Scoop

Since the late 1990s, dirt bag riders with dark circles under their eyes have been whispering about the North Umpqua Trail. Just a few years later, the 70-mile trail (80 if you count the hiker-only segment) gets top billing in all the mountain bike pubs because it's so awesome. But just to be clear, awesome doesn't really begin to describe it.

Here's how to start getting your head around a 70-mile trail: Due to administrative convenience, the trail's epic length, and radically varied ecosystems, North Umpqua Trail 1414, unlike most trails, is referred to in segments. There are 11 segments, ten of which you can ride. The upper segments are described in ride 65. The lower five segments—Marsters, Calf, Panther, Mott, and Tioga—are linked to make up this ride. Of course any of the segments of the trail can be ridden either as out-and-backs or as one-way rides, but then you'd have to go home without having conquered the North Umpqua. So how to ride this beast? I suggest two epic days in August. Conveniently, Eagle Creek Campground, located just about half way along the trail, accommodates this. Ride the upper 39 miles one day, camp at Eagle Creek, and then ride the lower half of the trail (this ride) the following day. It's a brutal weekend, with some long shuttles, so start planning and training now.

Now there's also another way to divide up the trail—poison oak. The upper segments (ride 65) have essentially no poison oak (you'll find some in the Deer Leap and Jessie Wright segments). The lower half, however, beginning with Marsters and running through Tioga, is packed with it. Not every inch of the way, but there's more than enough to get into trouble with. And poison oak is nasty stuff, a plant most of us don't want anything to do with, which makes it hard when it grows right alongside the trail for long stretches. While riding through corridors of the stuff, just remember:

Poison oak

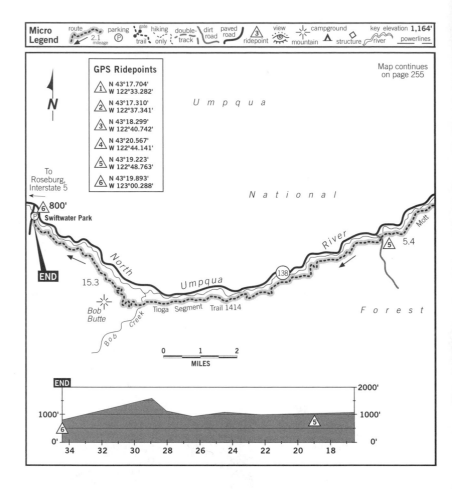

Micro Legend

route • 2.1 mileage • parking (P) • gate • hiking trail • only • double-track • dirt road • paved road • 3 ridepoint • view mountain • campground • key structure • elevation **1,164'** • river • powerlines

GPS Ridepoints

△1 N 43°17.704'
W 122°33.282'

△2 N 43°17.310'
W 122°37.341'

△3 N 43°18.299'
W 122°40.742'

△4 N 43°20.567'
W 122°44.141'

△5 N 43°19.223'
W 122°48.763'

△6 N 43°19.893'
W 123°00.288'

Map continues
on page 255

U m p q u a

N a t i o n a l

To
Roseburg,
Interstate 5

△6 **800'**
Ⓟ Swiftwater Park

END

15.3

North

Umpqua *River* Mott

138

△5 5.4

Bob
Butte

Bob Creek

Tioga Segment Trail 1414

F o r e s t

0   1   2
MILES

END 2000' — 1000' — 0'

6 ... 5

34 32 30 28 26 24 22 20 18

Don't look where you don't want to go. To review: the no poison oak North Umpqua (ride 65) and the poison oak North Umpqua (this ride). I recommend immediate washing with soap and water or with a proven poison oak remover like Tecnu after a ride like this—or even slathering it on beforehand.

Driving Directions

From Interstate 5 at Roseburg, take State Highway 138 eastbound. Just after milepost 22, find Swiftwater Park Road on the right. Leave a vehicle at

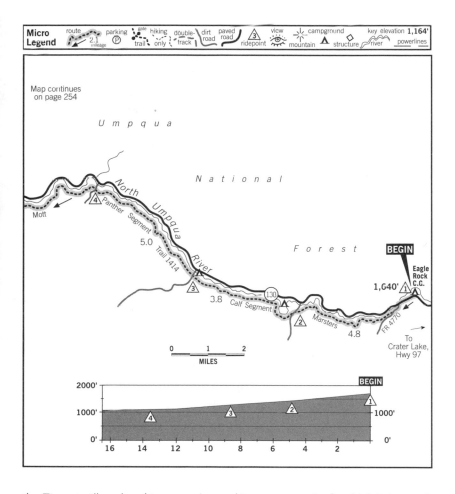

Map continues
on page 254

the Tioga trailhead parking area (no parking pass required), which is located just across the river from the highway. Continue east on Hwy 138. After about 28 more miles, right at milepost 50, find FR 4770 on the right. This is the trailhead for the Marsters segment, and you can park along this road. However, the ride description begins from Eagle Rock Campground, which is located 0.7 mile farther east on Hwy 138.

Still feeling fresh on the lower North Umpqua Trail

The Ride

From Eagle Rock Campground, ride west on State Highway 138. At **0.7** mile, just before crossing over the river, find FR 4770 on the left. This nondescript gravel road marks the start of the Marsters segment. Pedal along the road, just above a Chinook salmon spawning bed called Weeping Rocks. At **0.9** miles, take the singletrack on the right. Though the route follows the river and there's only one significant climb along its entire lower half—at Bob Butte most of the way through the Tioga segment—the trail constantly elevators from riverside to high up on the bank and back again. So don't spend all your energy in the first few miles cranking up each and every 100-foot climb.

Marsters is a fun segment, roller coastering up and down. You might appreciate the wide tread since a steep cliff drops off toward the river for much of the way. In some spots the exposure, airy and sheer, will add 20 or 30 beats to your heart rate, which is probably already running at full capacity. The forest is dominated by hemlock and Douglas fir, with an understory of fern. At **4.7** miles, the trail ends at a dirt road—turn left and immediately cross Calf Creek. At **4.8** miles, the trail starts up again on the right. The Calf segment, which begins here, has been one of the easier sections of this epic trail. However, it re-opened in late 2007 after being closed because of a fire, and some sections are now rough and rocky. Note: Given heavy snowfall in winter 2008, this segment could be closed again. You can detour around it via Hwy 138 to Panther trailhead. The trail follows the river as it loops south at Horseshoe Bend. From here, you traverse west, sometimes alongside the churning rapids, other times well above the river.

At **8.6** miles, reach a dirt road and the end of the Calf segment. Just across the road, find Panther trailhead. The trail climbs steadily then, beginning around **9** miles, traverses the side hill, up and down, into deep stands of Douglas fir, hemlock and western red cedar, then out into open areas near the river where alder and vine maple grow. Just beyond the **12**-mile mark, you'll hit a very steep climb—a walk for many. From here until the beginning of the Mott segment, the trail can be overgrown and brushy, especially with

North Umpqua River

poison oak. So beware. At **13** miles, ignore an unmarked trail on the left. Soon after the trail drops close to the river and winds around a rock corner.

At **13.6** miles, reach a T at a paved road. Ride straight across the road to begin the Mott segment of Trail 1414. (Note: There's a pit toilet and fresh water available at the Mott trailhead. If you cross the historic Mott bridge to Hwy 138, turn left, and ride about one-half mile, you'll find an inn with food and drinks. Crossing the bridge also accesses Riverside Trail 1530, which runs along the north bank of the North Umpqua River.) A favorite of fishermen, the Mott segment has many unmarked trails that drop down to the river. So be sure to stay on the main trail. And watch out for hikers. At **14.1** miles, ignore a trail on the left.

At **15.5** miles, cross over a bridge. Though it looks like all the rest, this bridge was the site of author Zane Grey's fishing camp. The trail romps through this area, rolling but mostly level alongside the river, into the forest, and back out again. The tread is sometimes duff, but often rocky. Though it's not brushy—thankfully—poison oak is everywhere. When the trail forks at **17.6** miles, stay to the right and cross Cougar Creek. Ignore another trail on the left at **17.7** miles. From here, it's a tough climb before descending back toward the river. Pass by the Old Growth Interpretive Loop Trail on the left at **18.3** miles and then again at **18.6** miles.

At **18.8** miles, reach a T at a paved road and turn right. Ignore a trail on the right as you ride down the road. At **19** miles, arrive at Wright Creek trailhead, which is located immediately south of the bridge that spans to Hwy 138. The 15-mile Tioga segment of North Umpqua Trail begins from this trailhead. Note: There are no bailouts from here on out. For the next few miles the trail ripples through the forest, past fat old growth and through canyons of bonsai ferns, an eddy here, a fast run there.

Around the **26.5**-mile mark the singletrack follows one side of an old double-track. At **27.1** miles, the tread is now a full doubletrack, climbing gently. Stay to the right. When the doubletrack divides at **28.3** miles, bear right, following the North Umpqua Trail signs. Immediately pass under a set of powerlines. From here the trail whorls around a sidehill to Bob Creek, **28.6** miles. After crossing over the creek, the pain begins without delay. While the climb from Bob Creek up to the top of Bob Butte isn't long, it's extremely steep, and the loose tread doesn't help. It's also routed up a tree-less slope, and the heat can be punishing. **WOOF!** Gain the top of the butte at **29.3** miles, then glide into a beautiful and much cooler forest of fir and hemlock with a fern understory.

Jockeying for position on the Marsters segment

From here the trail is wide and smooth as it undulates through the forest. At **33.7** miles, stay to the right. Ride straight through a four-way at **33.9** miles. Just after the **34**-mile mark, ignore two trails on the right and then one on the left, continuing along the main trail. At **34.3** miles, reach the parking area at end of the Tioga segment to complete the ride.

Gazetteer

Nearby camping: Eagle Rock
Nearest food, drink, services: Roseburg

Trapped within the concrete gridwork of the city? Unless you plan to put in some miles on the Leif Erikson Trail at Forest Park (ride 74), cartwheel down some of the fire lanes there (Firelane 1, ride 75), or spin out Springwater Corridor to play on the trails at Powell Butte (ride 76), you'll need to throw your bike on the rack and start driving. The good news is that you don't have to burn through too much gas to reach a bunch of trailheads, and the variety of the trails you discover might surprise you, from root-strewn routes in the lowlands to rocky zip-fests in Mount Hood's fir forests.

You can head west to Tillamook State Forest for a number of zippy, lunging trails near the summit of the coast range. In addition to Tillamook Burn (ride 69), both Gales Creek (ride 67) and Storey Burn (ride 68) are new routes. Think your quads are too big for the Tillamook? Try Standard Grade (ride 70), which offers up one of the most brutal climbs anywhere.

Want to bring the family? There are a number of mellower rides in this section. Check out Banks-Vernonia Trail (ride 72) or go carve some fun turns at Hagg Lake (ride 71).

Heading eastward, you quickly ascend into the evergreen mountains near Mount Hood. Here you'll find numerous options, from short, easier routes like the Crosstown Trail (ride 80) and Timothy Lake (ride 81) to expert on Flag Mountain (ride 79).

But if you steer east on State Highway 224, you'll head toward some of the most alluring trails in this section of KTTO. Nothing will cure the blues like a good romp down Dry Ridge's 4,000-foot descent (ride 82). And tackling the rock jungle gym on the scenic trail to Red Lake (ride 84) is frustrating on some days, exhilarating on the others.

The Portland United Mountain Pedalers (PUMP) and Salem's Merry Cranksters manage to get a fair amount of trail work accomplished between rides. PUMP is one of the primary reasons that the trail around Hagg Lake was reopened back in the 1990s, and they continue making great trails available. The more low-key Cranksters, meanwhile, keep adding to that maze of trails near Molalla River (rides 77 and 78), and more are coming. If you do much riding in the northwestern corner of Oregon, or even in southwest Washington, sign up with one of these clubs.

Distance 12-mile out and back

Route Ragged creekside singletrack

Climbs Some frustration and pain; high point: 2,550 ft, gain: 1,630 ft

Duration Fitness rider: 1 to 2 hours; scenery rider: 2 to 4 hours

Travel Portland—39 miles

Skill Intermediate

Season Spring, summer, fall

Map Tillamook State Forest Trail Guide: Gales Creek Trail

Rules CURRENTLY CLOSED FOR TRAIL RE-ROUTE—call for current conditions.

Manager Tillamook State Forest, 503-357-2191

Web www.oregon.gov/ODF/TSF/trails.shtml

Who Will Like This Ride

What is it about the magnetism of creekside trails?

The Scoop

WHOA! Floods in December 2007 washed out a 2-mile chunk of this trail. Needless to say, it's currently closed. As KTTO goes to press, it's uncertain

exactly when the trail will re-open. The current best guess is summer 2009. Call for current conditions.

Gales Creek is an intermediate ride in distance and skill level, but the constant ups and downs, the grade on some of the steeps, and the creek ford could prove too much for an out-of-shape intermediate rider. Try Storey Burn (ride 68), instead. The other issue here is the less-than-sexy destination—a dirt road. (Another beautiful creekside trail just broke your heart.) But I

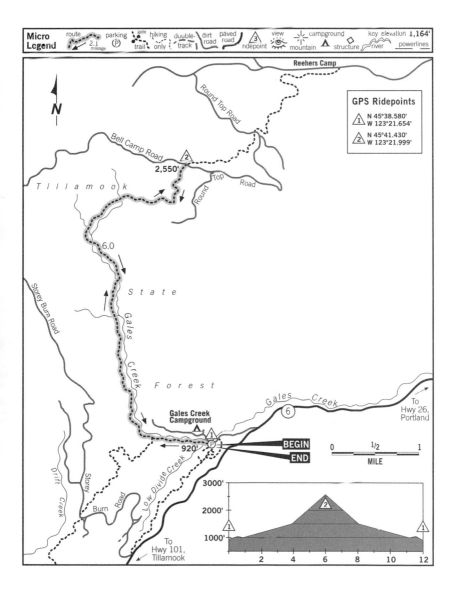

Gathering no moss on the Gales Creek Trail

know you, you're interested in exploring the country, checking another trail off the list, throwing your tires on singletrack you've never ridden before. If you're looking to add distance and difficulty, try combining this with Storey Burn or Tillamook Burn (ride 69). Or, continue on past the turn-around point described here at Bell Camp Road and ride on to Reehers Camp, about 3.5 miles farther. Note: Gales Creek Campground is closed and the road gated November through April. If you ride this trail when the campground is closed, park at the entrance along State Highway 6—don't block the gate—and ride down to the second day-use parking area to begin. This will add about one and a half miles to the ride.

Driving Directions

From Portland, drive about 20 miles west on US Highway 26 to its junction with State Highway 6. Take Hwy 6 westbound. Pass milepost 36 and set your odometer to zero. At 0.9 mile, turn right on a gravel road toward Gales Creek Campground. At 1.6 miles, park in the first day-use area on the left.

The Ride

From the parking area, take Gales Creek Trail. The way ascends at a moderate rate then drops. Just after crossing a creek at **0.8** mile, reach a T and go right, continuing out Gales Creek Trail toward Bell Camp Road. Right along the creek, up on the bank, then back down again, constantly climbing and dropping, the ragged trail throws in challenging sections here and there. But it's all ridable.

At **3** miles, cross over the wide creek on a bridge. The trail crosses back over the creek about a half-mile farther. At **4** miles, the trail crosses the creek again, but this time there's no bridge. After fording the creek, you find the route is steeper and rocky in places. The trail widens to what looks like an old road which hasn't been used in years, and ascends at a hectic pace. **WOOF!** Reach Bell Camp Road at **6** miles (ridepoint 2). Turn around here and return to the trailhead at Gales Creek Campground, **12** miles.

Gazetteer

Nearby camping: Gales Creek
Nearest food, drink, services: Forest Grove, Portland

Distance	7.8-mile loop
Route	Forest singletrack
Climbs	Moderate, plus some; high point: 1,980 ft, gain: 1,060 ft
Duration	Fitness rider: 1 hour; scenery rider: 2 to 3 hours
Travel	Portland—39 miles
Skill	Intermediate
Season	Spring, summer, fall
Map	Tillamook State Forest Trail Guide: Storey Burn Trail
Rules	None
Manager	Tillamook State Forest, 503-357-2191
Web	www.oregon.gov/ODF/TSF/trails.shtml

Who Will Like This Ride
You have a half-day hall pass.

The Scoop

Here's a moderate loop beginning from Gales Creek Campground. It'll make you feel good about your mountain biking—it's never too challenging, but you'll feel as though you deserve those pints after the ride. And you'll enjoy 98% singletrack. The climbs push but don't crush, and the descents throw in some challenge but don't require body armor. You might consider combining this

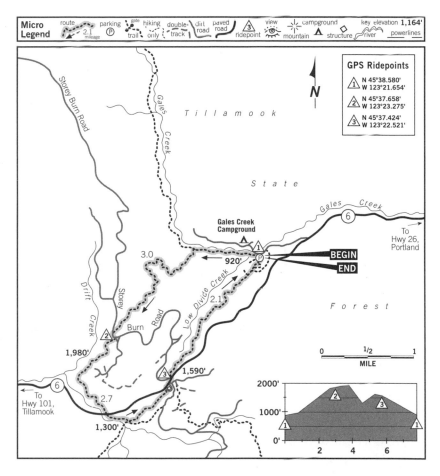

ride with Tillamook Burn (ride 69) or Gales Creek (ride 67). Note: Gales Creek Campground is closed and the road gated November through April. If you ride this trail when the campground is closed, park at the entrance along State Highway 6—don't block the gate—and ride down to the first day-use parking area on the left to begin. This adds about one and a half miles to the loop. Note 2: Don't ride this trail when wet. Try the nearby Wilson River Trail instead.

Driving Directions

From Portland, drive about 20 miles west on US Highway 26 to its junction with State Highway 6. Take Hwy 6 westbound. Pass milepost 36 and set your odometer to zero. At 0.9 mile, turn right on a gravel road toward Gales Creek Campground. At 1.6 miles, park in the first day-use area on the left.

The Ride

From the parking area, take Gales Creek Trail (you'll return on the Low Divide Trail, which also heads out from this same trailhead). The trail climbs moderately then descends. Just after crossing a creek at **0.8** mile, reach a T and go left on Storey Burn Trail. The trail climbs steadily—maybe too steadily—and as it does, the forest changes from birch and alder to fir and hemlock with a thick understory of fern. Pass a small waterfall and continue up.

An old school stiffy leads the Storey Burn Climb

At **2.9** miles, the trail seems to end at a dirt road. Bearing slightly to the left, cross the main dirt road to a lesser road, and climb this road for a few hundred feet. Reach Storey Burn trailhead at **3.0** miles (ridepoint 2). From here, hop on the trail and ride it down. It's a fun descent along a steep side slope through fir forest. At **4.5** miles, the trail whips underneath Hwy 6. After a steep drop, arrive at a four-way at **4.7** miles—turn left on Historic Hiking Trail. Put it in your granny gear again and churn up the wide trail.

Getting ready to bunny hop the creek

You've topped out when you reach Hwy 6 at **5.3** miles. **WHOA!** Haul your bike over the railing, bear right, and ride along the highway. Pass the Department of Transportation sheds and then Beaver Dam Road on the right. From here, carefully cross the highway to a large gravel parking area on the north side. At **5.7** miles (ridepoint 3), Low Divide Trail to Gales Creek Campground begins from the back of the parking area. Walk the plank! The trail plunges down in the tight, lush Low Divide Creek valley. Stay on the main trail. At **7.6** miles, reach a fork and go left. Arrive back at the trailhead parking at **7.8** miles.

Gazetteer

Nearby camping: Gales Creek
Nearest food, drink, services: Forest Grove, Portland

69 TILLAMOOK BURN

Distance	8.1-mile loop (12.7-mile option)
Route	Rough, winding, unpredictable singletrack
Climbs	Tricky, rarely too steep; high point: 1,900 ft, gain: 600 ft
Duration	Fitness rider: 1 hour; scenery rider: 2 to 3 hours
Travel	Portland—45 miles
Skill	Advanced
Season	Spring, summer, fall
Map	Tillamook State Forest Trail Guide: Historic Hiking Trail
Rules	None
Manager	Tillamook State Forest, 503-357-2191
Web	www.oregon.gov/ODF/TSF/trails.shtml

Who Will Like This Ride
The more bumps, roots, and rocks, the better.

The Scoop
What is it with Tillamook Forest and burns? Back in the 1930s, this area went up in flames in one of the biggest fires ever in Oregon. Now, the maturing forest has grown back, and you can either set the trail on fire with your speed, or flame out on the rocks and roots. This singletrack loop, known both as the Historic Hiking Trail and Nels Rogers/Gravelle Brothers Trail, straddles the crest of the Coast Range in Tillamook State Forest. Though the trail crosses a multitude of dirt roads and random trails, it's fairly well signed by name and also with brown carbonate bike signs. In case of a serious bonk, those signs will lead you to calories. The ride's elevation gain checks in at the easy end of moderate—just 600 feet—but the trail climbs and drops incessantly—it's almost never level. Of course, elevation change is our friend, and gravity makes the heart grow stronger. The constant ups and downs, combined with a challenging root- and rock-strewn trail, make this a tough ride, despite its short length. Note: Don't ride this trail when wet. Try the nearby Wilson River Trail instead.

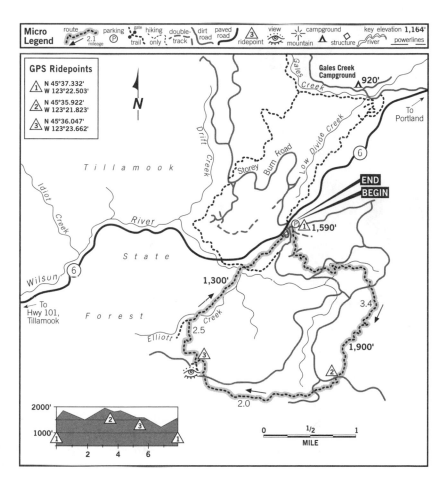

Driving Directions

From Portland, drive about 20 miles west on US Highway 26 to its junction with Hwy 6. Take Hwy 6 westbound. Pass milepost 36 and set your odometer to zero. At 0.9 mile, pass by the gravel road to Gales Creek Campground on the right. At 3.7 miles, reach the summit and turn left on Beaver Dam Road toward Rogers Camp trailhead. At 3.8 miles, turn left at the T. At 3.9 miles, reach Rogers Camp trailhead and park in the dirt lot.

Sucking air at the top of the first climb

The Ride

From Rogers Camp trailhead, take the steep, narrow dirt road that heads up to the south, away from Hwy 6. At **0.1** mile, turn right onto a singletrack—Nels Rogers Trail. The tough climb continues: steep with just enough roots to keep you focused. The trail levels, passes straight through a four-way, then climbs again. ***WOOF!*** Reach a high point at **0.6** mile and cross a dirt road. From here, the trail twists and corkscrews—more roots—down to a dirt-road crossing at **1** mile. At **1.1** miles, reach a fork and go left, cross over a creek, then arrive at a T—turn left. At **1.6** miles, pass straight through another four-way. At **2.0** miles, cross a gravel road. Beyond this point, the trail crosses numerous roads, both dirt and gravel. Follow the brown carbonate signs that point the way.

Climb, descend, then climb again to another high point at **3.1** miles. Go straight through the four-way, then descend the fast, hard-packed trail. It's a fun romp. Reach a gravel road at **3.4** miles and turn right. After about fifty yards, turn left to regain the trail and continue the fast descent. After another short climb, through fir trees with a salal and Oregon grape understory, cross a gravel road. The trail, rocky and root-strewn here, drops and weaves, crosses several more dirt roads. **WHOA!** Reach a four-way at **5.5** miles and take a hard right turn. (The trail on the left leads to University Falls.) The trail drops and climbs and drops again, then cruises down to a T—go right. The trail, now quite wide, crosses over Elliott Creek at Piranha Crossing, **6.1** miles.

The route follows an old roadbed, descending to a low point at **6.9** miles. Turn right and ride across a series of bridges. From here, the wide trail climbs away from the creek at a hectic rate. Ride straight through a four-way at **7.1** miles. **WOOF!** Reach Hwy 6 at **7.7** miles. From here, haul your bike over the railing, turn right, and carefully ride along Hwy 6 for a couple hundred yards past the Oregon Department of Transportation gravel shed. At **7.8** miles, turn right on Beaver Dam Road toward Rogers Camp trailhead. Turn left at the T, and return to the trailhead at **8.1** miles.

Option

Not quite long enough for you? Start the ride at Gales Creek Campground (see ride 69). Park in the first day-use area on the left. Take Low Divide Trail straight up toward Hwy 6. At the **2.1**-mile point, cross Hwy 6 and ride up to Rogers Camp trailhead, **2.3** miles, then follow the Tillamook Burn loop. At Beaver Dam Road, immediately before the end of this loop, cross back over Hwy 6 (rather than riding up to Rogers Camp trailhead). From the large gravel parking area on the north side of the highway, take Low Divide Trail back to the campground. This creates a 12.7-mile lollipop.

Gazetteer

Nearby camping: Gales Creek
Nearest food, drink, services: Forest Grove, Portland

Distance	23.8-mile loop
Route	Rocky dirt-road ascent, dirt- and paved-road descents
Climbs	Absurdly steep; high point: 3,200 ft, gain: 2,320 ft
Duration	Fitness rider: 2.5 to 3.5 hours; scenery rider: 4 to 6 hours
Travel	Portland—45 miles
Skill	Advanced
Season	Spring, summer, fall
Map	Tillamook State Forest Map & Guide
Rules	None
Manager	Tillamook State Forest, 503-357-2191
Web	www.oregon.gov/ODF/TSF/Recreation.shtml

Who Will Like This Ride

Your quads control your frontal cortex, and not the other way around.

The Scoop

Want an adventure challenge and a great workout? You've got it. Standard Grade is the only difficult ride in this book that doesn't head out onto singletrack. Still, the dirt-road climb up to Standard Grade will hurt you. I promise. It's easily the toughest four-mile segment in this book. This big, fat loop tracks both dirt and paved roads and affords a few long views of Mount Hood. But Standard Grade isn't as much about views or lack of dirt trails as it is about plumbing the depths of your brain's wildest hallucinations and testing your legs' quiver point.

Driving Directions

From Portland, drive about 20 miles west on US Highway 26 to its junction with State Highway 6. Take Hwy 6 westbound. Pass milepost 36 and set your odometer to zero. At 0.9 mile, pass by the gravel road to Gales Creek Campground on the right. At 3.7 miles, reach the summit and park in the wide gravel pullout on the right.

The Ride

From the wide gravel pullout, at the crest of the Coast Range, ride west on Hwy 6. The highway descends at a fast rate as it follows the course of the Wilson River. During all but the warmest months, start out with a windbreaker because this paved-road descent, combined with the deep, shaded valley, can leave you chilled. Stay on the highway. At **5.1** miles (ridepoint 2), turn right on Elk Creek Road. At **5.5** miles, pass a parking area on the left, then cross over Elk Creek. Continue up the road, ignoring a trail on the left and then riding around a rusted cable that blocks the road to motorized use.

From here, the road heads straight up, following West Fork of Elk Creek as it rounds the east side of Elk Mountain. Climbing 550 feet per mile, the road is absurdly steep. Loose drainage berms and a minefield of death-cookies, however, pose the real challenge, so plan on a four-mile hike-a-bike. This climb will make you feel like a test rat, prove the inadequacy of Cliff Shots, and evoke curses aimed at this book, as well as the inventors of the mountain bike. It's tough. Needless to say, that windbreaker is history.

WOOF! With hallucinations crescendoing, ignore a faint road on the right and then pass around an old gate at **9.7** miles. At **9.9** miles, there's a wide turnout that affords long views of Mount Hood, Mount Jefferson, and

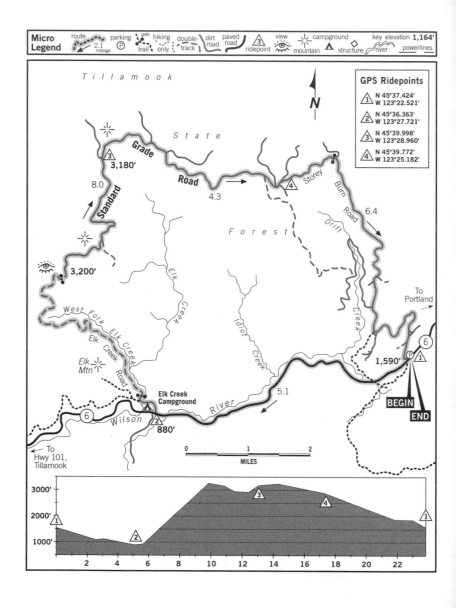

Mount Adams. This is the ride's high point. From here, the road—Standard Grade Road—bends left and traverses along the top of the ridge, rolling easily. Ignore a private road on the right at **11.9** miles. When the road divides at **13.1** miles (ridepoint 3), bear right and ride east on Standard Grade Road. At **14.3** miles, pass Kenny Creek Road on the left. At **14.5** miles, reach a fork and bear right, staying on the main road.

At **16.6** miles, the road forks—go left, then bypass a lesser road on the right a short distance farther. At **17.4** miles (ridepoint 4), pass a road on the left, followed by one on the right. Immediately reach a fork and stay right onto Storey Burn Road. The road descends around the top of a clearcut, then climbs to a yellow gate. Ignore the road back to the left at the gate. From here, Storey Burn Road descends at a fast rate, and it's fun. But watch out for vehicles on the road. Stay on the main road as you drop, passing numerous lesser roads on both the right and left. At **21.4** miles, after ignoring a lesser road on the left, reach a fork and bear left. At **21.9** miles, pass by two lesser roads on the right. When the road divides at **23** miles, bear right. Ignore a road on the right at **23.2** miles. Reach the gravel pullout along Hwy 6 to complete the loop, **23.8** miles.

Gazetteer

Nearby camping: Gales Creek
Nearest food, drink, services: Forest Grove, Portland

Distance	14.1-mile loop
Route	Rolling singletrack, short paved sections
Climbs	Short ups and downs; high point: 420 ft, gain: 220 ft
Duration	Fitness rider: 1 hour; scenery rider: 2 to 3 hours
Travel	Portland—36 miles
Skill	Intermediate
Season	Spring, summer, fall
Map	Henry Hagg Lake information brochure
Rules	Entrance fee required; closed November through March
Manager	Washington County Parks, 503-359-5732
Web	www.co.washington.or.us/deptmts/sup_serv/fac_mgt/parks/hagglake.htm

Who Will Like This Ride
You enjoy love-hate relationships and rides close to home.

The Scoop
Hagg Lake makes a great mountain-bike access story: The trail was closed to bikes for a number of years, but thanks to trail and advocacy work by the Portland United Mountain Pedalers (PUMP) and a small group of local Hagg Lake cyclists, the trail is now open for mountain-bike business. Just don't ride this loop in wet weather, or it may be closed again. The trail undulates its way around the lake, climbing and dropping, winding and zipping, stopping and starting. You'll hate it; you've love it. Some sections of trail are rutted, others can be overgrown (watch for poison oak!), still others are blissfully fun. There are many many spur trails along the way—used by fishermen to get from the road down to the lake—so it's easy to get off the main route. Don't fret because you can't really get too lost—stay close to the lake but don't go down to the lake. Take the advice of one local rider who takes a slightly different route around the lake every time out. That's okay. Note the trails and routefinding on the west side are considerably more difficult. Beginners and families may want to consider riding out and back on east side, where the trail is smoother and the route less frustrating.

Note also that the lake is super popular with the fishing and boating crowd, and can be packed on summer weekends, so plan and ride accordingly.

Driving Directions

From Portland, there are numerous "best" routes to Hagg Lake, depending on your starting point. The key is getting to Forest Grove at the junction of State Highway 8 and State Highway 47. Here's one route: Take US Highway 26 westbound for about 20 miles. Bear left on State Highway 6 and proceed about 2.5 miles. Turn left on Hwy 47, now heading south toward Forest Grove. Drive about 7 more miles, then stay on Hwy 47 as it passes to the east of the center of Forest Grove (the old Hwy 47 zigzags through town). Stay on Hwy 47, passing straight through the junction with Hwy 8. About 5 miles south of this junction, turn right on Southwest Scoggins Valley Road toward Hagg Lake. Set your odometer to zero. Pass through the toll booth. At 3.5 miles, turn left on Southwest West Shore Drive. Cross over the top of the earthen dam; then, at 4.3 miles, park at Elks Picnic Area, a large gravel parking area on the right.

The Ride

From the parking area, take the paved road away from the dam. About a hundred yards beyond the parking area, turn right onto the single-track. Note: Because of constant trailwork and the many secondary trails, the route that follows can change—stay on the main trail and follow any detours. The trail zips and rolls clockwise around the lake. At **0.4** mile, pass straight through a four-way. At **0.7** mile, reach a fork and go left At **0.9** mile, stay to the left again at the fork. Ride straight through a four-way at **1.1** miles. After a mile of sharp climbs and descents, pass through a confusing section of trail at **2.1** miles—stay on the main trail, keeping the picnic tables on the right. At **3.3** miles, the trail ends at a T with the paved circumference road—turn right. At **3.4** miles, the trail begins again on the right.

Stay to the right as you ride through a small picnic area at **3.7** miles. Pedal across a large paved parking area at **4** miles. At the far end of the paved lot, the dirt trail starts up again. At **4.6** miles, reach a T and turn left, climbing. The trail almost immediately divides—turn right. Just before reaching the paved

Trail work at Hagg Lake

circumference road, **4.9** miles, turn right. At **5.2** miles, the trail kisses the paved road on the left. Reach a T with the road at **5.4** miles and turn right. The paved road descends and then climbs. At **6** miles (ridepoint 2), find a gravel pullout on the right. The trail begins again at the edge of this pullout. At **6.4** miles, turn right just before reaching the paved road. After about fifty yards, reach a T and again turn right.

At **7.2** miles, bear right at the fork and then ignore a trail back on the left. When you reach a T at the circumference road again, **8** miles, turn right. At **8.2** miles, bear right to retake the singletrack. Over the next mile and a half, stay to the right at each of four intersections. At **10.6** miles, pop out at a parking area along the paved road—bear right, then immediately

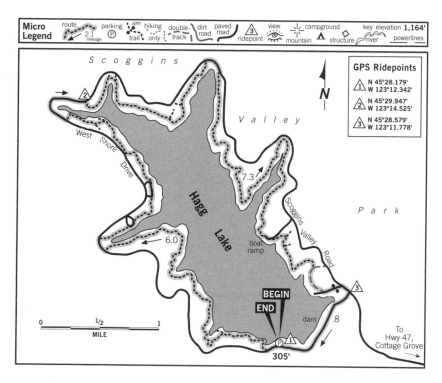

Micro Legend — route, 2.1 mileage, parking ⓟ, gate, hiking trail only, double-track, dirt road, paved road, ③ ridepoint, view, mountain, campground, ▲ structure, ◇ river, key elevation **1,164'**, powerlines

GPS Ridepoints

① N 45°28.179'
W 123°12.342'

② N 45°29.947'
W 123°14.525'

③ N 45°28.579'
W 123°11.778'

S c o g g i n s

V a l l e y

West Shore Drive

Hagg Lake

7.3

6.0

boat ramp

Scoggins Valley Road

P a r k

BEGIN
END

dam .8

To Hwy 47, Cottage Grove

0   1/2   1
MILE

305'

go right again to continue on the singletrack. At **11** miles, reach a fork and go left, climbing. At **11.9** miles, the trail ends at a paved boat ramp. From here, curve around to the left, then turn right onto the singletrack. Reach a T at **12.1** miles and turn right. Turn right at a second T a short distance farther. At **12.5** miles, ride straight through a four-way. When you arrive at a wide gravel path at **12.9** miles, go right and descend. The trail ends for good at a paved spur road at **13.1** miles. Turn left and climb past the gate. At **13.2** miles, reach the main road around the lake and descend. Take the next right (ridepoint 3). Follow the road as it crosses the dam at the southeast end of Hagg Lake. At **14.1** miles, reach the large gravel parking area on the right to complete the ride.

Gazetteer

Nearby camping: Gales Creek, Champoeg State Park
Nearest food, drink, services: Forest Grove

72 BANKS-VERNONIA TRAIL ⊙

Distance	28-mile out-and-back (shorter options)
Route	Paved rail-trail with one gravel section
Climbs	Mostly gradual; high point: 1,160 ft, gain: 580 ft
Duration	Fitness rider: 2 to 3 hours; scenery rider: 4 to 5 hours
Travel	Portland—27 miles
Skill	Beginner
Season	Year-round
Map	Oregon State Parks: Banks-Vernonia Trail Guide
Rules	None
Manager	Oregon State Parks, 800-551-6949
Web	www.oregonstateparks.org/park_145.php

Who Will Like This Ride

Either you want to put in some fast, flat miles or bring the family out for an easy jaunt.

The Scoop

Since most of the route is paved, I've listed the Banks-Veronia as a one-wheeler, despite the length. This ride is intended for families, so disregard the twenty-eight-mile length and turn around when intuition says you should. Managed by Oregon State Parks, the Banks-Vernonia State Trail is the prototypical rail-trail: wide, easy grades, and long sweeping turns. The trail begins in the town of Banks, south of US Highway 26, and meanders all the way north to Vernonia, covering twenty miles one-way. Up until now, the first seven miles from Banks have been somewhat difficult to follow because the trail was routed out onto county roads in numerous locations. However, by 2010 the entire route should be on its own dedicated path. The following description leaves out the first seven miles and begins just north of the hamlet of Buxton at the Buxton trailhead. From here to the Vernonia turnaround the route is all paved save for one two-mile section near Tophill. This section will likely be paved sometime before 2010.

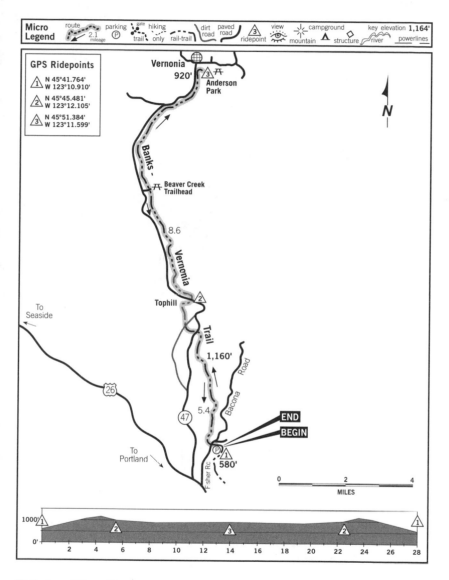

Micro Legend
route 2.1 mileage | parking Ⓟ | gate hiking trail only | rail-trail | dirt road | paved road | ▲3 ridepoint | view 👁 | mountain | campground | structure ◇ | river | key elevation **1,164'** | powerlines

GPS Ridepoints

▲1 N 45°41.764'
W 123°10.910'

▲2 N 45°45.481'
W 123°12.105'

▲3 N 45°51.384'
W 123°11.599'

Vernonia
920' ▲3
Anderson Park

N

Banks -

🎋 Beaver Creek Trailhead

8.6

Vernonia

To Seaside

Tophill ▲2

Trail

1,160'

26

47

5.4

Bacona Road

END
BEGIN

To Portland

Ⓟ ▲1
580'

Fisher Rd

0   2   4
MILES

1000' ▲1   ▲2   ▲3   ▲2   ▲1
0'
2 4 6 8 10 12 14 16 18 20 22 24 26 28

Driving Directions

From Portland, drive about 26 miles west on US 26. Just past Manning, turn right on Fisher Road toward Buxton, and set your odometer to zero.

Preparing for a future of singletrack

As you pass through Buxton, bear right on Bacona Road. At 1.4 miles, turn right to the trailhead for Banks-Vernonia Linear Trail. At 1.5 miles, park in the Buxton trailhead parking area on the right.

The Ride

Facing the paved trail, which is at the back of the parking area, turn right and pedal northwest. After crossing Bacona Road, the trail gradually ascends through slow, arching railroad turns. At **3.2** miles, cross a gravel road. After an easy climb, reach the ride's high point at **3.5** miles. The paved trail becomes gravel as you approach Tophill. From the crest, the trail descends then loops over Hwy 47 on the Horseshoe Trestle, **5.4** miles (ridepoint 2).

At **6.9** miles, the trail becomes paved again and the riding easy. Pass by Beaver Creek trailhead, a nice picnic spot, at **8.1** miles. Cross a road at **8.4** miles. From here, the trail closely follows Hwy 47 (also known as Nehalem Highway) along Beaver Creek. It's a nice, gradual descent into Vernonia. Beaver Creek flows into the Nehalem River, and around the **12.5**-mile mark, the trail follows the river as it bends east toward its endpoint at Anderson Park. At **14** miles (ridepoint 3), reach the north end of the trail at Anderson Park, along the Nehalem River in Vernonia (another nice picnic spot). Turn around here and ride back to Buxton trailhead, **28** miles.

Option

Twenty-eight miles sounds pretty intimidating, especially for beginning cyclists. You can always turn around and pedal back to Buxton trailhead. Decide the amount of time you want to be out riding and then turn around after you've been out about 40 percent of the total time (the second half of a ride often takes longer).

Gazetteer

Nearby camping: Gales Creek, Champoeg State Park
Nearest food, drink, services: Vernonia, Forest Grove

🛞 73 SCAPPOOSE ⚙️⚙️⚙️

....

Distance	2 to 12 miles
Route	Maze of winding singletrack, some dirt roads
Climbs	Lots of up and down, high point: 810, gain: 270 ft
Duration	All riders: 1 to 5 hours
Travel	Portland—13 miles
Skill	Intermediate
Season	Year-round
Map	USGS Dixie Mountain, Oregon
Rules	None
Manager	Private property
Web	Try Googleing Scappoose mountain biking

....

Who Will Like This Ride
Freeriders, explorers, and cross-country riders who dream in spirograph.

....

The Scoop
So I actually wrote up a 6-mile ride route description for Scappoose. And if you've ridden out there, you will understand the absurd and obsessive quality of such an endeavor. It became the guidebook version of War and Peace.

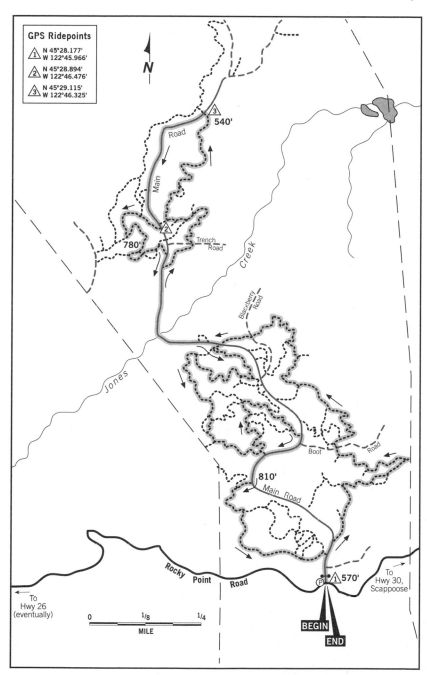

GPS Ridepoints

△1 N 45°28.177'
    W 122°45.966'

△2 N 45°28.894'
    W 122°46.476'

△3 N 45°29.115'
    W 122°46.325'

N

Main Road

③ 540'

② 780'

Trench Road

Creek

Jones

Blackberry Road

Boot Road

810'

Main Road

Rocky Point Road

P ①570'

To Hwy 30, Scappoose

To Hwy 26 (eventually)

0   1/8   1/4
MILE

BEGIN
END

That's because the area contains a frenzy of trails, interconnecting in mind-bending combinations. And, of course, that's the fun at Scappoose—exploring every little segment of the whorling, winding, whoop-ass singletrack. It's a blast. I've since dispensed of the long ride description because you'll have more fun without it. I have, though, highlighted a suggested route on the map. Use it for spatial reference—I'm sure the trailbuilders will make it obsolete soon enough. The trails here run the gamut from meandering sideslopes to wickedly fast (though short) descents to easy, who-knows-where-this-goes noodling. And don't forget the freeriding! From primitive teeters to tasty

Playing on the structures near ridepoint 2

skinnies to big jumps, it's all here. The main dirt road that bisects Scappoose is the spine of the riding area and your primary frame of reference.

Driving Directions

From Portland, take Highway 30 west toward St Helens and Scappoose. Just after milepost 17 (but several miles before reaching the town of Scappoose!), turn left, following the sign for Rocky Point Road. Set your odometer to zero. There's an immediate T—turn left on Rocky Point Road. The paved road climbs steeply. At 1.1 miles, find a blue gate on the right—that's the starting point of the ride. Park by the gate, if there's room, or in one of the small pullouts above the gate.

....

Starting the Ride

Here's how I like to start my Scappoose session: Ride around the blue gate and up the dirt road beyond. Ignore an old doubletrack on the right and then a trail on the left. At **0.1** mile, find a trail on the right that climbs away from the road—take it. After a short climb, reach a fork and bear right, passing a primitive teeter before dropping into a shallow draw. Shift down and climb again, past Oregon grape, fern, and salal. *WOOF!* The way levels at **0.3** mile. Just beyond, the trail braids apart, then reconnects—stay to the left. At **0.4** mile, reach a T and turn left. Ignore a trail on the left at **0.5** mile, then noodle across the ridge top before descending. Bear left as you pass a series of jumps below on the right. At **0.6** mile, below another set of big ramps on the hillside to your right, bear right and descend to a dirt road. The trail continues on the opposite side of the road. You're on your own.

Wondering what's around the next corner at Scappoose

Gazetteer

Nearby camping: Gales Creek

Nearest food, drink, services: Scappoose, Portland

74 LEIF ERIKSON

Distance	22-mile out-and-back (shorter options)
Route	Wide dirt and gravel trail
Climbs	Gentle; high point: 760 ft, gain: 440 ft
Duration	Fitness rider: 1.5 to 2 hours; scenery rider: 3 to 4 hours
Travel	Portland—2 miles
Skill	Beginner
Season	Year-round
Map	Green Trails: Forest Park
Rules	None
Manager	Portland Parks and Recreation, 503-823-2223
Web	www.portlandonline.com/parks/

Who Will Like This Ride
Families, hybrid riders, or fitness riders preparing for weekend epics.

The Scoop
Forest Park, designed by the Olmsted brothers at the start of the twentieth century, is the largest city-bound wilderness park in the United States. Trails, fire lanes, and old roads crisscross the vast area that's bordered by the Willamette River to the northeast and Skyline Boulevard at the top of the ridge to the southwest. Bikes are prohibited from nearly all the trails in the park, but the fire lanes and dirt roads are open and make for good riding (if there can be such a thing without singletrack). The ride along Leif Erikson Drive, a gated dirt road, is the one moderately graded mountain-bike route in the park. It's great for beginners and families, but given the lack of mountain-bike opportunities close to Portland, many intermediate and advanced riders get their workouts on the Leif. The park's loose, rocky fire lanes also attract many riders (see ride 75), and the stories of cartwheeling endos are legend.

Driving Directions
From Northwest 25th Avenue and Northwest Thurman Street in Portland, set your odometer to zero and proceed northeast on Thurman. At 1.2 miles, Thurman ends at a green gate. Park here.

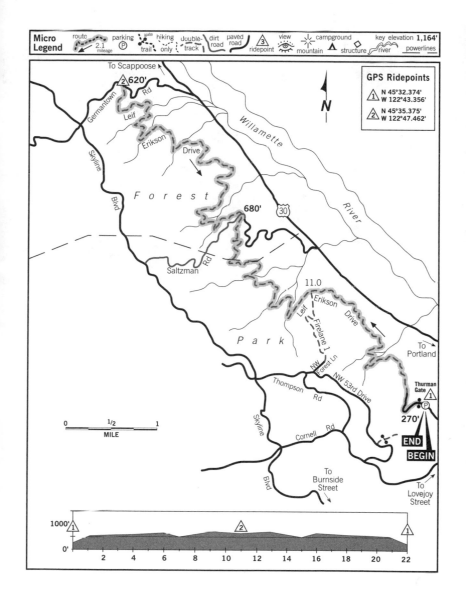

Spinning out the miles on Leif Erikson

The Ride

From Thurman Gate, the route heads into the thick deciduous forest, known to most Portlanders as Forest Park. Leif Erikson Drive, an old road turned trail, winds in and out of the folds of the steep, northeast slopes of the Tualatin Mountains. The grades are easy despite the steepness of the hillside, and the hard-packed gravel tread provides good purchase, making the pedaling easy. Numerous trails (closed to bikes) and fire lanes (open to bikes) take off from the main road. At **6** miles, when Leif Erikson crosses Saltzman Road, ride straight through the four-way intersection. From here, the way narrows and becomes more intimate. At **11** miles (ridepoint 2), reach a trailhead along Germantown Road. Turn around here and pedal back to the Thurman Gate, **22** miles.

Option

Make this ride any length you want by just turning around and riding back to Thurman Gate.

Gazetteer

Nearby camping: Gales Creek, Champoeg State Park
Nearest food, drink, services: Portland

Distance	7-mile loop
Route	Wide dirt and gravel trails, paved road
Climbs	Very steep; high point: 1,020 ft, gain: 750 ft
Duration	Fitness rider: 45 minutes; scenery rider: 1 to 2 hours
Travel	Portland—2 miles
Skill	Intermediate
Season	Year-round
Map	Green Trails: Forest Park
Rules	Bikes uphill-only on Holman Lane
Manager	Portland Parks and Recreation, 503-823-2223
Web	www.portlandonline.com/parks/

Who Will Like This Ride
You don't have much time but... must go riding.

The Scoop

Families and beginners should stick with Leif Erikson Drive (ride 74) because of its gentle grades and elastic distance (it's out and back, so you can turn around at any time). Despite the short distance of this route, it's designed for fitness riders without a lot of time on their hands. Get a workout in and get home. And Forest Park, the largest city-bound wilderness park in the United States, makes it perfect for that application. Of course you can dial up the mileage by riding your bike from home, or by adding some Leif Erikson miles onto the ride. Because you need to get those miles, right? The one-way grunt up Holman Lane—short, perhaps, but relentlessly steep—qualifies as an official ass kicker. Can you say "maximum heart rate"? One more note: The Firelane 1 descent isn't for anyone who hasn't mastered his or her brakes.

Driving Directions

From Northwest 25th Avenue and Northwest Thurman Street in Portland, set your odometer to zero and proceed northeast on Thurman. At 1.2 miles, Thurman ends at a green gate. Park here.

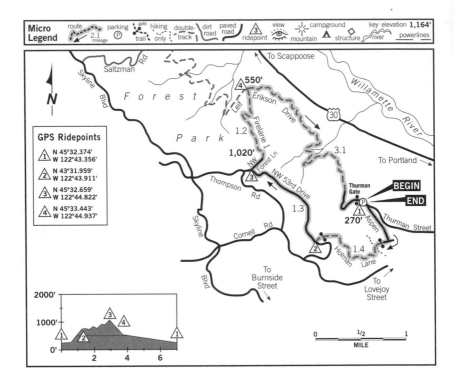

The Ride

To begin, turn around and ride away from Thurman Gate on Aspen Ave., a residential street. Follow Aspen as it winds and curves through the neighborhood. At **0.6** mile, reach a T at NW Raleigh and turn right. Half a block farther the street ends at a gate. Beyond the gate is Holman Lane, a wide dirt path. Per city park regulations, bicyclists are supposed to walk the next 200 yards to the junction of Holman Lane and Wildwood Trail. Reach the junction at **0.7** mile, hop back on your bike, and start the climb up Holman.

WOOF! The grade eases slightly at **1.2** miles. Ignore a trail on the right as you crest the top. At **1.4** miles, ride around a gate. A few pedal strokes farther (ridepoint 2), Holman Lane ends at a T at NW 53rd Drive—turn right. NW 53rd Dr., which is paved, rolls up and down along a high spine of the Tualatin Mountains. Pass by trailheads on the right at **1.6** miles, **1.7** miles, and **2.1** miles. Crest the second hill at **2.4** miles, traverse for a short distance, then begin descending.

The Holman climb begins

WHOA! At **2.7** miles (ridepoint 3), take a sharp right onto NW Forest Lane (Firelane 1). This street looks like a private drive and is easily missed. Still on pavement, though narrow and less traveled, NW Forest Lane climbs toward the top of the ridge. At **2.9** miles, pass over the top. Stay on the main road, which becomes dirt just past the crest. Ride around a gate at **3.1** miles. NW Forest Lane has officially become Firelane 1. Now check your brakes and quick release skewers. The descent is eye-watering steep—watch out for hikers and dog walkers! Pass by another Wildwood Trail trailhead at **3.4** miles. Just beyond this point, reach a fork and bear right, angling down. At **3.9** miles (ridepoint 4), Firelane 1 ends at a T at Leif Erikson Drive—turn right. (Add some mileage by turning left and riding an out-and-back spur.) Leif Erikson Drive, wide, hardpacked dirt, spins south-east along the contours of Forest Park. Return to Thurman Gate at **7.0** miles to complete the loop.

Gazetteer

Nearby camping: Gales Creek, Champoeg State Park
Nearest food, drink, services: Portland

76 POWELL BUTTE

Distance 6.7-mile lollipop

Route Singletrack with some doubletrack; views

Climbs Short and not too serious; high point: 610 ft, gain: 370 ft

Duration Fitness rider: 30 minutes; scenery rider: 1 to 2 hours

Travel Portland—10 miles

Skill Intermediate

Season Year-round

Map Portland Parks and Recreation: Powell Butte

Rules None

Manager Portland Parks and Recreation, 503-823-2223

Web www.portlandonline.com/parks/

Who Will Like This Ride

You need a place to test ride what might be your sweet new bike.

The Scoop

The old Powell Butte ride is out, and the new Powell Butte ride is in. As it should be. This out-and-back tour of the park is all dirt and more single-track than my last effort in the first edition of *Kissing the Trail Northwest & Central Oregon*. The route's short, but you'll like it. Powell Butte rises up out of the east Portland flats, between the Columbia and Willamette Rivers, to the whopping height of 612 feet. So how bad can the hill climbs be? Numerous hiking, equestrian, and bicycling trails spread out across the 570 acres here, and though there's a limited amount of ultra sweet singletrack, it's a worthwhile place to break a sweat and feel the flow of a dirt trail. Some Portlanders use the Springwater Corridor, a paved rail-trail, to access the butte. And that's a good thing.

Driving Directions

From Portland, head east on SE Powell Boulevard (US Highway 26). About 3.3 miles after passing under Interstate 205, turn right on SE 162nd Avenue and set your odometer to zero. At 0.5 mile, reach the parking area.

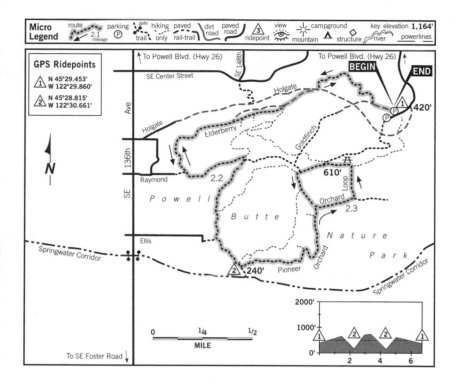

Micro Legend route 2.1 mileage, parking ℗, gate, hiking trail, paved trail only, dirt road, paved road, ③ ridepoint, view, mountain, campground, ⛺ structure, river, powerlines, key elevation **1,164'**

GPS Ridepoints
① N 45°29.453' W 122°29.860'
② N 45°28.815' W 122°30.661'

To Powell Blvd. (Hwy 26)

SE 148th

SE Center Street

Holgate

BEGIN

END

Holgate

℗ ℗ **420'**

Ave

Holgate

Elderberry

Goldfinch

136th

Raymond

2.2

⛺ **610'** Orchard Loop

Orchard Loop **2.3**

SE

P o w e l l

B u t t e

N a t u r e

P a r k

Ellis

Springwater Corridor

Orchard

Springwater Corridor

② **240'** Pioneer

0   1/4   1/2
MILE

2000'
1000'
0'
② ② ①
2   4   6

N

To SE Foster Road

The Ride

From the lower parking area, take the service road that exits past the No Parking signs. Ignore the horse access road on the right. Then, less than 200 yards from the start, find a singletrack on the right and take it. After a few rollers, reach a T at Holgate Trail and go right. Immediately, the wide trail divides—stay to the left, now on Holman Trail. When you reach a funky four-way at **0.7** mile, take Elderberry Trail. The route is mostly forested now. Arrive at an unmarked fork at **0.9** mile and go right. Ignore a trail on the left a short pace farther.

At **1.1** miles, bear left, continuing down Elderberry Trail. Stay left again at **1.4** miles, ignoring an access trail on the right. At **1.6** miles, turn right to cross over the creek, then bear right again, now descending on Cedar Grove Trail. Bypass a hiker-only trail on the left. At **2.1** miles, bear left at the fork, now reaching the low south side of Powell Butte, near Springwater Corridor,

Finding a good line at Powell Butte

a paved rail-trail. At **2.2** miles (ridepoint 2), take the second left turn on Pioneer Orchard Trail, which is unmarked, and begin climbing.

The trail, wide and hard-packed, ascends at a steady, then hectic, rate. Ignore a faint trail on the left at **2.6** miles. Cross over the creek and continue up. At **2.8** miles, the forest gives way to grassy meadow. A short distance farther, reach a fork and bear right onto a doubletrack. When the path forks again, **3.1** miles, turn left. Pass through a 5-way, and pedal up toward the old walnut orchard at the top of the butte. As you crest the top, **3.4** miles, bear left and ride alongside the old trees. On a clear day, check out the mountain views from here—Hood, Adams, and St. Helens. Pass by a paved trail on the right, then at **3.6** miles, turn left. From here, descend back toward Pioneer Orchard Trail. At **3.8** miles, reach a fork. You've completed a loop around the top of Powell Butte. Now bear right, drop back into the woods on Pioneer Orchard Trail, and retrace your tracks back to the parking area, **6.7** miles.

Gazetteer
Nearby camping: Ainsworth State Park
Nearest food, drink, services: Portland

77 MOLALLA RIM ◯◉◯

Distance	6.9-mile lollipop
Route	Singletrack with some dirt-road connections
Climbs	Some steep, most rolling; high point: 1,520 ft, gain: 760 ft
Duration	Fitness rider: 1 hour; scenery rider: 2 hours
Travel	Portland—37 miles; Salem—40 miles
Skill	Intermediate
Season	Spring, summer, fall
Map	Molalla River Trails: Loop Trails
Rules	Closed November through April
Manager	Bureau of Land Management, Salem District, 503-375-5646
Web	www.blm.gov/or/index.php

Who Will Like This Ride

A squirrel in another life, you loved chasing other squirrels around and around and around and around...

The Scoop

The Molalla River Recreation Area, owned and managed by the BLM, makes a great trail-use success story. Molalla River Watch (an environmental group), a couple of mountain-bike clubs (Salem's Merry Cranksters and Portland's PUMP), and others have worked together with the BLM to create an outstanding, shared-use trail system. These groups have collaborated on the planning and construction of many of the trails, which range from easy roadbeds to steep, nasty singletrack. And they continue with monthly work parties—sign up for one. About twenty miles of trails crisscross the area and more are slated. This process of trail building and increasing trail use has had the collateral benefit of deterring (though not eliminating) trailhead theft and illegal dumping along the river. The route described below uses Rim Trail and Huckleberry Trail to circle the Loop Trails area at Molalla, but with the crisscrossing maze of great trails here, exploration is the real fun.

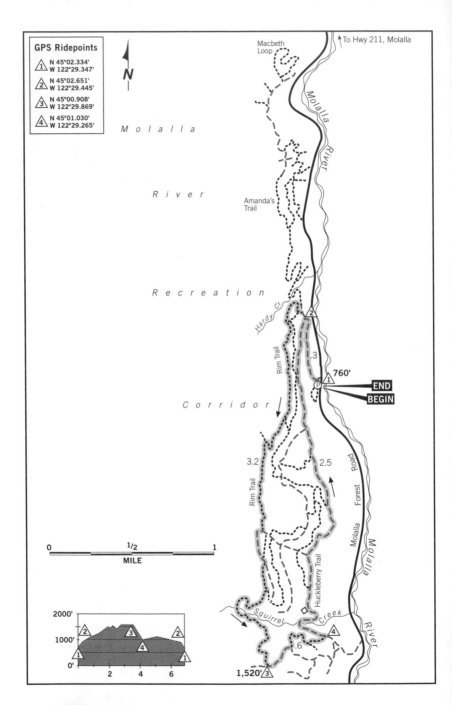

GPS Ridepoints

△1 N 45°02.334'
W 122°29.347'

△2 N 45°02.651'
W 122°29.445'

△3 N 45°00.908'
W 122°29.869'

△4 N 45°01.030'
W 122°29.265'

N

Molalla

River

Recreation

Corridor

Macbeth
Loop

To Hwy 211, Molalla

Molalla River

Amanda's
Trail

Hardy Cr.

Rim Trail

2

.3

P 760'

END

BEGIN

3.2

2.5

Rim Trail

Molalla Forest Road

Molalla River

Huckleberry Trail

Squirrel Creek

4

.6

1,520' 3

0   1/2   1
MILE

2000'
1000'
0'

2   4   6

The singletrack begins soon

Driving Directions

From Portland, drive south to Oregon City. From Oregon City, drive a little more than 12 miles south on State Highway 213, turn left on South Molalla Road, and set your odometer to zero. After 3 miles, reach a stoplight in the town of Molalla and turn left on East Main Street (State Hwy 211). At 3.6 miles, turn right on South Mathias Road, heading south toward Feyrer Park. At 3.9 miles, bear left on South Feyrer Park Road and continue to follow the signs toward Feyrer Park. At 5.6 miles, pass Feyrer Park, cross Molalla River, and reach a T—turn right on South Dickey Prairie Road. At 11.2 miles, turn right on Molalla Forest Road, following the Molalla Recreation Corridor sign. At 14.8 miles, turn right into the Hardy Creek trailhead parking area.

From Salem, drive northeast on Hwy 213 toward Molalla. Turn right on Hwy 211 and drive through the town of Molalla. On the eastern outskirts of town, turn right on South Mathias Road toward Feyrer Park and set your odometer to zero. At 0.3 mile, bear left on South Feyrer Park Road and continue to follow the signs toward Feyrer Park. At 2 miles, pass Feyrer Park, cross Molalla River, and reach a T—turn right on South Dickey Prairie Road. At 7.6 miles, turn right on Molalla Forest Road, following the Molalla Recreation Corridor sign. At 11.2 miles, turn right into the Hardy Creek trailhead parking area.

The Ride

The wide trail, which begins next to the BLM kiosk, hogs through a thicket of blackberry before climbing steeply up the hillside. At **0.3** mile (ridepoint 2), reach a T and turn right. When the trail divides at **0.4** mile, bear left on Rim Trail and keep climbing. Immediately bypass a singletrack on the left and continue up the main trail. Around **0.5** mile, the trail narrows to singletrack and heads south. The trail is hard-packed and smooth, and it ascends the wide ridge—a mixed forest to the east, pastureland to the west—in fits and starts. At **0.7** mile, stay to the right at a fork. When the trail forks at **1.4** miles, bear right to remain on Rim Trail. Ignore a trail on the right at **1.6** miles.

At **2.1** miles, reach a T and turn right, climbing up a wide trail. Bypass Bear Woods Trail on the left at **2.3** miles. Almost immediately, turn right on a singletrack, following the Rim Trail sign. At **2.5** miles, reach a fork and bear right. The trail drops sharply, then climbs again. The erratic, hard-scrabble tread may force a few short pushes. At **3.5** miles (ridepoint 3), reach a fork and go left on Bobcat Trail, a wide trail that descends eastward. **WHOA!** At **3.7** miles, turn left on Squirrel Creek Trail, which is easily missed. From here, the trail corkscrews steeply down the side of the ridge. At **3.8** miles, turn left to remain on the singletrack. When the trail dumps out at a dirt road, **4.1** miles (ridepoint 4), turn left. The road, known as Huckleberry Trail, traverses north. Pass Annie's Cabin on the right and numerous trails on the left. At **5.8** miles, after a series of easy undulations, the road descends at a fast rate. At **6.6** miles (ridepoint 2), reach a fork and turn right. Descend to the trailhead to complete the ride, **6.9** miles.

Gazetteer

Nearby camping: Feyrer Park
Nearest food, drink, services: Molalla

78 MOLALLA NORTH

Distance	5.8-mile figure eight
Route	Wide and narrow trails
Climbs	Up and down, some pushing; high point: 1,110 ft, gain: 350 ft
Duration	Fitness rider: 1 hour; scenery rider: 2 hours
Travel	Portland—37 miles; Salem—40 miles
Skill	Advanced
Season	Spring, summer, fall
Map	Molalla River Trails: North End Trails
Rules	Closed November through April
Manager	Bureau of Land Management, Salem District, 503-375-5646
Web	www.blm.gov/or/index.php

Who Will Like This Ride

You like to leave the damn book in the car and just explore the trails.

The Scoop

The trails accessible from Hardy Creek trailhead along the Molalla River are divided into three areas: South End Trails, Loop Trails, and North End Trails. South End Trails are still being assessed, planned, and constructed, while the Loop Trails, like Molalla Rim Trail (ride 77), are fun, heavily used, and ridable by most intermediates. Meanwhile, the trails in the north end are generally more advanced, rocky and technical in places, and traversed less frequently. They also, generally, shed water better than South End trails. This route tours the North End Trails, and includes Macbeth Loop, an intimate, twisting singletrack that's one of my favorites at Molalla. But, with about twenty miles of trails for all ability levels, the high exploration potential is really the reason to head out to this trail system. Big thanks should go to Molalla River Watch, the Merry Cranksters, and Portland United Mountain Pedalers for the vision, stewardship, and endless work they've put into the trails, as well as to the BLM for being open to a multi-use system. Note: Despite a marked decrease in car prowls, vehicles parked at this trailhead—as at many trailheads—still get broken into occasionally.

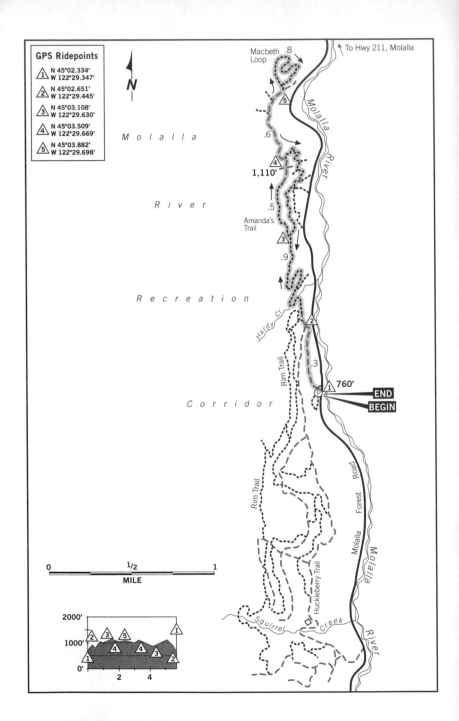

GPS Ridepoints

△1 N 45°02.334'
  W 122°29.347'

△2 N 45°02.651'
  W 122°29.445'

△3 N 45°03.108'
  W 122°29.630'

△4 N 45°03.509'
  W 122°29.669'

△5 N 45°03.882'
  W 122°29.698'

N

To Hwy 211, Molalla

Macbeth Loop

.8

△5

.6

△4

1,110'

.5

Amanda's Trail

△3

.9

Recreation

Hardy Cr.

△2

.3

760' △1 END

BEGIN

Corridor

Rim Trail

Rim Trail

Huckleberry Trail

Molalla Forest Road

Molalla River

Squirrel Creek

Molalla River

M o l a l l a

R i v e r

0   1/2   1
MILE

2000'

1000'

0'

2   4

Bridge over Hardy Creek

Driving Directions

From Portland, drive south to Oregon City. From Oregon City, drive a little more than 12 miles south on State Highway 213, turn left on South Molalla Road, and set your odometer to zero. After 3 miles, reach a stoplight in the town of Molalla and turn left on East Main Street (State Hwy 211). At 3.6 miles, turn right on South Mathias Road, heading south toward Feyrer Park. At 3.9 miles, bear left on South Feyrer Park Road and continue to follow the signs toward Feyrer Park. At 5.6 miles, pass Feyrer Park, cross Molalla River, and reach a T—turn right on South Dickey Prairie Road. At 11.2 miles, turn right on Molalla Forest Road, following the sign for the Molalla Recreation Corridor. At 14.8 miles, turn right into the Hardy Creek trailhead parking area.

From Salem, drive northeast on Hwy 213 toward Molalla. Turn right on Hwy 211 and drive through the town of Molalla. On the eastern outskirts of town, turn right on South Mathias Road toward Feyrer Park and set your odometer to zero. At 0.3 mile, bear left on South Feyrer Park Road and continue to follow the signs toward Feyrer Park. At 2 miles, pass Feyrer Park, cross Molalla River, and reach a T—turn right on South Dickey Prairie Road. At 7.6 miles, turn right on Molalla Forest Road, following the sign for the Molalla Recreation Corridor. At 11.2 miles, turn right into the Hardy Creek trailhead parking area.

The Ride

The trail begins near the BLM kiosk. After cutting through a thicket of blackberry, the wide, rocky trail climbs steeply up the hillside. At **0.3** mile (ridepoint 2), reach a T and turn right. When the trail divides at **0.4** mile, bear right on Looney's Trail. After a short level stretch, the trail narrows and switchbacks down to cross over Hardy Creek. From here, the trail climbs steeply out of the drainage. Reach a fork at **0.7** mile and bear left. The trail is loose and rocky, and the section between the creek and the wide trail along the top of the old clearcut at **0.9** mile will be a hike-a-bike for most. At **1.2** miles (ridepoint 3), reach a fork and bear left. At **1.3** miles, bear left onto Amanda's Trail and ride back into the woods.

At **1.6** miles, ride straight through a four-way. Ignore Mark's Trail on the right at **1.7** miles (ridepoint 4), continuing straight on Amanda's Trail. From here, stay on the main trail, ignoring two trails on the left as you gently descend. At **2.3** miles (ridepoint 5), reach a fork and turn left on Macbeth Loop. After a few spins of the pedals, reach a faint, unmarked fork and bear left. The trail, fun and winding, alternates between short climbs and descents and slow noodling through the forest. At **3.1** miles (ridepoint 5), reach the same faint, unmarked fork and bear left (although I'd recommend a couple more circuits around Macbeth Loop). A short glide farther, reach a T and turn right, ascending on a wide trail.

During the easy climb, ignore two trails on the right. At **3.7** miles (ridepoint 4), turn left on Mark's Trail and begin a twisting descent. When the trail forks at **4.0** miles, go right. Reach a T at **4.1** miles and turn left. Reach another T at **4.2** miles and turn right. A short distance farther, reach a four-way and turn right on AmeriCorps Alley Trail. (Note: some riders prefer to take a leftie and drop down to Molalla Forest Road here or at one of the previous intersections.) From here, the trail winds steeply up the hillside, and short sections may have to be walked. During the ascent, the trail becomes Clifford's Crossing Trail. At **4.6** miles (ridepoint 3), reach Amanda's Trail and bear left. At **4.9** miles, bear left again and descend—ignoring a lesser trail on the left—back to Hardy Creek. Cross the creek at **5.3** miles and climb south. After bypassing a trail on the right, turn left at **5.5** miles (ridepoint 2) and descend. Reach the trailhead at **5.8** miles to complete the figure eight.

Gazetteer

Nearby camping: Feyrer Park
Nearest food, drink, services: Molalla

Distance	6.7-mile loop
Route	Steep singletrack with short gravel road connector
Climbs	Straight up at times; high point: 2,500 ft, gain: 820 ft
Duration	Fitness rider: 1 hour; scenery rider: 2 to 3 hours
Travel	Portland—47 miles; Bend—107 miles
Skill	Advanced
Season	Summer, fall
Map	Green Trails: Government Camp
Rules	None
Manager	Mount Hood National Forest, Zigzag District, 503-622-3191
Web	www.fs.fed.us/r6/mthood/recreation/trails/zigzag/

Who Will Like This Ride
Your projects require a high degree of difficulty but a short attention span.

The Scoop
Expert riders might enjoy this as the second ride of the day, or hit it during a late afternoon drive to somewhere else. The Flag Mountain loop is just too short and too steep to be a real destination trail. But the climb—**WOOF!**—and the descent—Yikes!—double-down the challenge. The route begins from Camp Creek Campground along US Highway 26, climbing on singletrack and roads to Flag Mountain Trail. Once on the unmarked trail, you'll do a lot of walking unless you weigh 100 pounds, and 99 of them are in your quads. The narrow tread—through salal and Oregon grape—and

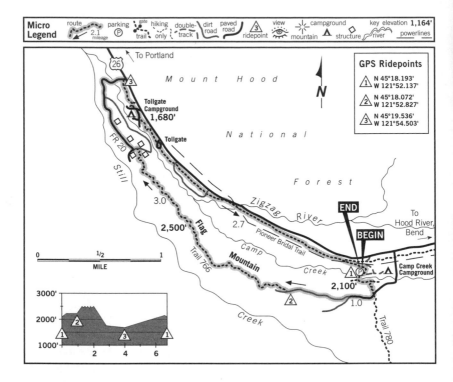

the intimate forest take away some of the pain. From the top of the narrow, fin-shaped mountain, the coquettish descent—nearly vertical in spots—can entice you into kissing the trail.

Driving Directions

From Portland, drive east on US 26. After about 43 miles, pass through the town of Zigzag. Just past milepost 47, turn right on Forest Road 150 toward Camp Creek Campground. At the campground kiosk, turn right. A quarter mile from the highway, reach a small day-use parking area on the right, signed Still Creek Trail 780.

The Ride

From the day-use parking area, cross the bridge over Camp Creek on Still Creek Trail 780. The trail forks on the opposite side of the bridge—turn left. At **0.1** mile, take the right fork and begin a short but steep climb.

....

Reach a paved road at **0.3** mile and turn right. When the road divides at **0.5** mile, bear right. Now gravel, the road descends and then climbs. **WHOA!** At **1** mile (ridepoint 2), take an unmarked and easily missed singletrack on the right. The narrow trail immediately heads straight up at a discouraging rate. It's a hike-a-bike to the **1.3**-mile point. From here—on the eastern fin of Flag Mountain—the trail flutters up and down the edge of the long, narrow mountain, dropping and ascending at a hectic rate. At **2.1** miles, pass a rocky viewpoint: Mount Hood and the Zigzag River valley.

Just after a cliff on the left, the trail drops precipitously, and you'll need to shake that big butt over the back wheel or it'll be you and the trail doing kissy-face. Pass by some cabins at **2.9** miles. Just around the corner, the trail ends at a dirt road—turn left. Thirty yards farther, turn right onto FR 20, paved. Stay on the paved road as it winds past cabins and descends to a bridge over Zigzag River. At **4** miles (ridepoint 3), just before reaching US 26, turn right onto an unmarked singletrack. At **4.2** miles, ignore a trail on the left and then immediately ignore one on the right. A few pedal strokes farther, reach a paved road and turn left. At **4.3** miles, reach the entrance road to Tollgate Campground and turn right, paralleling US 26. The paved road into the campground forks at **4.4** miles—bear left and immediately take the singletrack on the left. Pedal east on the trail, still paralleling the highway, and ignore several trails on the right that access the campground.

At **4.5** miles, pass through a paved parking area at the historic Tollgate. Continue straight on Pioneer Bridle Trail. Cross a dirt road at **4.6** miles. The trail becomes a doubletrack here. Stay to the left and you'll soon pick up the trail again. Cross dirt roads at **4.9** and **5.2** miles. The trail runs along-side the highway for a short stretch. Just after crossing the Zigzag River on a wood bridge, the trail eases to the right, following powerlines, and the highway is no longer visible though it's still audible. After crossing another road, **5.6** miles, the trail is a wide, rocky rough-and-tumble. Cross another road at **6.5** miles. At **6.6** miles, reach a five-way intersection under power-lines: Take the singletrack just to the right of the powerlines. Reach a fork at **6.7** miles and turn right. Drop down a narrow trail to the parking area immediately below to complete the ride.

Gazetteer

Nearby camping: Camp Creek, Still Creek
Nearest food, drink, services: Zigzag, Government Camp

80 CROSSTOWN TRAIL

Distance	5.8-mile out-and-back
Route	Wide singletrack
Climbs	Easy, moderate grades; high point: 3,960 ft, gain: 340 ft
Duration	Fitness rider: 30 minutes; scenery rider: 1 to 2 hours
Travel	Portland—54 miles; Bend—100 miles
Skill	Beginner
Season	Summer, fall
Map	Green Trails: Government Camp, Mount Hood
Rules	National Forest Recreation Pass needed at Glacier View trailhead
Manager	Mount Hood National Forest, Zigzag District, 503-622-3191
Web	www.fs.fed.us/r6/mthood/recreation/trails/zigzag/

Who Will Like This Ride
You often have 16-inch wheeled bikes on the back of your car.

The Scoop
The name says it all—this is an easy (though not boring) trail intended for beginners and families. It's a great introduction to singletrack. From Summit Ski Area at Government Camp, climb a short distance under the chairlift before the frolicking traverse begins. The trail is wide, smooth, and hard-packed, but there's plenty of zip and sway to keep your interest. It's heavily traveled, so watch out for other users.

Driving Directions
From Portland, drive east on US Highway 26. Just after milepost 52, pass Ski Bowl West on the right. At milepost 54, turn left onto Government Camp Loop at the village of Government Camp. Immediately bear right into the large paved parking lot at the foot of Summit Ski Area.

The Ride
From the large parking area in front of Summit Ski Area, ride toward the base of the chairlift. Follow the brown carbonate hiker/biker signs that mark the trail. Climb for a short distance under the chairlift. At **0.2** mile, the

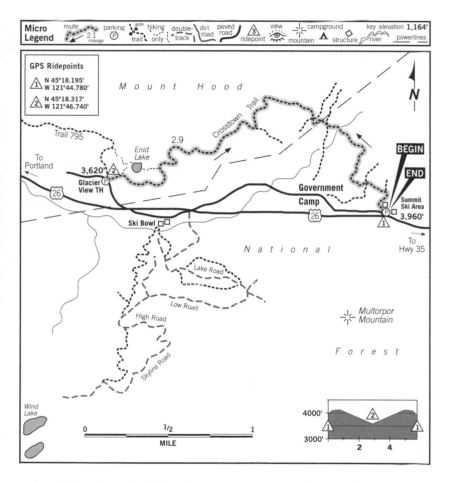

trail switchbacks to the left and traverses into a pine forest. Ride straight through the four-way at **0.3** mile. Stay on Crosstown Trail. Wide and non-technical, the trail rolls and swells. At **0.9** mile, go straight at the four-way to stay on Crosstown Trail. Proceed straight through another four-way a short distance farther.

At **1.5** miles, reach a T and turn right, heading toward Glacier View Sno-Park. The trail, zippy and fast, gradually descends from a pure pine forest into a mixed pine and fir forest. When the trail divides at **2.5** miles,

Starting out from Summit Ski Area

bear left. After a couple more turns in the trail, pass by a fen on the right. Reach a fork at **2.8** miles and veer left to stay on the main trail. At **2.9** miles (ridepoint 2), the trail kisses a paved road near Glacier View Sno-Park. Crosstown Trail ends here; Pioneer Bridle Trail, a more challenging trail, picks up and continues west. For this ride, turn around here and retrace your route. Remember: The elevation gain on the return trip will make the going somewhat slower, but it's not too tough. Return to Summit Ski Area at **5.8** miles.

Gazetteer

Nearby camping: Still Creek, Camp Creek
Nearest food, drink, services: Government Camp, Zigzag

81 TIMOTHY LAKE

Distance	8.4-mile out-and-back (15-mile option)
Route	Wide singletrack along lake
Climbs	Essentially flat; high point: 3,270 ft, gain: 70 ft; views
Duration	Fitness rider: less than an hour; scenery rider: 1 to 2 hours
Travel	Portland—79 miles; Bend—100 miles
Skill	Beginner
Season	Summer, fall
Map	Green Trails: High Rock
Rules	None
Manager	Mount Hood National Forest, Zigzag District, 503-622-3191
Web	www.fs.fed.us/r6/mthood/recreation/trails/zigzag/

Who Will Like This Ride
You like wide flat, comfortable trails.

The Scoop

I designed this ride for beginning mountain bikers. The trail is hard-packed and almost flat but with enough roll to keep it zippy, and first-time singletrackers will love it. Kids will love it too. Intermediate and advanced riders will probably want to choose the longer option that circles the lake. Or head somewhere else. Either way, Timothy Lake is a lovely place, with long views of the surrounding Cascades across the water. On summer weekends the lake can be packed with fishermen, the campgrounds full of kids, and the trails crowded. So ride carefully.

Driving Directions

From Portland, drive about 56 miles east on US Highway 26. Just after passing Ski Bowl, Summit, and Timberline Ski Areas, pass by State Highway 35 on the left. Continue 10 more miles east on US 26. Just past milepost 66, turn right on Forest Road 42 (Skyline Road) toward Timothy Lake, and set your odometer to zero. At 8.7 miles, turn right on FR 57 and continue toward Timothy Lake. Pass four campgrounds on the right, then bear right

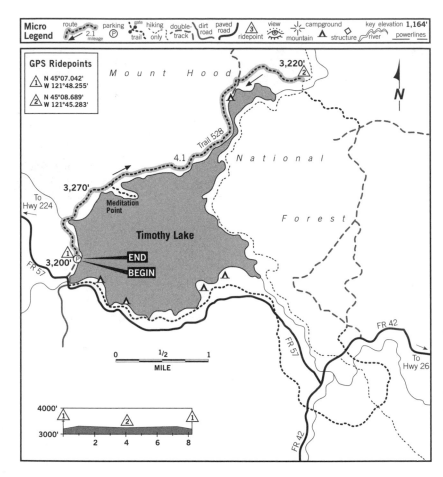

to cross the short dam at 12.2 miles. Immediately beyond the dam, turn right on a dirt road. Bear to the right and then left, then park at the trailhead, 12.6 miles.

The Ride

Timothy Lake Trail 528 takes off from the trailhead at the lakeshore. The trail, wide and smooth, rolls easily through a grand fir forest and affords numerous views of the lake. At **0.9** mile, go straight through a four-way. At **1** mile, reach a fork and bear left (the short spur to the right out to Meditation

Timothy Lake with Mount Jefferson in the distance

Point is a great addition). The wide, level trail has a surprising amount of zip, and it'll bring a smile to even expert cyclists. At **2.7** miles, ignore a lesser trail on the right. Beginning at **3** miles, ride past a campground on the right. Cross the campground road at **3.5** miles and continue on Trail 528. Ignore another trail on the right at **3.6** miles. After some more noodling through a nice forest, reach a T with the Pacific Crest Trail at **4.2** miles (ridepoint 2). Turn around here and retrace your route back to the trailhead, **8.4** miles.

Option

The Pacific Crest Trail runs north and south along the east side of Timothy Lake, and bikes are prohibited on the PCT. However, if you turn right onto the PCT at the **4.2**-mile mark, cross the bridge, and immediately bear left on Trail 537, you can follow Trail 537, a combination of singletrack and old roadbeds, to make a loop around the lake. Ride toward Joe Graham Horse Camp at FR 42. As the trail crosses FR 42, bear left and follow Trail 522. Trail 522 crosses the PCT and becomes Trail 534. Stay on Trail 534 as it recrosses FR 42, passes the historic ranger station, and crosses FR 57. From here, Trail 534 passes by (and through) four campgrounds and finally ends at FR 57 next to the dam at the west end of Timothy Lake. Turn right on FR 57 and cross the short dam. Immediately across the dam, turn right on the dirt road and pedal back to the trailhead. The entire loop clocks in at about 15 miles.

Gazetteer

Nearby camping: Pine Point, Hoodview
Nearest food, drink, services: Government Camp

Distance	19.3-mile one-way shuttle (38.3-mile epic option)
Route	Dirt-road and singletrack ups, epic singletrack descent
Climbs	Strenuous then sick; high point: 5,000 ft, loss: 4,000 ft
Duration	Fitness rider: 2 hours; scenery rider: 3 to 6 hours
Travel	Portland—62 miles
Skill	Advanced
Season	Summer, fall
Map	Green Trails: High Rock, Fish Creek Mountain
Rules	None
Manager	Mount Hood National Forest, Clackamas River District, 503-630-6861
Web	www.fs.fed.us/r6/mthood/recreation/trails/clackamas-river-conditions

Who Will Like This Ride

When someone says a trail's dangerous, well, all the more reason to ride it.

The Scoop

A cursory glance at the ride stats above caused the BMXer to salivate, the single-speed cyclist's head to spin, the weekend warrior's legs to stop aching. What sweet music: a 4,000-foot descent! No such luck. The ride up

Lake Serene

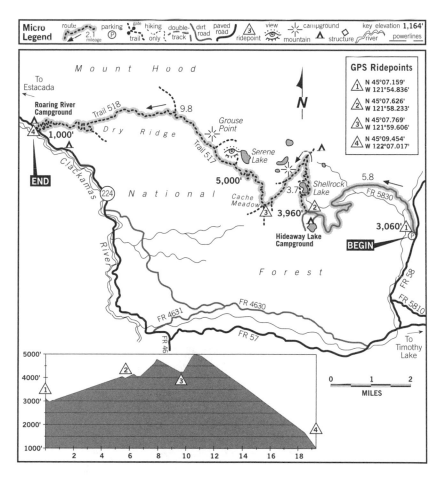

Micro Legend: route, 2.1 mileage, parking (P), gate hiking trail, hiking only, double-track, dirt road, paved road, ridepoint (3), view, mountain, campground, structure (A), river, key elevation **1,164'**, powerlines

Mount Hood

To Estacada

Roaring River Campground

Trail 518   9.8

Dry Ridge

Grouse Point

Trail 517

Serene Lake

1,000'

GPS Ridepoints
1. N 45°07.159' W 121°54.836'
2. N 45°07.626' W 121°58.233'
3. N 45°07.769' W 121°59.606'
4. N 45°09.454' W 122°07.017'

N

END

Clackamas River

224

5,000'

National

Cache Meadow

Shellrock Lake

5.8

FR 5830

3.7

3,960'

Forest

Hideaway Lake Campground

3,060'

BEGIN

FR 58

FR 5810

FR 4631

FR 4630

FR 57

FR 46

To Timothy Lake

Elevation profile: 5000', 4000', 3000', 2000', 1000' — marked points 2, 3, 1, 4 across miles 2, 4, 6, 8, 10, 12, 14, 16, 18

0   1   2
MILES

to Grouse Point—past Shellrock Lake and Cache Meadows—and then down Dry Ridge ends up being much more difficult than the nineteen miles and eye-popping descent would indicate. The route climbs about 2,000 feet on dirt road and singletrack, several miles of which are a probable hike-a-bike. There are some nice views and the forest is beautiful, but the descent isn't always buffed out—it can be ragged, sometimes overgrown, and hairball, which is why the Forest Service warns mountain bikers against riding this trail. But let's face facts, you don't turn down a nine-mile, 4,000-foot descent, whatever the conditions. Just get in some semblance of shape first. Now if you really want to ratchet up the calorie burn, try the epic option. Just be certain to bring along enough water and plenty of sweet doughy things to propel your sorry ass around the entire loop.

Driving Directions

From Portland, drive southeast on State Highway 224 (Clackamas Highway). About 17.5 miles past Estacada, between milepost 41 and milepost 42, leave a car at Roaring River Campground on the left. Continue southeast on Hwy 224. About 26 miles past Estacada, turn left on Forest Road 57, and set your odometer to zero. At 7.3 miles, turn left on FR 58. At 10.3 miles, reach the junction of FR 58 and FR 5830. Park in the gravel pullout at this junction.

The Ride

Starting from the junction of FR 58 and FR 5830, pedal up FR 5830. After a very short descent to cross a Shellrock Creek tributary, the road heads west and climbs toward Frazier Mountain. The gravelly road, exposed to the sun most of the way, ascends at a steady rate. After about **3.5** miles, the road bends to the left, crosses the creek, and switchbacks up toward Hideaway Lake. At **5.4** miles, pass the entrance to Hideaway Campground on the left. Stay on the main road to a crest, then descend to find Shellrock Lake Trail 700 on the right at **5.8** miles (ridepoint 2).

The trail climbs through a clearcut, then traverses into a fir forest. After a short descent, reach a fork at **6.3** miles and turn right to cross the creek. Now you need to wind counterclockwise around the east side of Shellrock Lake. The trail is indistinct in spots as it passes through several campsites and past a few trail spurs. Just keep going around the lake to a fork at **6.6** miles, then bear right toward Frazier Turnaround. From here, it's a hike-a-bike as the rocky, root-strewn trail climbs away from the lake. If the mosquitoes are out, this segment of trail tests the limits of your frustration. **WOOF!** Reach a T at **7.5** miles and turn left on Trail 517 toward Cache Meadow. The trail, an old road, wide and rocky but ridable, edges around the scree slopes along the east face of Frazier Mountain.

At **8.2** miles, you'll gather some momentum (at last!) as the wide trail heads downhill. **WHOA!** At **8.4** miles, reach an easily missed fork and turn left on Grouse Point Trail 517. The singletrack corkscrews down toward the mosquito quag of Cache Meadow. It's a fast, somewhat technical descent that's over all too quickly. When the trail divides at **9.2** miles, go right and cross the swampy meadow. After passing a shelter, reach a four-way at **9.5** miles (ridepoint 3) and turn right, continuing on Trail 517. The trail wends along the east side of Cache Meadow before heading up the steep bank toward Grouse Point. This climb is another probable hike-a-bike. *WOOF!* At **10.5** miles, the trail crests the route's high point and noodles along the top of the ridge.

Arriving at Shellrock Lake

At **10.7** miles, the trail divides. The short spur to the right leads to a viewpoint: Check out the view down to Lake Serene, as well as the long views of Hood, St. Helens, Adams, and even Rainier. Now go back and take the left prong. Be sure you've taken a good break—a forearm massage wouldn't hurt either—because it's here that the romping nine-mile, 4,000-foot descent begins. Reach a fork at **11.4** miles and go left. The trail, overgrown in places, loose and rocky in others, cuts a steep, accelerating traverse down the wide ridge. *WHOA!* Brakes, in fact, are necessary because when you reach a fork at **13.6** miles, you need to bear left on Dry Ridge Trail 518 toward Roaring River Campground. And without brakes you'd miss the turn. The trail whips westward, dropping at a rapid rate. Wheee! Your tear ducts will open up—even with glasses—and your ears will pop.

Hit the first switchback at **15.7** miles. The trail forks on a scree slope at **16.2** miles—turn right and head toward Hwy 224. From here, the trail is quite technical, narrow and steep, ragged and rocky, as it drops off the precipitous western prow of Dry Ridge, and short segments may need to be walked. **WHOA!** The narrow tread switchbacks and hugs the fern-covered slope. It's this section that prompted the Forest Service to discourage mountain bikers. **At 19.1** miles, reach a four-way, turn left, and walk down to Roaring River Campground. Take the campground road out to Hwy 224 to complete the ride, **19.3** miles (ridepoint 4).

Dry Ridge Epic Option

Only one car to work with? Begin the ride at Roaring River Campground to create an epic loop. From the campground, pedal south on Hwy 224. At **7.6** miles, go left on FR 4631. At **10.1** miles, go right on FR 4630, and stay on the main road. At **14.8** miles, turn left on FR 57. At **15.9** miles, go left again on FR 58. At **19** miles, after lots of ups and downs but mostly ups on paved and gravel forest roads, reach FR 5830 on the left, then follow the directions above. The full loop clocks in at **38.3** miles.

Gazetteer

Nearby camping: Roaring River, Fish Creek
Nearest food, drink, services: Estacada

 **RIVERSIDE**

Distance	8.2-mile out-and-back
Route	Winding riverside singletrack
Climbs	A few sharp rises; high point: 1,530 ft, gain: 130 ft
Duration	Fitness rider: less than an hour; scenery rider: 1 to 3 hours
Travel	Portland—52 miles
Skill	Intermediate
Season	Summer, fall
Map	Green Trails: Fish Creek Mountain
Rules	None
Manager	Mount Hood National Forest, Clackamas River District, 503-630-6861
Web	www.fs.fed.us/r6/mthood/recreation/trails/clackamas-river-conditions

Who Will Like This Ride
You like rolling riverside trails.

The Scoop
Riverside National Recreation Trail 723, a beautiful winding singletrack, runs along the east side of the Clackamas River through pockets of old growth. Downriver, it should be noted, the eight-mile-long Clackamas River Trail 715 is closed to mountain bikes—don't mix them up. It's too bad that Trail 715 is closed, but the same pressures that closed that trail are in play here as well. Ride gently and be a courteous trail user. And: Don't park in the campground or you'll be charged a fee.

Driving Directions
From Portland, drive southeast on State Highway 224 (Clackamas Highway). About 26 miles past Estacada, Hwy 224 becomes Forest Road 46 as you pass Ripplebrook Campground on the left. Cross Oak Grove Fork of Clackamas River and bear right on FR 46; then immediately turn right into Rainbow Campground. Park here.

Riverside Trail 723

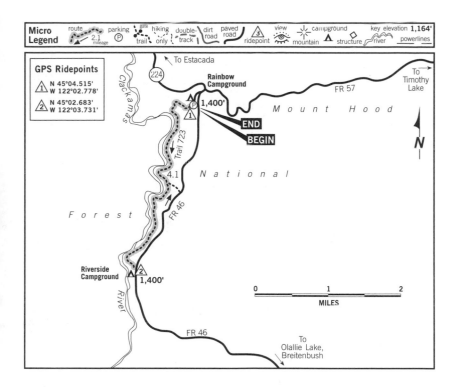

The Ride

Riverside Trail 723 begins from the far end of the campground loop road. The trail winds, up and down, through a dark forest. After winding along the Oak Grove Fork of the Clackamas River, the trail meets the main channel of Clackamas River and heads south. There are a few narrow bridges and wood walkways where you may need to walk. At **2** miles, the trail kisses the river then heads up the bank. Reach a fork, **2.5** miles, and bear right. From here, the trail levels out somewhat and meanders. Reach another set of stairs at **4.1** miles (ridepoint 2). Riverside Campground is located just beyond the stairs. Turn around here and pedal back to Rainbow Campground, **8.2** miles.

Gazetteer

Nearby camping: Rainbow, Riverside
Nearest food, drink, services: Estacada

84 RED LAKE ◉◉◉◉

Distance	15.5-mile loop (12.5-mile option)
Route	Gravel-road ascent, rocky singletrack; views
Climbs	More technical than steep; high point: 5,380 ft, gain: 820 ft
Duration	Fitness rider: 2 hours; scenery rider: 3 to 5 hours
Travel	Portland—84 miles; Salem—84 miles
Skill	Advanced
Season	Summer, fall
Map	Green Trails: Breitenbush
Rules	None
Manager	Mount Hood National Forest, Clackamas River District, 503-630-6861
Web	www.fs.fed.us/r6/mthood/recreation/trails/clackamas-river-conditions

Who Will Like This Ride
During weekdays you play on the structures at Blackrock or Scappoose.

The Scoop
Olallie, as in Olallie Lake, a prominent feature of this route, is the Chinook word for "berries." I'm wondering what the Chinook word for "rock jungle-gym" is, because that's what the riding is like here. If you have the skills, this is a great loop, past many sweet mountain lakes and through a beautiful pine

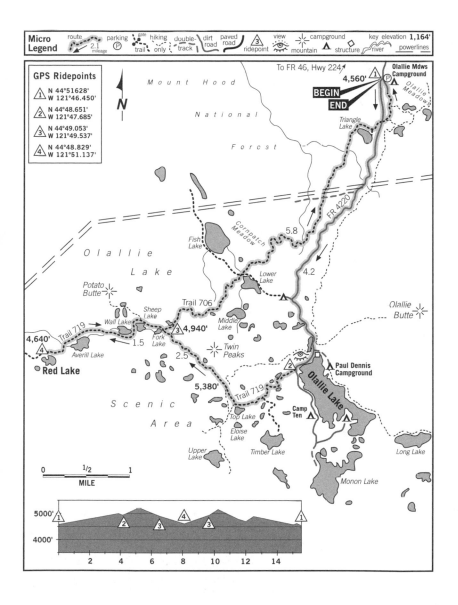

Micro Legend
route — 2.1 mileage — parking P — gate — hiking trail only — double-track — dirt road — paved road — △3 ridepoint — view 👁 — mountain ☀ — campground ☀ — structure △ — key elevation **1,164'** — river — powerlines

GPS Ridepoints
△1 N 44°51628' W 121°46.450'
△2 N 44°48.651' W 121°47.685'
△3 N 44°49.053' W 121°49.537'
△4 N 44°48.829' W 121°51.137'

M o u n t   H o o d

N a t i o n a l

F o r e s t

To FR 46, Hwy 224
BEGIN
END
4,560' △1 P Olallie Mdws Campground
Olallie Meadow
Triangle Lake

Cornpatch Meadow
Fish Lake
5.8
FR 4220
4.2
Lower Lake

Olallie
Lake

Potato Butte
Trail 706
Olallie Butte
Sheep Lake
Wall Lake
△3 **4,940'**
Middle Lake
Trail 719
4,640' △4
Fork Lake
1.5
Averill Lake
Red Lake
Twin Peaks
△2 Paul Dennis Campground
2.5
5,380'
Trail 719
Olallie Lake
Camp Ten △
S c e n i c
Top Lake
Eloise Lake
A r e a
Upper Lake
Timber Lake
Long Lake
Monon Lake

0   1/2   1
MILE

5000' △1 △2 △3 △4 △3 △1
4000'
2   4   6   8   10   12   14

forest. But the trail demands some riding chops, and even with them you should prepare for several miles of hike-a-bike. The uneven, rock-covered trail climbs and drops and climbs, and even the descents can be slow. The trail never really gives you the opportunity to open it up, a bummer because you miss the speed, which would come in handy against the millions of mosquitoes who call this place home.

Driving Directions

From Portland, drive southeast on State Highway 224 (Clackamas Highway). About 26 miles past Estacada, Hwy 224 becomes Forest Road 46 as you pass Rainbow Campground. Stay on FR 46 toward Olallie Lake Scenic Area. About 22 miles past Rainbow Campground on FR 46, turn left on FR 4690 and set your odometer to zero. Stay on FR 4690, ignoring several roads on either side. At 8.3 miles, turn right on FR 4220. At 9.9 miles, bear right and park at the entrance to Olallie Meadow Campground.

From Salem, drive east on Hwy 22 toward Detroit. Just after crossing the Breitenbush River, turn left on FR 46. Proceed about 24 miles northeast on FR 46, then turn right on FR 4690 and set your odometer to zero. Stay on FR 4690, ignoring several roads on either side. At 8.3 miles, turn right on FR 4220. At 9.9 miles, bear right and park at the entrance to Olallie Meadow Campground.

The Ride

From the entrance to Olallie Meadows Campground, pedal up FR 4220 toward Olallie Lake. The gravel on the road is sometimes loose, making traction difficult, but the grade isn't too steep. Stay on the main road as you climb. Pass under some powerlines at **1.3** miles. Bypass the entrance to Lower Lake Campground on the right at **3.1** miles. Reach a fork in the road at Olallie Lake, **3.9** miles, and bear right to remain on FR 4220. Mount Jefferson peeks up over the ridge across the lake. At **4.2** miles (ridepoint 2), turn right onto Red Lake Trail 719. White and gray granite boulders, scattered over the landscape, mute the greens of low mountain hemlock and pine, and the trail climbs awkwardly through these big rocks. At **4.9** miles, reach a fork and go right. The trail skirts by a series of ponds, then passes a lake at **5.2** miles. At **5.3** miles, reach a T and turn right. Ride straight through a four-way at **5.5** miles. The climb ends a short distance farther as the trail cascades through a mogul run of granite.

The trail eases into a flat, pine-forested swale between Twin Peaks, Double Peaks, and Potato Butte; at **6.7** miles (ridepoint 3), it forks. Bear left, continuing out Red Lake Trail 719. (Note: From here, the route spurs out to Red Lake and then returns to this intersection, a three-mile out-and-back that you can skip by turning right on Trail 706 and picking up the directions below beginning at the **9.7**-mile mark.) The narrow trail, a jungle gym of rocks and roots, passes four lakes on the way to Red Lake. At **7** miles, reach a fork and bear left. Stay on the main trail. At **8.2** miles (ridepoint 4), reach Red Lake, a great place for a picnic. Turn around here and take Trail 719 back to the junction with Trail 706, which you reach at **9.7** miles (ridepoint 3).

At the trail junction at **9.7** miles, turn left and ride northeast on Trail 706 toward Lower Lake. After a few tire rotations, pass a lake on the left. Unless you are both technically skilled and very fit, the next four miles require a fair amount of pushing. **WOOF!** Crest a high point at **10.3** miles and begin a technical descent, again punctuated by huge rocks. Reach a four-way at Lower Lake, **11.6** miles, and continue straight ahead toward Triangle Lake, several miles ahead. (Option: You can bail out here by turning right and riding to Lower Campground and then down FR 4220. This shaves two miles and a fair amount of hike-a-bike from the ride.) Cross an easy ridge and drop to Cornpatch Meadow at **12** miles. The hike-a-bike continues as you ascend another ridge.

The trail, ragged in sections, climbs and falls in sharp, irregular spikes. At **13.5** miles, cross a dirt road and then pass under a set of powerlines. The trail is faint here and difficult to follow; meanwhile, the ups and downs continue to force the occasional push. There's a horse camp at Triangle Lake, so watch out for equestrians. The trail swings around the north side of Triangle Lake at **14.6** miles. At **14.8** miles, reach a fork and bear left. Cross FR 4220 at **14.9** miles, continuing down Trail 706 on the opposite side. The trail immediately divides—go left. At **15.1** miles, when the trail divides again, bear left. Arrive at the south end of Olallie Meadows Campground a short distance farther. Pedal north and reach FR 4220 at **15.5** miles to compass the loop.

Gazetteer

Nearby camping: Paul Dennis, Camp Ten
Nearest food, drink, services: Detroit, Estacada

ABOUT THE AUTHOR

Zilly's been on a lot of trails. Author of 11 guidebooks, he's ridden, written about, and mapped over 500 trails across the West. And sampled many more. He grew up hiking and skiing in Washington's Cascades and Olympics and, at age 19, spent 10 months touring around the country by bicycle. He now writes, rides, and obsesses over maps from a home base in Seattle.